"I'M STILL HERE":

a letter to my children about family violence,
sexual abuse, surviving and thriving

ELIZABETH DUTTON-SCOTT

BALBOA
PRESS
A DIVISION OF HAY HOUSE

Copyright © 2013 Elizabeth Dutton-Scott.

All rights reserved. No part of this book may be used or reproduced by any means, graphic, electronic, or mechanical, including photocopying, recording, taping or by any information storage retrieval system without the written permission of the publisher except in the case of brief quotations embodied in critical articles and reviews.

Names and places have been changed to protect the privacy of those mentioned in the book. The author's name is a pseudonym. The story is true.

Balboa Press books may be ordered through booksellers or by contacting:

Balboa Press
A Division of Hay House
1663 Liberty Drive
Bloomington, IN 47403
www.balboapress.com
1-(877) 407-4847

Because of the dynamic nature of the Internet, any web addresses or links contained in this book may have changed since publication and may no longer be valid. The views expressed in this work are solely those of the author and do not necessarily reflect the views of the publisher, and the publisher hereby disclaims any responsibility for them.

The author of this book does not dispense medical advice or prescribe the use of any technique as a form of treatment for physical, emotional, or medical problems without the advice of a physician, either directly or indirectly. The intent of the author is only to offer information of a general nature to help you in your quest for emotional and spiritual well-being. In the event you use any of the information in this book for yourself, which is your constitutional right, the author and the publisher assume no responsibility for your actions.

Any people depicted in stock imagery provided by Thinkstock are models, and such images are being used for illustrative purposes only.
Certain stock imagery © Thinkstock.

Printed in the United States of America.

ISBN: 978-1-4525-8138-5 (sc)
ISBN: 978-1-4525-8139-2 (hc)
ISBN: 978-1-4525-8140-8 (e)

Library of Congress Control Number: 2013915736

Balboa Press rev. date: 09/09/2013

Memory & Healing

Memory is:

- an illusion of reality but is believed to be an accurate account of the past . . .
- a fleeting moment of an image from the past . . . a series of photographs segmenting our lives . . .
- an attempt to make sense of our lives . . . to be successful we join those snap shots creating our own movie . . .
- the feeling we are left with when we remember . . .
- Carol Burnett, as she writes to her children:
"Memory is a tricky thing. It all has to do with our own point of view, which always puts us center stage . . . but I don't think it matters that much one way or the other, because what I really wanted to do was let you know my take on it all . . . to share my feelings with the three of you. And if I succeeded, even a little, it was worth it." "One More Time" . . . p355

Healing is:

- Cure
- Recovery
- Restore
- Rebuild

SEARCHING
by
Elizabeth Dutton-Scott
1973

I search in my mind
    To find you,
But instead, many doubts and anxieties
I reach out
        you are not there.
I search for you
        I don't find you.
In my dreams I wonder why
        I cannot find you.
The obstacles mount
        why can't I find you?
Why are you so hard to discover,
        will I ever find you?
What is it that compels me to
        keep searching?
Why can't I be satisfied
        with who I am?
Or do I know?
Perhaps I am crazy.
Or do I search because
        inside I know that I am not.
I flounder like a baby
        learning to swim
Thrashing, gasping, reaching
        Reaching out,
But
        you are not there—yet.

Effects of Trauma

My understanding from the books I have read is the following:

The diagnosis of Post Traumatic Stress Disorder (PTSD) is not confined to war veterans. I learned it is also from other forms of trauma: a terrorist attack, illness, sexual assault, sexual molestation, common assault, bullying, wife battering and any other trauma that changes a person's life, behaviour and mental/emotional stability.

The effects of abuse or trauma are determined by the emotional state of the person prior to the trauma. Usually the victim experiences a period of about two weeks of reliving the trauma (flashbacks) through frightening images, nightmares and anxious moments. This is called Post Traumatic Stress. But if after a few weeks, those symptoms continue, Post Traumatic Stress Disorder is usually the diagnosis. If multiple and varied abuses occur repeatedly over time and effects of the abuse are not resolved with each abuse, Complex Post Traumatic Stress Disorder (CPTSD) will likely be the diagnosis.

A traumatized person sees the past and the future running parallel with the present. The victim can have flashbacks that become chronic and may continue to live in a state of fear and anxiety as if being traumatized every day. The sense of danger is constant even when there is none. A traumatized person lives with the fear that the abuse won't stop and is constantly waiting for the next shoe to drop. Living in this relentless state of fear can escalate to the point that the abused will shut down emotionally, be depressed, withdraw from human encounters, become addicted to drugs or alcohol, commit suicide, or become violent towards others and could use a weapon to stop the abuse, the pain and the fear.

Prologue

I began writing this book following my presentation to colleagues of Victim Assistance, about family violence and sexual abuse based on my history. I wanted to address the question, why?

Why do so many women, including myself, put themselves in violent situations and stay there to be abused, physically, emotionally and psychologically? From my experience, research and beliefs about myself, this book, my story, is about my struggle to survive during multiple abusive relationships and sexual abuse, to thriving and offering support to others who are facing similar challenges.

Before writing this book, I believed that if I didn't think about the abuses I could carry on living without the feelings associated with abuse. But my body and mind continually presented challenges that prevented me from achieving peace. I could not make sense of anything about me. I had difficulty understanding why I could not move forward with my life and be happy.

After all, I am: educated, compassionate, have a sense of love and gained respect from the people who know me. I understand the 'battered wife syndrome', as well as the effects of child sexual abuse. But still, I have felt lost. I had to find a way to move on from surviving to peace with myself and the world. I no longer wanted to be suspicious of others and my surroundings. I didn't want to live in fear. I didn't like being on alert all the time. And I did not want to feel shame and guilt any longer.

As I sat in front of the computer waiting for inspiration and the first words to type, my mind became cluttered with flashing images of dramas in my life and inexplicable feelings. Where do I begin? I had seventy-one years to sift through. Did I have anything worthy to say that hasn't already been said? Will I hurt anyone? Would I remember the pain and feel violated again? Would there be a release from past emotions?

I could see chapter headings and parts of the activities in them, but remembering details in those segments was hazy and distorted. However, the message was the same: I had been abused, violated and dehumanized. I was sad, angry, confused, fearful, guilty, filled with shame and I survived.

I have lived with self-loathing and fear most of my life. I lived with fear of being hurt by perpetrators disguised as family, friends and lovers. I carried the heavy burden of guilt because I abandoned my children in so many ways when I was with them and after I left forty-four years ago. Perhaps, as I wrote, I would develop healthy feelings toward myself and self-reproach would vanish. It might be like crying; tears would eventually stop and reason and balance would arrive. I had to try because living this way was not living.

I thought of my children, who have not been a part of my life for more than twenty years. What had their father told them about me? I wondered what they told themselves about me and why I wasn't a part of their lives. I wondered if they were angry and struggling with their own feelings and behaviours. I wondered if they had questions they found impossible to answer.

I decided to write to them through this book, this memory of my life and my understanding of how it has affected me and my behaviour and how I suppose it has affected them, based on the science of human behavior that I have read. Perhaps, I thought, others would see a part of themselves in my story and begin the journey to going beyond surviving to thriving. And hopefully, my story would give greater insight for the victim assistants and first responders of family violence and sexual abuse.

Once I committed to writing my story, I did not want to stop, no matter how it made me feel. This was a challenge, like so many I have had over the years and overcome. Maybe writing my story would reveal a sense of peace.

Chapter One

My Search for Understanding Began in 1989 When . . .

I was meditating in a cool room, lying on a soft, comfortable bed. As I listened to my breathing I felt my body and mind relax. I began imagining myself above the tree line of a mountain, in the centre of a circle surrounded by everyone who helped me feel safe. The air was sweet, the sun warm and the birds were high in the sky floating peacefully among the fluffy white clouds. A gentle breeze caressed my body.

As if the clouds had turned black and lightning struck, I was suddenly catapulted from these serene thoughts and feelings, to a grotesque image. My body had shrunk to the size of a baby. I was choking, I couldn't breathe and I couldn't get away. I opened my eyes and the image was gone, but the feelings of helplessness and fear lingered.

I knew enough about child sexual abuse, that this image scared and concerned me. Was I abused as a baby and this was a flashback? At that moment I felt sure I had been sexually abused. I needed to yell, to scream, to fight.

I ran outside and onto the open prairie; where the wind blew strong. I joined the howling wind as it raged around me, pulling my hair, the swirling sand biting my skin and scratching my eyes, deafening me to all sounds but our mutual wailing. Together we moaned of all the offences perpetrated on me throughout my life and sent the fragmented messages to be carried in the particles of dust to unknown places.

Exhausted, I returned home and remained quiet for the rest of the day. When I felt less fearful, I decided I needed to know who I was.

Extensive research lay before me to understand my life, the source of my pain and find ways to move forward toward happiness. Years of therapy, self-help books, and other forms of self-awareness exercises helped me understand fragments of my behaviour, but they were not enough. I was still unhappy. Possibly, hopefully, writing my history would provide answers. That's what this book is about.

To write my story, I begin with the beginning . . . .

Chapter Two

My mother and father met near a military base early in 1940. She was working at a hospital as a nurse's aide in training and he was in army boot camp. Mom was nineteen, tall and slender with blue eyes and long blonde hair that gave her the nickname 'Blondie'. She was dating 'Jerry' at the time and would often go to dances that were organized for the soldiers. It was there that she met my dad. He was twenty-three, six feet tall, with black hair in a pronounced widow's peak and soft blue eyes. Mom said he looked a lot like Robert Taylor, the heartthrob actor of the times.

When Dad noticed mom, he walked across the floor and asked her to dance. They both loved dancing and apparently dad was very good, having been a student of the Arthur Murray Dance Studio in his home town. People would stop and watch them as they glided across the dance floor. That was the end of Jerry. Most dates were to a dance hall where they usually stayed until late into the night. That was a problem for mom. The hospital dorm had a curfew. To avoid being caught, she had to climb through the window of her room.

Many years after dad died, mom said he was gentle, well-mannered, but not romantic. She said it was difficult for him because he came from parents who weren't very affectionate. His life's path was marked before he enlisted. He would have to be: a "proper" son of English parents; married to someone who met their approval; obedient to their wishes. He was considered an excellent soccer player on a team coached by his father. At home, he created lovely functional pieces of furniture that have never been duplicated.

Mom came from a family who enjoyed music. Her mother was a graduate of the Royal Conservatory of Music. Her father was a self-taught tenor. The entire family could play instruments and sing. Some siblings created bands in their adult life. Mom played the piano, organ and harmonica and composed music and lyrics. She was an exceptional athlete while in school, winning awards for track and field. To this day, her eighth grade picture hangs in her former elementary school. She was the eldest daughter of a large family of eleven. That meant she was the second mother to the rest of her siblings; a demanding role for a young girl.

After a short courtship, dad and mom married on March 30, 1940. He wore his uniform and mom wore a plain blue princess line dress purchased by her maid of honor, Sandy, who was marrying mom's brother Patrick, in a double wedding. Mom and Sandy stood as witnesses for one another. Dad's army buddy, Arnold, was dad's witness. I adored Uncle Arnold, but in recent years I suspected he was inappropriate with me. Mom's parents were the only others in attendance.

Dad invited his parents, but they didn't respond, nor did they send a gift or any other acknowledgement of this very important event in his life. I can only imagine his disappointment.

After the ceremonies, they all went out for dinner at a local restaurant. During the short time they were together as husband and wife, they lived in a furnished one bedroom apartment. Just before dad was shipped out to England six weeks later, mom discovered she was pregnant with me. Mom could not go back to nursing because she was married. She didn't have a job to support herself, so Dad arranged for her to move to live with his parents, whom she had never met.

According to mom, living with dad's parents was very difficult for her. When they were with friends; whether or not mom was within ear shot, they would express their displeasure in dad's choice for a partner. Her life was hell under these circumstances. She was: pregnant, miles away from her own family and friends and fearful for her husband's well-being.

On the 20th of February 1941, I came into this world of chaos and emotion. World War II was raging, my father was overseas, there was tension between mom and his parents, my mother felt trapped, she cried all the time from loneliness and I was colicky.

My father's parents, like many of their generation, didn't approve of handling a baby unless it was for the purposes of feeding, bathing or changing a diaper. They insisted mom do the same with me. It was their way and there were no exceptions. Perhaps this tension I lived with explains the stomach problems I have experienced my entire life, which rise to greater levels during times of high stress.

My mother told me recently that dad's parents didn't think much of me at first, however, when their friends spoke of my beauty, they changed their attitude. After that, every Sunday morning grandma would take me to their bed to snuggle awhile. Then grandma would leave me with grandpa while she went into the kitchen to prepare breakfast. When it was time for my feeding, mom went to their bedroom to get me. As she approached the bedroom doorway, she saw grandpa, inappropriately handling me. He had a defense, but mom didn't accept it. She picked me up and vowed never to let me enter their bedroom again.

When I was older and stayed overnight at grandma and grandpa's house, I would sleep with grandma, tossing and turning throughout the night, disturbing her sleep, while grandpa slept on the couch, his long slim body extending over the end of the sofa.

I understand now, why grandpa slept on the couch, if in fact he had abused me. But to this day, I question my mother's interpretation of the incident. She was sexually abused by an uncle when she was a young girl and perhaps she read something into the scene of grandpa and me in bed that morning that wasn't really accurate. I may never know the truth. I do recall that he was crude when it came to women, making insulting remarks about their bodies. While clenching his jaw and holding a slithery smile, he said that during the time he and grandma went on a cruise, he found,: "the best time was sitting on the deck with a drink of rye in hand, a beer in the other, watching the women go by", as well as other crude comments about their bodies.

I also have inappropriate photographs of myself taken by grandpa. In the picture, I am not of school age, dressed in leotards and a blouse, bending over with my bum facing the camera. When I looked at that photo years later, I was repulsed and threw it away.

We stayed with grandma and grandpa for the first three years of my life until mom got a job at Boeings Aircrafts producing airplanes for the war. This was her opportunity to remove us from any chance of further abuse for both of us. We moved to a rooming house where the landlady agreed to be my sitter. Shortly after we moved in, mom discovered the woman treated me unkindly and we moved again, to stay with the Castel's, people mom found through a newspaper ad. They cared for me while mom worked. My mother had many moments where she knew what to do to keep me safe; but in this case, I wonder now, why mom would leave me with total strangers after I had already allegedly been abused.

The photographs of me during my early years were similar to the images seen in the old movies of Shirley Temple of the same age. I looked like a chubby blue eyed doll: clean, frilly, cute, curly blonde locks of hair and according to my mother, I was also well behaved. She said I used to cry if I got my hands dirty. Considering the difficulties mom had with my grandparents, I can't help wondering if she thought that by keeping me looking perfect and behaving perfectly, they would finally approve of her.

CHAPTER THREE

In the spring of 1945, when I was four years old, a stranger called daddy, came home. "Daddy" was the man in a picture that rested on the side board in the dining room. Before my bedtime, grandpa would carry me on his shoulders around the table so I could say good night to "daddy". I had no idea "daddy" had two legs and two arms, walked and talked. I just liked being bounced around on grandpa's back.

When the train carrying the troops arrived, mom broke through the crowd and swung her arms around a man in a uniform. As she reached to put her arms around him, her slip was exposed under the hemline of her dress. I saw that indiscretion before I noticed "my daddy". "Look", I said pointing, "mommy's slip is showing", a common expression, usually spoken in a whisper, in those days.

This stranger scooped me into his arms and the newspaper photographer took our picture. That evening, a large image of the three of us appeared in the paper. The caption under the picture names this man as "Gnr. Alick Dutton". I looked wary of this man. After dad died I got a copy of the photograph and someone had torn mom's image from the photo. Probably dad did it when they divorced years later.

When I learned to read, I used to tell my friends that my dad was a general in the army but of course he wasn't. He was a gunner. That was all I knew of this man for most of my life. I didn't know where he had been and why he hadn't been a part of my early life. Until the month before his death in 1990, I struggled for his acceptance.

According to some research I have read, girls born while their fathers were fighting the war had difficulty relating to men. That certainly was true in my case. Dad made attempts to establish a fatherly relationship with me in his own way, but these attempts were met with great trepidation and resistance on my part.

For example, when he was cutting up a tree for firewood he would ask me to sit on the log to hold it in place. But as a child I wanted to play, so I would complain to my mother who would come to my defense and tell dad that I was a girl and shouldn't be doing things like that.

When I struggled with arithmetic, he tried to help. His father was a capable mathematician who had taught dad short cuts in calculating figures. Dad tried to teach them to me, but I knew my teachers would not accept his methods. I was required to show how I arrived at the answer, only by the procedure the teacher taught. Dad would yell; I'd cry, and my mother would make an effort to mediate.

After a few of those scenes, dad stopped trying to "help". I never did do well in math.

Dad picked on me at the dinner table. "Sit up straight", "don't put your elbows on the table", "stop fidgeting", "eat up". Before dinner was over, I was often in tears. The nagging was relentless, and in an attempt to ease the pressure, my mother began preparing supper for me at lunch time. In the evening, I would have something simple so I could leave the table quickly and not have to endure his wrath. Whenever he tried to teach me anything I would end up in tears and he would stomp off in frustration.

When I was about six years old, I began dance lessons. I was pretty good too. In fact, my instructor told mom I could do anything I wanted in the dance field because I was that good. Later in life, I became a very graceful ballroom dancer.

However, I had trouble distinguishing right from left. Dad decided he would "help". He had me stand in the kitchen while he sat on the wood box by the stove. He would yell: "Where's your left arm? Now where's your left foot?" I couldn't remember that the left arm was on the same side as my left foot! He'd yell at me until I was shaking and the more he yelled the more confused I became. I felt like I was being interrogated. It was as if my inabilities were a direct reflection of his ability to be a good father. To this day, on occasion, I find myself wondering if I've identified my left from my right when the need arises.

He attempted to be physically violent toward me on two occasions. The first time was when I was about thirteen. I don't recall what caused his anger, but, while grasping a roasting pot, he stretched his arm as high as he could until his veins bulged ready to bring it down on me, but instead, he stopped short of my head. I was shocked and terrified. I went outside and away from him.

The other time was much later when I was seventeen. We were having a disagreement. His face was contorted in anger, his body inches away from mine as he raised his open hand. I stood tall and rigid as I looked into his hateful eyes and said: "Don't you dare". His arm dropped. I turned, walked out of the house and went to a movie where I was in shock, afraid, sad, lonely and crying. As I look back over the years, there were many times where I showed courage and determination that were not part of my consciousness at the time.

Dad had another form of abuse that led me to believe I should be afraid of him, but that was a few years down the road when our family's life was turned upside down.

These experiences and others kept us apart emotionally. We couldn't relate to each other without tension. I was constantly wondering if he liked me. I thought that perhaps if I could be more like him, think like him, behave like him, have no thoughts of my own so they didn't clash with his, then he would accept me.

Oh course he did do the right thing from time to time, but the wall that had been created was impenetrable. The emotional connection between us was non-existent. He said he loved me only once when his mother died and I was in my thirties.

He did have his moments of caring. When I left Monty, my first husband, and living on my own in another city, I phoned dad and told him I was having trouble dealing with the loss of my children. He and my brother Mathew drove three hours one Sunday to be with me. We had dinner, talked and he went back home. When my family needed emotional support following a tragedy, dad came and stayed until we were stabilized.

Twice he averted a disaster. I was quite young as I played on a beach unaware that the tide had started moving in. When mom and dad looked up they saw I was surrounded by water. He ran out and carried me back. The other time was when we went to a riverside picnic and swimming area. I was just learning to swim. I went out into the water a little too far and was being swept away. Dad jumped in and saved me.

Tenderness wasn't part of dad's way, usually. When I was about thirteen, I saw in him a moment where I felt loved. I developed the mumps. I was so sick and in so much pain. When the one side healed, the other side swelled. I felt like this was never going to stop. Dad came home one evening when I was crying. He tenderly touched my face and said something about it hurting. I nodded and he comforted me with a hug. That was a first that I remember.

The month before he died was a time I value. During Easter weekend, I visited my sister, who lived a few blocks away from dad. I intended to make an effort to visit him for a few hours. The short visit turned into a full day and led to another visit the next day to enjoy more of the same. I don't know what had changed between us, perhaps age, perhaps we were both ready. It was a time together when we talked freely without tension.

I cried uncontrollably at his funeral. I had only two days with him during which we were able to treat each other with respect. There would be no additional opportunities to discover more about him. I cried for what I hadn't had all those years. I cried for what I wished we could have had.

After his funeral, I was given a photo of my younger self. It had been in dad's wallet. I stared at the frayed and creased photo of myself in a two piece bathing suit: fifteen years old, slender and attractive. It has taken a long time to accept that this photo was an indication of his love for me. I have difficulty understanding the distance between us, because I don't know his story as I know my own, but now I can accept him as he was without strong feelings of blame, anger, frustration and disappointment.

Our first home, as a family, after dad had returned from the war, was an apartment in tenement housing. It was dark and dingy with a long communal porch. I don't recall playing with other children. I just know that I often entertained myself. There was a deep construction hole in the lot alongside our building where I often played. Following a rain, the hole would fill and I'd use a piece of construction wood to float on the water like a raft. In my own world of make-believe I'd be on an adventure with not a care in the world. I was four years old. If I wasn't in that site, I'd wander down the street toward the park in search of someone to play with.

Grandpa, had arranged an inside job for dad when he returned from the war, but after all those years of living in the open, dad couldn't handle the four walls. He drifted from one job to another, totaling seven in the first year. Some of them included delivering: baked goods, dairy products and the mail, but he couldn't settle into any of those jobs. He managed to stay a little longer as a supervisor at a furniture manufacturing plant using his knowledge from school when he made furniture in shop class. As an adult with a family, he made all our furniture. Some pieces are still being used by family members. In the end, he was happiest when he began a career as a bartender, probably because it fed his alcoholism.

Dad's army buddy, Arnold, had a mop of dark slightly curly hair that fell onto his forehead. He was a good looking man about the same build and height as dad. I don't know when I first met 'Uncle' Arnold, but I recall one time when I was four and we were still living in tenement housing. It was dark outside and I had been in bed for a while. He woke me and told me he had something to show me. It was Hallowe'en and he had fireworks to set off, just for me. He crouched down so I could sit on one of his knees while he lit the fireworks, one after the other as we watched in awe the explosions in the sky.

There were many more visits with Uncle Arnold. I became more attached to him than I was to my father. Mom told me he took me out for ice cream quite often. My next recollection of him was when I was about seven years old. He came over to our house one evening and he had a woman with him. He introduced Lindsay to my parents and announced they were getting married. Shocked and hurt, I ran to my room crying. He had promised to marry me when I was old enough! I didn't speak to him for a very long time.

Mom didn't like Uncle Arnold. She said he was totally about himself and his pleasures. He flirted with all the wives of his buddies, including her. She said she always felt uncomfortable around him and in later years she feared he may have abused me. Often a molester will shower their victim with gifts, treats and a promise to marry his victim so they have a bond that won't be broken.

I discovered while writing this book that my whole life wasn't always about my sadness. There were good times, good memories. Dad's mother, was like a second mother to me. If I wasn't 'helping' her in the kitchen, she was always available when I needed support or help.

When grandma baked, I 'helped'. Pies were the most difficult. I had wet sticky pastry dough clinging to my hands, up my arms and most times on the floor.

Grandma didn't have a washing machine. All the laundry was done on a scrub board in the bath tub. As I often watched her, she'd quietly listen to me chatter away about my adventures outside with my imaginary friend.

I was about eleven years old and babysitting my two sisters, when my puppy went missing. I phoned grandma who asked if I had looked under the bed. "Yes, he's not there" I babbled uncontrollably. Grandma travelled for an hour across the entire city to my rescue and found the puppy under my bed peering at us from a dark corner, snuggled against the wall with her tail thumping the floor.

Grandma often took me to lunch and a movie on Saturdays. In the late 1940s, Saturday matinees were for the kids; cartoons, an episode of a serial, usually 'cowboys and indians', followed by the main feature. Grandma would endure the entire two hour session in a theatre full of screaming, fidgeting children. And she endured even more when one afternoon at the Exhibition, after a ride on the "Tilt-a-whirl", she vomited all the junk food she had consumed.

Grandpa was the one who taught me how to tell time. I was probably four or five. He'd sit me on his lap, with his large pocket watch in hand, patiently pointing the hours and minutes. I became his shadow in the garden as he tended to his flowers, digging holes in the fall for the bulbs and removing them in the spring after they'd flowered. He pruned the plumb tree and set fire to the tent caterpillars' web that clung to the finer branches. I watched in amazement as the nest was engulfed in flames.

From time to time, mom would take me to visit her grandparents, the McDougals. I seldom saw great grandma because she was always in bed, which in my immature mind made her seem very mysterious. I didn't know until just recently that she had cancer and dementia.

Grandpa McDougal was special to me. He was big and tall, old and wrinkled with white hair and a kind face. It's obvious to me now they didn't have much money. He had lost his assets as a successful rancher during the thirties. But at the time, I didn't care; I was spending time with my great grandpa McDougal.

I was fascinated with how he made toast. He didn't have a toaster so he put the slices of bread on the surface of the wood stove. When it was ready, he'd pour a cup of tea and we'd sit at the table next to the window and visit. If my mother had made toast that way, I'm sure I would have refused to eat it. I was probably five or six. When grandma McDougal died, grandpa sent me her gold heart locket. Special memories.

Chapter Four

While writing this book I often asked my mother to remember segments of my life when I was young, that I could not remember. I asked her about my emotional or physical problems when I was very young. She recalled that when I was about five, she noticed a drastic change in my behavior. I withdrew and became very quiet, more than usual. She said that one day when I sat on the toilet I began crying because it hurt to pee. The doctor said I had picked up a parasite. Several painful penicillin shots were required. I wonder now, if that was a sexually transmitted disease from an abuser.

I began wetting my bed. I would wake through the night curled up at the foot of my bed because the sheets and blankets were wet. In the bathroom I imagined a hand would reach up from the toilet and grab me. I always made sure I left the door open in case I had to make a quick get-a-way. As an adult, when I went into a public bathroom stall, I wondered if anyone was watching me. Was I doing this in view of the public? Had I removed my underwear?

When I was about six years old, I began dance lessons. We wore white and red checkered costumes as our regular dance wear along with the typical black tap shoes with the heavy metal pieces on the sole of the toe and heel. I loved dancing. I felt like I glided across stage with a sense of freedom. My class was beginning to learn ballet when my emotional problems interfered with my dancing. My teacher said I wasn't focusing on the routines. Eventually I dropped out.

I began to have terrifying nightmares and felt anxious most of the time? *One of the nightmares began with me running away from someone. He would be so close I could feel the warmth of his hands. My body would tense, I stopped breathing, then, I would levitate and begin flying above his reach just as I woke.* Each nightmare left me frightened and feeling alone.

The most traumatic nightmare filled my sleep with terror. *The room was suddenly filled with snakes. There was no escape, no room to move and barely enough space to breathe. They filled every corner and crevice of the room and me. The images and feelings of those snakes slithering against my body, around my face, between my legs have been unforgettable. They were everywhere. Slimy, sinister, indifferent.*

The nightmares were always there in the black of the night, unexpected, yet familiar.

The family doctor referred me to play therapy for diagnosis. I recall standing in a line of boys and girls, stripped down to our underpants. One by one the doctor examined us. I was embarrassed. The doctor and nurse chuckled when they saw my attempts to cover my nakedness with my skinny arms. Their behaviour further humiliated and shamed me.

For several days, I remember being excused from class and went to this place where I was involved in play therapy: finger painting, folding pieces of paper and telling how many pieces I had with each fold and coloring with crayons. The counselor was concerned about one particular painting I had done. It was the picture of a hand, palm down on the page, sliding down the page with blood trickling down, and all my coloring was outlined in black.

The sessions were difficult for me because I was afraid I was going to make a mistake. I didn't understand there was no right or wrong in any of the tasks they gave me. After a number of sessions a diagnosis was sent to my doctor that I had pent up anger and control issues. Long term therapy was recommended. Dad's parents took control. They refused to believe there was anything wrong with me. So I didn't get help.

The snakes were in my nightmares well into my adult life whenever I was under duress or emotionally distraught. The last time I had such a nightmare was as recent as 2009 when I was restricted to bed for four months unable to move without extreme sciatic pain.

The nightmares about snakes made no sense. I couldn't understand why I was haunted by them. In a dream, snakes can be considered a phallic symbol, but what did they mean in my case? What was the connection? I already realized I had spent most of my life in a state of anxiety. Where these snakes a symbol of the source of my anxiety?

My search for answers proved to be a long journey compounded by other traumas, more anguish and mental and emotional imbalances, creating a myriad of feelings and behaviours that ruled my life. They became part of who I have become. I was nine when I was in play therapy and much later I was in therapy sporadically through the years to the present time. I had managed to change some things about myself, but I just couldn't get a grip on why the flashbacks wouldn't stop.

Perhaps there was more to remember? Perhaps I just needed to understand how and why these things happened to me. Perhaps I had a sign on my forehead that said "abuse me". Perhaps, perhaps, perhaps. So many questions. I would learn the answers later in life.

Chapter Five

I didn't have any sisters or brothers yet. Apparently mom was told she shouldn't have any more children due to medical issues. But one day, mom and dad brought home a six month old baby boy. Their intention was to adopt him. Suddenly I was no longer the centre of attention. I became jealous. Dad never did take to me and now he was giving his attention to this boy they named, Mark. Maybe he had always wanted me to be a boy. It felt that way. However, I overcame my resentment of this baby and often would rise in the morning to heat his bottle and feed him.

A disturbing memory was how my parents dealt with one of Mark's problems. I remember seeing him in a high chair crying and screaming. When he was like this he would eventually hold his breath. Mom or dad would throw cold water in his face to startle him and get him breathing again. I was always afraid when that happened. I saw cruelty in their behaviour.

In 1948, even less attention was given to me when mom brought home a baby girl, Betty. Now there were four of us and the tenement housing was too small. We had to move. Our first house was perfect. I had my own bedroom, a nice lawn in the front to run through the sprinklers on a hot summer day. The back yard was divided into a vegetable garden and space for a shed that stored my second hand bike and garden tools, until it burned down one summer day destroying my precious bike.

The house was also big enough that on the eve of Christmas, grandma and grandpa Dutton would stay overnight to be with us Christmas morning. Mom, grandma and myself, would sleep in one bed and I guess, dad and grandpa shared a bed upstairs. I'd wake when the sun hadn't begun to light up the sky and ask if Santa had come yet. Grandma would say "probably". That's when I was allowed to get up and bring my stocking stuffed with a coloring book, crayons and of course candy to bed until a reasonable hour for the adults to rise. Dad and grandpa, having had too much to drink the night before, would stumble down the stairs to a room full of electric energy, their hair disheveled and eyes only partly opened. They'd reach for the egg-nog and that's when the fun began.

I started school (1948) while living in that house. Mom accompanied me on my first day showing me how to get there on my own. We entered the alley from our backyard, which lead directly to the school grounds. The next day I was without the comforts and safety of my mother. On one side of the alley were houses, but on the other side was a spooky, dark forest. I was certain something was watching me in the dense recesses of the bush. After one long scary walk to school I decided I was too uncomfortable walking the alley and for the rest of the school year, I made those extra steps around the block of houses to travel the sidewalk.

The dark brick school building had been established for a number of years. It looked tired. This was an old neighborhood with tall trees to the right of the building and small shabby housing on the left side. The largest part of the school yard was near the girl's entrance. The other side was for the boys with their entrance to the building.

One bright morning I was following alongside a high dense hedge that surrounded a small house, kicking loose stones onto the unkept boulevard. I was almost to the intersection, across from the school, when a man in a beige trench coat suddenly appeared from around the corner of the hedge. His tall frame bent over me. I looked up as he asked: "My daughter is afraid to go to school on her own, can you come with me and take her to school with you?" My response, thank goodness was: "you know where the school is, why don't you bring her yourself?" and I walked on to the school grounds, firm in my walk, but feeling his eyes on me until I was among my school mates. I don't recall feeling upset during the day. School time went on as usual. Over dinner I revealed to my parents, what had happened that morning?

I was in a deep sleep when my mother gently woke me: "come, talk to the policeman about what happened this morning." Blurry eyed and uncertain, I took mom's comforting hand and walked with her into the living room. The policeman, in his dark blue suit, sitting on the couch, invited me to sit beside him. I was dwarfed by his size. But his voice didn't reflect his bulk. Calmly the officer spoke quietly, asking me to give a description of the man I met in the morning and relay what he said. I told him what I remembered and returned to bed drifting back to sleep.

A few days later the police reported to mom, that this man was dangerous and had been apprehended. I wasn't sure what that meant, but mom said the policeman thanked me for helping. Now, I am grateful to my intellect and courage that I didn't go with the "dangerous man". Where did that strong self-assurance come from? Where was it when I needed that self-protection years later?

After that experience, I was keenly aware of my surroundings front and back, checking the road and the other side of the street. One day during my diligent cross checking, I saw someone behind me. When I looked, a man in a beige trench coat was following. Or, at least I thought he was. He looked too much like the "bad man". I walked faster, he was getting closer. I became frightened. I couldn't get far enough away from him, so I took the first gate to someone's house, ran up the steps and rang the doorbell. No response. I pounded on the door with my little fist. My heart was beating fast, certain he would grab me off the porch between the beats of my heart. Finally, a sleepy woman, her grey hair tousled from her night's sleep, opened the door slightly. She peered out from the behind the door with her head barely visible while in exasperation and fear, I told her a man was chasing me. In a low voice and annoying gestures with the flick of her hand, said "go around to the alley and don't bother me". Shocked and wanting to push her aside and enter her house and safety, I reluctantly did what I was told. I gathered what bravery I had left and went to the scary alley. Nothing further occurred. I didn't bother telling my parents. Perhaps I already felt defeated by the old woman's gruff response to my pleading.

When Mark was around two, I came home and he was gone as mysteriously as he had arrived. No one told me he was leaving or why. I was glad he was gone; maybe attention would return to me . . . I thought. I told a friend how I felt. She told mom. "Ah, why would you say that", with that tone in her voice to inject a guilty feeling in me as was her usual way of discipline. Mom never slapped or spanked me, I never had "time outs", but, she knew how to make me feel guilty. And I did.

Mom told me years later Mark was not well. He had a mental disability, dragged one leg, was cross-eyed and he had become violent.

Mom was probably busy with the new baby and unable to give him the attention he needed. The message to me though, at that age, was that when you aren't perfect, you get sent back. However, that rule didn't last.

In 1949, fourteen months following Betty's arrival, Ellen was born. There was something different about this baby; but I wasn't privy. No one talked about her condition in front of me. She was always bound up in her blankets with only her head visible.

When Ellen was still considered a newborn, mom and dad took her away, leaving Betty and I with grandma and grandpa. I would later learn; mom and dad took Ellen to a special hospital out of town for reconstructive surgery on her arms and hands. Her condition was caused by an anti-nausea pill mom took during her pregnancy. Jacquie's condition was similar to thalidomide babies born the following years. There were many more trips and surgeries to follow. My job, at the age of eight, was to help mom with the babies.

Ellen's life was not easy. Mom's mission was to make Ellen strong to withstand the discrimination and pain brought on by ignorant people. Mom insisted that Ellen struggle to find ways to deal with daily activity and told us we couldn't help her. But, Betty was to watch over her at school. Apparently Betty didn't think that was such a great idea and often was mean to Ellen as siblings can be. I don't remember much about how Ellen interacted in the family. She seemed to be away so much that is was almost like she wasn't part of the family.

Only once in her young life did she cross me. I was about seventeen and I had left my purse in the living room. I discovered that my money was gone and that same day, Ellen came home with an expensive glass ash tray. Mom questioned her and Ellen admitted she'd taken my money. Mom got dad's belt, took Ellen to the garage and struck her so often, Ellen told me years later, that she couldn't go to school for days because of the bruising and pain. I may not have seen this happen but I felt it. I felt the tension, the sadness, the anger. And I was scared and sorry for Ellen.

Radio was a wonderful form of entertainment when I was a child. In the evenings and on Sundays, we all listened to the big shows like: Edgar Bergan and Charlie McCarthy, Amos and Andy, The Hornet,

The Shadow and Inner Sanctum (the last two would scare me, but I listened anyway). When I was very little; I'd press my ear against grandma's big radio and wonder how all those people fit into that box. When I was a little older, I had a routine of listening to radio shows that I loved. Roy Rogers and Dale Evans were my heroes. If I was outside playing, mom would call me saying that Roy Rogers was going to be airing in five minutes. I'd run home and sit glued to the radio. When it was over, I'd return to play with my friends.

Every Saturday, I'd listen to "Eaton's Good Deed Club" sponsored by Eaton stores. It showcased talented children and encouraged us to be kind and helpful. Someone had to write in to the show to tell of a good deed by a child they knew or the child could do this on their own. They rewarded good deeds with: first a Good Deed pin, then ribbons to hang on the pin for each good deed performed. But there was a bigger prize once all the ribbons were awarded. I already had two ribbons but I coveted the watch. That was for a special deed. I listened faithfully to the show, hoping in some mysterious way, my name would be called. But with every airing, I was disappointed.

Then it happened. I heard my name. Not quite able to believe what I heard, I pressed my ear to the radio, my eyes wide open as if I would hear better than if they were closed. The announcer was reading a letter. A letter my mother had sent describing the things I did for her when she had two babies to care for. I was ecstatic, jumping up and down and screeching "I won!" A few days later, grandma took me to the radio studio to pick up my watch. I wore it with pride until years later when it stopped working.

Shortly after the birth of my new sister, Ellen, dad lost his job. For a short time there was no money coming into the family until he began working at the furniture factory. They barely had enough money to raise three young children, especially with Ellen's special needs. I added to their problems.

It was a warm sunny day. My neighbor and I were playing tag in the back yard; dad was tending to the vegetable garden and mom was in the house. To escape the touch of my playmate, I ran up onto a stack of lumber by the fence. I began to slip.

As I grabbed one of the fence boards, it gave way causing me to fall onto my back on the graveled alley. My left arm slapped the ground and twisted. I lay motionless until dad picked me up and carried me into the house. A bone was protruding at the elbow. Our next door neighbor came over after hearing the commotion and held my arm while we waited for someone to drive me to the hospital.

The emergency room was packed with people suffering from various conditions. Someone put an ice pack under my arm while mom and I waited hours for a doctor to examine me. X-rays revealed extensive damage. My injury was called an "inside out elbow" which meant the bones at the elbow were sticking out. My arm was not only broken, but, I had nerve damage. Two surgeries and I still had no sensation in my arm from the elbow down. A neurosurgeon was scheduled for my third surgery. If this didn't work, they would amputate.

No one told me when surgeries were going to be performed. A nurse would just show up one day and stick needles in me. After the second surgery, no one said I was going home, so I lay in bed watching the nurse come into the ward each day with needles and fearing that one of them would be for me. Days went by and then, without warning, the nurse came to my bed with her tray of needles. I hated them and didn't understand why I had to tolerate this pain.

Preparation for this surgery is well entrenched in my memory. They had to freeze the nerves leading to my arm. I am sure the needle was very long and fat. Someone thrust it into the left side of my neck. Shocked, I screamed, gyrated, kicked and pleaded with them to stop. They continued to sink one painful needle after the other into my neck. I couldn't stop them and I couldn't run away. I became frozen, like wild prey downed by its predator. Moments later the dreadful stinky mask was placed over my nose and I slipped into the drugged darkness.

The surgery worked and shortly there was talk of sending me home. Halloween was approaching and I wanted to be a part of it and no longer face the fear and pain of needles and surgery, but my appendix had other ideas.

In disbelief, the nurse with the tray of needles came to my bedside, again. I was trapped in this awful place. The appendix had erupted and removal was compulsory. This meant another surgery, more needles and disappointment; I may not go home for trick or treating.

The day before Halloween, the doctor agreed to send me home. I was ecstatic. I was out of this tortuous place. I left the hospital after weeks of surgeries and recovery; my stomach stitched and my arm in a cast and sling for the next three months.

On about the third month, I was playing at school and a school mate ran toward me, slamming her body against mine. She didn't mean to hurt me, but her force caused a crack in my cast at the elbow. I was terrified. She looked frightened. I thought maybe I would have to go through surgery again. I cried all the way home. Mom took me to our family doctor who then ordered X-rays. There was no damage, in fact, the cast could come off!

The process, if you've even seen it done, is scary. The doctor used an electric saw that cut through the cast. I was certain he'd cut my arm off so I was pulling away from him as he was trying his best to hold onto my arm.

When the cast was removed, we all discovered that I couldn't extend the lower part of my arm. It had been in the cast so long that the muscles had shortened. The doctor pulled on my arm in an attempt to extend it, while I pulled back, fighting him all the way. It was clear my arm was not going to open. For the next several weeks at home, I had to carry mom's iron in my left hand to encourage the muscles to stretch. Eventually the "treatment" worked and I have never had trouble with that arm since. Apparently, the surgery made medical history in the successful treatment of an "inside-out elbow".

At that age I wasn't aware of the cost of medical care, so when I heard my mother tell friends that my broken arm cost them $1000, I felt guilty that I had caused more financial difficulties for them. Mom told me recently that the costs were absorbed between the doctors and the hospital.

Individual families in their backyards would customarily set off fireworks on Hallowe'en. I had finished my rounds in the neighborhood with my friends and was ready for the fireworks display. Dad wasn't home yet, so mom, Betty and Ellen watched from the kitchen window, while I set off the fireworks. Not the best thing for an 8 year old, but I did okay until the final rocket. It didn't go off. I was curious.

I cut the rocket open and laid the tiny parts on the porch table. I lit a match, bent over and poof! The full power of all those tiny particles, that when combined make a large dazzling explosion in the sky, flared-up in my face. The brilliant flash momentarily blinded me. I ran into the house screaming, certain I was scarred for life and might never see again. Mom applied a cool wet towel to my face and looked closer. "Look at your face in the mirror, it's okay". I was too terrified to look, thinking my whole face was gone. As it turned out, my eyebrows and lashes were singed but there was no damage to my skin or eyes.

Feeling relieved, I changed gears and proceeded to devour my cache of sweets. It was shortly after my encounter with fireworks, that an article appeared in the newspaper reporting an incident where a rocket; instead of going up in the air, spun through the crowd and killed someone. I think it was that same year that City Council declared fireworks would be banned except in approved areas set off by professionals. I never set off the fireworks again until I was an adult.

Chapter Six

A few years later, we moved to a brand new housing development for veterans. The house was bright, clean and fresh. The streets were wide, young trees were set and the grass seed in the front of each house had just begun to sprout. It was 1951, the year our family expanded.

In May, Mathew was born. Finally, a boy for dad. This was the time I discovered the anatomical difference between a boy and a girl. Our family was very private when it came to our bodies. I had never seen mom or dad without clothes. When mom was changing Mathew's diaper, I asked: "how do you know it's a boy?" Her response quickly and quietly pointing: "What's down there". I was satisfied with the answer and needed no further information, but I also got another message: talking about "down there", was embarrassing.

I made three friends fairly quickly: Marilyn, across the street, Nancy next door and Lorie across the alley.

When Lorie and I got together we were a bad mix. We did nothing that was good for us or, as it turned out, not good for someone else.

She and I learned to smoke. When I babysat my siblings, Lorie would steal tobacco and papers from her parents and come to my house. We'd spend hours learning how to roll a cigarette, then more hours smoking ragged roll-your-owns, one after the other, certain our parents were unsuspecting. After all, dad smoked, so there wouldn't be a change in the smell of the house. However, we managed to burn a few holes in the tablecloth. When mom asked me what was going on, I told her we were experimenting for a science project. Nothing further was mentioned.

When I stayed overnight at Lorie's, we shared her single bed. By that time I had stopped wetting the bed, but she hadn't. In the morning we'd be soaked in her urine.

We often played doctor, pretending to torture each other. The "victim" would struggle and cry out in pretend pain. There seemed to be no boundaries to our "play". The more pretend pain we could inflict the better.

I made friends with a boy in my class that lived close by. Greg seemed like a nice kid but he and Lorie didn't get along. I don't know what their problem was, but they argued and physically fought. The last time Greg would be allowed to enter my house was the time they were fighting by the front door. I guess his hand, which was likely intended for her face, missed her and swung to the side, going through the thick window of the door, creating a noise loud enough that my neighbor heard it. He rushed over and called an ambulance.

Greg came to school a few days later with a thick bandage on his hand. He required a lot of stitches to save his thumb. He told me then, he was forbidden to come to my place any more. I felt very sad and scared for Greg and myself. What kind of anger did he carry that caused so much rage at the age of eleven that he could shatter a plate glass window with his fist? That evening also ended the baby-sitting sessions with Lorie. I would have to entertain myself while babysitting my siblings.

Marilyn and Nancy were quiet, well-mannered girls. We would draw on scraps of paper, color in a coloring book or play with our dolls. It was quite a contrast to Lorie. Often Nancy and I would create a play, usually something with a moral ending. We'd go from house to house in our block and invite kids to come and watch. It only cost a penny. We would perform in my backyard or Nancy's, providing snacks for everyone, usually dry bread with pieces of apple. When the Red Cross had a fund raising campaign, Nancy and I donated our small fortune to the cause. It could not have been very much because we only had an audience of five or six kids at each performance.

My sisters and I often played in dad's car. Dad parked it by the curb in front of our house which was situated at the top of a hill. My sisters would take the roles as mother and child and I was the dad who was driving us to a picnic. I would wiggle the steering wheel, press the pedals and move the gear shift. One day, the car suddenly began to move, slowly at first, and then it began to pick up speed. Fortunately for us, our neighbor came bouncing out of his house, ripped the driver's door open and pulled the emergency brake. We were barred from using the car as a toy.

I loved softball and did very well. Usually, in the evenings and on weekends a bunch of us would get together at our school and play. It was near supper time and mom needed something at the store which was a few blocks away, across from the school. I was to return home directly, no detours.

Probably an hour later, I was standing in the batter's box when I saw dad passing by in his car. A shock of electricity pierced my gut; I dropped the bat, picked up the groceries and began to run. I kept yelling "daddy", but he kept moving until he rounded the corner and was out of sight. I'm sure he knew I was calling. I ran the rest of the way home, terrified I'd be in trouble. Not much was said except the usual: "when I say come right home, I mean come right home!"

When I was about ten, I had a personal victory. I had never taken swimming lessons, not because I was afraid of the water, I loved it. Mom and I spent many summer hours on the beach from the time I was a baby. When I was older I taught myself how to swim, usually under the watchful eye of my grandmother. I observed accomplished swimmers, how they moved their arms, rolled their head and body to one side to grasp the air, sink that side into the water again and propel forward; over and over again. The trick was not to be exhausted by any undue splashing while paddling the feet. But, I hadn't yet trusted the ocean or myself to swim in deep water. I always swam parallel to the beach.

One summer I gathered my courage. Uncle Arnold and his wife, Lindsay, lived in a small seaside community. He was a lumberjack and spent many days in the forest away from home. She was lonely and asked if I could spend the summer with her.

The harbor accommodated many yachts; large and small, while the people on board were on vacation or celebrating a long weekend. The small yachts moored at the docks, while the larger ones anchored in the bay. Their presence gave the harbour a touch of elegance. I'd sit on the dock, gazing at these beautiful floating hotels and dream of a life that was theirs.

To entertain myself, I went swimming. I had the option of swimming in the ocean off the dock or the lagoon. I knew the dark waters off the dock were deep so I considered the lagoon. It was a huge pond, bigger than any swimming pool I had ever seen. It was fed by the ocean and barricaded by netting at one end to prevent jelly fish and large crabs from entering and endangering the children. The rest of the lagoon was surrounded by trees and shrubs and an outcrop of smooth flat granite that hovered over the water. There was no beach. The only way to go swimming was to jump off the rock, but, only if you were brave enough to get past the little pea crabs huddled together bathing in the sun.

At first I was wary of those little crabs crawling around. I didn't want to get bitten. But, the local kids encouraged me. My best bet was to take a running jump and cannonball into the water, avoiding the crabs entirely. With trepidation, I jumped over the crabs and into the waist deep lagoon water. Following that first jump, swimming in the lagoon was a part of my daily activities. I also discovered the crabs weren't interested in me anyway. In fact, they scattered whenever humans were around.

The dark waters around the docks intrigued me. I decided this was the place I could do it; I would learn how to swim in deep water. Every ten feet or so, there were ladders fastened to the dock leading to the water. I climbed down the ladder into the deep blue water, swam to the next ladder and climbed out. I had done it! Success! However, I did it with my eyes closed. I knew I had to open my eyes because that was the safest and only way to swim. I climbed down the ladder, entered the water, still gripping the last rung. I could feel my heart beating. This was scary stuff, but I was determined. I released my grip, took a few strokes, and then opened my eyes to a startling discovery. The sea was pitch black. I panicked. I gulped water. My arms began thrashing at the water. I realized, not only was I swimming in water over my head, but I couldn't see or touch the bottom. My strokes doubled and my legs worked harder to move me to the next ladder as if someone was chasing me. I never went back to the docks to swim, but, I had inducted myself into the prestigious position of swimming in deep water; going into the unknown and reaching beyond my fear.

People in the area were preparing for a regatta. Word had gotten out that I was a strong and well-formed swimmer. One day, a coach for the swim team approached and asked if I'd like to be a part of the team because, he said, I was really good. I said no, I was leaving for home in a few days, but also, I turned them down fearing I'd do poorly. I didn't believe I was good enough to help the team win. How unfortunate that I didn't ask my parents for more time.

Roller skating was a way to get from one place to another quickly, short of riding a bike. My skates were the kind that attached to your regular shoes with clamps that grasped the toe area and tightened with a key. A leather strap straddled the ankle. I skated everywhere I could; to the store for mom; by myself or with friends. During the winter, I changed to ice skating. I taught myself how to ice skate and could actually do fancy whirls and jumps. If we could have afforded figure skating lessons, I would have eagerly taken them.

Even though we lived in a brand new house, we still didn't have much money, so mom made a lot of my clothes. I was standing in line at school when a girl, who always wore pretty dresses, made a comment about my clothes being homemade and not purchased in a store like hers. I felt so ashamed and asked mom if I could have store bought clothes. I don't remember if I got them at the time, but I did later when I was a young teen.

After my brief friendship with Lorie, I concentrated on skills development in Brownies and then moved up to Girl Guides where I passed with the highest marks in the City. My reward was a survival pocket knife, presented to me at a school gathering.

While on vacation one year, we visited the Wilson's, family friends who had moved to a small city in the mountains. Mom and dad made the decision to move there. This decision was at great expense to me. It meant leaving my friends, my softball team, girl guides, a really nice house and the close proximity to my grandparents. I went along with the flow. It wasn't my decision, I didn't have a choice. I was twelve. On the other hand, I discovered, I could have a lot of fun there.

We lived, for a short while, in a cabin on the lake close to Wilson's house. This was a great place because I could spend every day on the beach and swimming. The motel owners had a St. Bernard dog that was trained to be protective of children. My brother often climbed all over that huge dog while he rested on the sand. For fun, we would go into the deep water and yell for help. He would toss my brother off and dive into the water to save us.

A month later, my folks found a large old farm house in the country, twenty-three miles from the city. This was a great place. It had: a neglected apple orchard, three cherry trees, a vegetable garden, a boat house with a dock and a great beach.

In March, my friend and I, in our bathing suits would soak up the sun on the deck until we were hot, cover our bodies with cold cream and jump into the glacial waters of the lake, jump out instantly and lie on the boathouse deck to warm up in the spring sun.

In July, we would sit in the cherry tree, well into the darkness of the night, watching the stars and eating "just one more".

Some nights we'd ride our bikes five or more miles to the drive in, sneak under the screen and sit on the mound with a speaker between us. Then we'd ride home in the dark with no reflecting clothes or lights on our bikes. We were lucky. The mountain roads have many blind corners and narrow shoulders. We would not have been visible to the best of drivers. I knew it was illegal to ride a bike without lights, but mom gave me a non-functioning flashlight and told me, if we were stopped to tell the police that the batteries went dead in my flashlight.

The house was a long distance for dad to drive every day to work and back, so my parents decided to move into town and buy an old Victorian house on a rent-to-own agreement. The two story house was very old. It had: a covered porch in the front, paint peeling from the siding and it smelled musty, but, it was roomy and close to the schools. I would no longer have to ride the school bus. To heat the house, rusty old water radiators sat under a window in each room. A large fireplace in the living room added extra warmth on cold stormy nights.

Being in the city meant mom could also get a job. She was first employed as a cook and waitress at the lunch counter of the local bowling alley. Shortly after she started there, she also became the manager. Later on, she was also certified to teach bowling on top of her other duties. Bowling was a part of mom's family achievements. Her grandfather, her brother and when I was an adult were champions in the sport.

Her day began by walking down the hill twelve or more blocks to work, then put in her eight or more hours and walk home to resume her job as homemaker, wife and mother. Mom had a history of respiratory illness and it's possible that all this work began a downward spiral to ill health.

Chapter Seven

In the fall, I entered grade eight. My life was expanding and I was busy. Sports became my world: soccer, basketball, (tallying five baskets in ten minutes of play from center line), swimming, ice skating and softball, qualified me as an accomplished athlete. On our softball team we gave one another nicknames. I had mentioned that my grandmother use to call me "Dizzy". And that was how I was identified by the team. This made me feel special. Like I was somebody and I was accepted.

In the winter we glided down hills on our sleighs or skated on the icy roads grinding down the sharp edges of our skates. But it was free fun. Sometimes, if there was money, I'd go to the movies on Saturday. Summer was spent packing a lunch and walking down the hill to the city park and beach. It wasn't the same as living on the house by the lake, but I was young, strong and didn't mind walking a mile or so to the lake.

I had just entered grade nine when my world and our family's world turned upside down. Daylight was approaching. My mother was coughing. I listened. She could not seem to stop. Still dressed in my night clothes I went to their bedroom and I watched her; hunched over, her arms wrapped around herself, trying to breathe. The distortion of her face told me the pain in her chest was unbearable. Her lungs were on fire, her belly swollen and she was exhausted. Looking into the darkness, she told me more recently, was like looking through water, cloudy, unable to focus. I was scared.

The family doctor was called. As he entered the house, he knew at a glance mom was in trouble. Removing his coat, he wrapped it around her, gathered her now ninety pounds and carried her to his car and to the hospital. My mother was gone and I became her replacement. I was fourteen. She was diagnosed with pneumococcus meningitis, a very serious illness in those days.

Soccer games ended, Christmas was approaching and Mom was still in the hospital. I was outside clearing the snow from the sidewalk when a woman came to the house with an armful of wrapped Christmas gifts and a turkey. She asked my name. I asked who she was. She said she was Santa's helper. Later we learned she was delivering on behalf of the Salvation Army.

Christmas without mom was a sad time. But with the charitable gifts, Christmas was bearable. On the weekend before Christmas dad went into the bush and brought home a Charlie Brown pine tree. We decorated, placed our Salvation Army gifts under the tree and lit the fire in the fireplace to set the mood. The younger ones weren't as affected by the absence of mom, or at least they didn't say anything, so they were excited. Dad cooked our Christmas dinner and we sat down to eat without mom.

In those days, children were not allowed to visit patients in the hospital, but mom was dying. Clothed in my best dress, a hat and gloves, just to look older, dad took me to the hospital. As I entered the public ward I searched the room for my mother. There were women lying in their beds at various stages of illness. My eyes fell upon my mother as she lay under a white sheet and blanket; pale, much smaller and looking worn-out. I knew she was very ill but I wasn't aware that she could die. Those details were kept to the adults. I just knew I had no mother to count on and I was in charge of my three siblings, ranging from three to seven years of age. And I had my own tale of woe.

I began to cry. I cried because I was a kid looking after kids and a house. I cried because I missed my mom. I cried because of what happened in school. I couldn't hold back my emotions.

As I began to unravel my story, mom watched the tears roll down my face. The scene was my home economics cooking class. We were preparing creamy eggs. The instructions were to cook this combination of milk and eggs in the top a double boiler. I stood by the stove slowly stirring the ingredients unaware that the bottom pan was getting very hot. Smoke began to rise from the rings of the stove sending a stench into the air and alerting my teacher. She rushed over lifting the pot from the overheated rings on the stove leaving the bottom of the pan welded to the rings. I had forgotten to put water in the bottom pot.

She burst into a fit of rage yelling on how stupid I was and ordered me to sit in the corner of the room and observe. Humiliated and embarrassed I sat on the cold hard chair, facing the room for everyone to see. Fear of other possible punishments filled my mind. My fellow students glanced at me from time to time as they continued to make their creamy eggs. The good thing was I didn't have to eat that sloppy mess. I loved scrambled eggs, but not this. Revealing my story to my mother and not knowing what she could possibly do, I left for home.

One of mom's roommates overheard my story and consoled my mother who was distraught. Later her roommate's son, my school principal, arrived and she let him have it. "How could you let Liz be treated that way" "do you know what she and her family are going through?" "You'd better do something about this". Embarrassed by his mother's outburst, he fled the room.

My mother told me that the home economics teacher had been chastised but she never apologized.

Shortly after New Year's, mom was diagnosed with tuberculosis of the lungs and when she was strong enough, she would have to go to a sanitorium, a long distance from our town. I could no longer visit her. Letter writing was the only method of communication. Getting mom to the sanitorium wasn't going to be easy. She was very sick and weak. Dad would have to take precious time off from work and that wasn't feasible. Mom would have to get there on her own. She took the train to her grandparent's house. When great-grandpa met her at the station, he saw how diminished she had become and carried her to his car and his home. Next day he took her to the station and said good-bye, certain this would be the last time he would see her.

Dad and I took shifts caring for the house and my siblings. He worked nights at the hotel bar, so it was my job to cook supper, clean the house and get the kids to bed. In the morning I went off to school, while he took care of the family and house until I got home, then he'd leave for work. On weekends, I cleaned the house. There was no time for socializing after school. I had a job to do and I had to arrive home on time.

I had no experience with the type of heating system we had in this old house and noises from the radiators scared me. To resolve the problem the stiff release valves had to be opened. When I was babysitting I was certain the radiators would explode. I'd call dad at the bar and he'd tell me to open the release valve, I'd do it, but I was concerned until he came home at two in the morning.

Finally he introduced me to his friend and next door neighbor, Shorty. This man was massive, at least that's the way my fifteen year old mind saw him. Dad told me to call Shorty anytime I was nervous and he'd come over to help me. Well, he was more than happy to "help" . . . . himself.

It was particularly cold this one evening. A snow storm was raging. The radiators were hot as a fire and . . . noisy. I went around releasing the air from the radiators, but they continued to make noises. I thought they were going to blow up. Scared I called Shorty. In short time, his dark burly body filled our doorway as the raging storm swirled snow around him. We went around to each radiator and he stopped the noises.

The last radiator was in the bathroom upstairs. I stepped into the bathroom to show him where it was. Shorty stood in the doorway filling it with his mammoth body. He took my tiny innocent hand in his, bent down like a giraffe to pluck a small morsel at a lower level of the tree and kissed me on the lips. My body stiffened. I froze. I was terrified. Why was he doing this? What next would he do to me? I couldn't breathe. Out of fear I did and said nothing. We walked out of the bathroom hand in hand down the stairs and he left the same way he came . . . filling the doorway then vanishing into the winter storm.

My body shook with fear and revulsion. I resolved never to call him again. It was easier to live with the scary noises. I never told dad out of fear of the unknown. Maybe it was my fault. Would dad believe me? And what would Shorty do to me if I told dad? And what would dad do? There were too many unknowns. All the options that I could think of might not have a good outcome for me.

From time to time dad would bring in a woman from the bar to clean house and make soup, bread, lunch and dinner for us. I loved those days. I'd walk into the house for lunch absorbing the delectable aromas, then inhaling the buns with butter that drizzled down my fingers into my palms. The soup contained vegetables I would never have eaten, but everything was so delicious, I devoured the soup to the last drop. When she was gone I was back doing the work that my mom would have done, including being available to my dad. At least that was the way it felt.

On this odd day that dad and I were home at the same time, I was in the kitchen washing dishes when he came behind me, pressed his body against my back, reached around with his left arm and with his hand, cupped my breast. I had seen him do this often with mom and I could see by her expression she was uncomfortable. The whole image was dirty, and now it was happening to me. I'm only fifteen and I'm his daughter! I felt like a wife. He immediately pulled himself away and said "Sorry, so sorry honey". It didn't matter how sorry he was, I still felt repulsed and petrified. He was my dad and he was supposed to protect me.

Now there was no one to help me when I got scared. I feared I would be compromised at any time. Shortly after, grandma came to stay with us for a few weeks. But when she was gone, I went back to my domestic duties, school and being anxious. I never told anyone about Shorty or dad's fondling, not even to my mother. Mom had arranged for me to go to my home room teacher for help, but I couldn't tell her either. I was afraid. I don't know of what. Just afraid. Now I trusted no one. I had nowhere to turn. I was trapped and helpless.

There were times when I took my anger out on my dog Lady, a sleak black and white beagle cross. She and I were connected at the hip, but one day she was underfoot. I screamed at her, opened the basement door and kicked her down the stairs. She stayed quietly there until I had calmed down and I let her up. I was so distraught by what I had done. We cuddled together for a long time while I cried.

Time passed, I had no mother, my father and I barely saw each other and I had taken on the responsibilities of an adult. Final exams were coming, but the school in their compassion and understanding promoted me to grade ten so I wouldn't have to go through the stress of writing exams. I probably wouldn't have passed anyway.

Chapter Eight

Dad knew a number of people because he worked in a bar in a small community. I guess he spoke with a couple about mom being in the hospital and that led to another change. The McPhees lived by the lake and on their property they had a summer cottage and offered it to us for the summer.

The cottage had two very small rooms and a bathroom. We kids would sleep in the bedroom and dad would sleep on the pullout couch in the other room that included a kitchen. The cabin was on the beach and close to McPhee's family home where they could help me out if I had a problem while dad was working. I became friends with their daughter, Beth. The four of us spent most of our time on the beach and in the water playing with the neighboring kids.

Beth had an older brother who was, most days, on the lake in his small outboard. The lake was calm, the sky clear and dad was home. The brother, I don't remember his name, asked me if I'd like to join him. That was exciting. I hadn't had an opportunity to ride in a small outboard motor boat. Eagerly I jumped in and immediately we sped off racing across the water. The wind whistled through my hair and the sun warmed my face. To talk meant to yell over the noise of the outboard, so I stayed silent.

When we were on the far side of the lake, he cut the engine. I didn't understand why we stopped. As I turned to ask what he was going to do he told me to sit in front of him. When I did, he reached around and fondled my breasts. Again I was frozen, just as I did with dad and Shorty. I was trapped in this tiny boat and a huge breadth of water between us and the safety of the beach. I don't know how long he did this, but eventually he removed his hand and started the engine to take me home. I guess he'd had enough of me and dropped me off at the beach.

What was happening to me? Did I have a sign on my forehead that says: "fondle me", "abuse me"? Now I know that, yes, I did in a way have that sign on me. Vulnerable children and adults have an air about them that is noticed by perpetrators. They watch the way we walk and talk. Our shoulders droop and we talk softly. They see in our eyes a weakness and know with gentle sweet talk, they can manipulate us into trusting them.

Dad was a contradiction and that confused me. He was inappropriate only once, but it was enough not to trust him any longer, but he also showed me compassion and understanding. I knew we were short on money so I was always careful not to waste any. I was in the dressing room at school after gym. I put my glasses on a shelf and without thinking, when I grabbed for my sweater, I swept my glasses off the shelf and onto the cement floor shattering them. I was on the verge of tears the rest of the day and terrified to tell dad. He simply said: "don't worry about it honey".

I did my best to be a homemaker. I had to learn to cook, but I had no one to show me; so the food was probably not very good. I knew for sure that the lemon pie I made hit that category without contention. Dad was at work and I decided to surprise him. I followed the instructions carefully, or so I thought. When I took the first bite I knew something was wrong. I realized I'd forgotten to put the additional two cups of water in the lemon mix! I felt like a failure and told dad I was sorry, but he simply said: "it's okay" and ate it.

One day I felt so sorry for dad. He usually did the laundry and with three very young children and one teenager, there was a lot of it. He filled the clothes line but still had more left to dry so he put them on the return line above. It wasn't a minute after he had hung everything that the whole line, clothes and all fell onto the dirt below. Not only did he have to repair the clothes line, but he had to redo the laundry.

During the time mom was away, dad was not faithful. At the cottage he would bring women home and when the lights were out, I'd hear them getting into bed. My instincts told me this was wrong, but I was a kid and didn't have the right to judge my father. But I was certainly developing an unhealthy attitude towards men. I wasn't certain what they did when they had us but I knew they were not to be trusted. I was lonely and often scared.

There was one week during the summer when the temperatures were extremely high for long time. People talked of a storm brewing. Dad was at work. Dark clouds were moving in. Rumblings could be heard on the other side of the mountains. The wind picked up, changing the ripples on the lake to white caps. The winds blew stronger, the waves higher, threatening the cottage as they crashed onto the beach. The bedroom window had been broken the day before and was covered with a tarp, but that was coming loose and flapping in the wind. Rain was soaking the bedding close by. The sky blackened and suddenly it lit up with multiple blinding flashes that filled the sky and the cottage rooms. The kids were sleeping, I think, and I was on guard, petrified. At any moment, I thought, the rising lake waters would flood the cottage, or maybe we'd be blown away, or the strong winds would bring a tree down on the cottage, or just as daunting, lightening would find its way into our rooms and electrocute us.

Lady, my dog, stayed close to my side trembling. When I moved, she moved. Then suddenly the rooms went dark. I flipped the light switches . . . nothing. I picked up the phone but it was dead. Now I couldn't call dad or the McPhees. Going outside was not an option. It was so dark I wouldn't be able to find my way to their house. We were alone and I was responsible for the safety of my sisters and brother. I couldn't see where I was going as I moved about the living room. I found a flashlight and Lady and I jumped into my bed in unison. I pulled the blankets over our heads and left the flashlight on so the lightning wouldn't be as bright or feel as menacing. I was even too scared to cry. Lady and I. Two bodies, terrified and leaving our lives up to fate under our dimly lit makeshift tent.

I guess dad came home after the storm; I don't remember. In the morning I saw why the power had failed. A huge tree that stood close to the cottage had fallen across the phone and power lines. The McPhees asked why I didn't go to their house for help, but under the circumstances, walking out into that storm was the last thing on my mind.

Chapter Nine

Mom was coming home! Dad had already moved us from the beach cottage to Mr. Reed's more spacious rental house, still close to the lake but up a gravel mountain road. We had no visible neighbors up or down from us and only one house directly across the gravel road. I loved our new home. It was an old cottage and still small; only two bedrooms for the six of us, but we managed. My siblings and I slept in one bedroom, two in each double bed. Mom and dad had the other bedroom next to us.

The house was nestled among tall trees and bush with a creek meandering through the yard carrying our own source of cold mountain water. Dad made a workshop out of the shed on the other side of the creek where he could be found making or fixing something. A clothes line hovered over the backyard from the house to a tree in the bush where it was attached. A path led through the bush and across the creek to our neighbor, Milly. If mom wasn't at home, she was likely at there.

Inside the kitchen, next to the bathroom, was a wood burning stove with an integrated water heater at one end. Above it hung a wooden clothes hanger on pulleys to bring it down to a reachable level to hang the freshly laundered clothes or wet snowsuits to dry.

The flooring was well-worn linoleum that was cold in the winter. Covering the lino in the living room was a thin faded rug. Most cleaning days, mom would sprinkle water on the rug, then sweep it with the corn broom (we didn't have a vacuum). Occasionally she would lift the rug, hang it on the clothes line and we'd beat the dirt out of it.

We had two sources of heat. The wood burning kitchen stove and a potbelly stove in the living room. During winter nights, the fires in the stoves would die making the mornings icy cold. Dad would rise in the morning before us and set the fires. When he called, we jumped out of bed and hovered around the stove while we dressed.

The garage stood alongside the steep gravel road to our house and the houses higher up the mountain. Dad would tear up the hill and make a slight turn into the garage. When I was learning to drive I mimicked dad's flurry up that hill except, when I turned off the gravel road to enter the garage I stepped on the gas instead of the brake and slammed the fender into the side of the garage, creating quite a stir. Fortunately, no one was injured.

Dad was a hard worker. He'd come home about two or three in the morning from his shift at the bar, then he'd get up when we all did, go outside and cut wood, clean the yard, work on his car, or anything else that needed his attention, then clean up and go to work. He never stopped.

I learned that year how poor we were. I often saw mom scribbling numbers on pieces of paper. Then she would sigh and walk away. She told me she was deciding on what debt she would be able to pay that month. I asked if I could figure it out. She must have been wrong I thought. When I added up the income and debt, I was shocked and scared that there was not enough money to pay the debts.

Somehow they did find the money to put an addition onto the house. It would be the same length as the house and extend over the backyard about fourteen feet. We'd then have three extra bedrooms and a heating system under the floor fueled by oil. I'd have my own room at one end and mom and dad at the other end. Between the two was a small room where my brother slept. My two sisters stayed in the original bedrooms.

There wasn't much I could do to help, but when Dad was shingling, I climbed the ladder and drove a few nails in place. It was kind of fun working alongside dad and learning a skill.

When dad had finished the addition, he began working on the original part of the house. But with any renovation, when work is done in one area, it creates a problem in another. Dad moved the kitchen sink to another part of the kitchen but then discovered the old sewer pipes were going to fail soon, so he had to replace them before he could finish working on the kitchen. In the meantime, a bucket was placed under the sink to catch the water, but if the bucket wasn't empty and someone turned on the tap or drained the sink, the bucket overflowed and water would be everywhere.

Mom had a soft heart for any drifter who came to the door asking for food. She'd ask him to wait outside while she made something, maybe no more than a peanut butter sandwich. The grateful drifter would leave once he had food in his hand. She could turn no one away.

With four kids, three under ten, a teenager and the two of them, laundry was an all day job. Mom had an old wringer washer. The only way to heat water was in the small tank at the end of the stove, so that meant winter or the heat of summer, the stove was on to heat the water. This meant that the wash water wasn't replaced very often. Once a load was wrung out, the clothes went into a metal laundry tub filled with fresh rinse water. While a new load went into the washer, she'd squeeze rinsed clothes through the wringer and hang them on the line outside. Over and over again, mom would do one load after another. If there were too many items to hang on the line or if it rained, the clothes stayed in the rinse tub until the clothes on the line were dry or the sun came out from behind the dark clouds.

It was here in this house, in this location, at this time, that my life became easier for a while. Mom was home I was free to be me.

Between spring and fall, I spent hours wandering through the bushes. There was an old fruit orchard across from us where I'd sit on top of a rock and gaze at the beauty of the lake and mountains in the distance.

When school was out for the summer, I'd jump out of bed before the sun rose, step into my bathing suit, gobble down breakfast, make a lunch, grab a towel and run down the gravel road barefoot, with my dog Lady by my side; cross the highway and be on the beach ready to swim, all within about twenty minutes.

I loved those mornings when the lake water was so still it looked like a giant mirror reflecting the mountains and sky. This was when nature was at its best. A soft warm breeze moved the leaves slightly and occasionally caused a ripple in the water; geese and ducks lazily dipped their heads into the shallow water's edge nibbling at the flora below. Sometimes the aroma of coffee and bacon cooking on a cottage stove nearby would hang in the air.

Slowly the screen doors would creak open and neighborhood kids wandered onto the beach in their pyjamas, their hair still dishevelled from the night's sleep. We'd sit on the soft sand and gaze at the water as the sun rose above the mountain tops across the lake slowly casting its warmth on the beach. When we were warm enough, we'd play in the water. Often, we'd fill a jar with sand and drop it off the far end of the wharf and dive in to see who could bring it to the surface first. Sometimes we'd test ourselves to see how long we could stay under water. We would dance around on the bottom, make faces at each other and when our eyes began to bulge, we'd surface and gasp for air, glass jar in hand.

In July and August, there were days the sand was so hot we'd have to run from the water to our towel with the least amount of weight on our feet to avoid burning them. When the temperature rose to 100 F or more, we'd seek refuge in the bushes on the side of the beach, but we never considered going home. When we got hot, we would run across the hot sand, dive into the water and play until we were cooled off, then hop across the fiery sand and settle onto our towels in the shade until we felt hot and jumped in the lake again.

I'd stay until the sun went behind the mountain tops about three o'clock, return home, weathered from playing in the water and soaking up the sun's rays, eat supper and go back to the beach and play games with neighbors until the mosquitoes chased us away and it was too dark to see each other.

The only thing that could top the summer days by the lake were the nights my friend and I slept on the beach. I'd lumber down the gravel road in my pyjamas, with blankets and a pillow. Somehow I managed to include newspaper and matches to set a fire close to the water's edge. We'd watch the flames dance and reflect on the water while it kept us warm; at least it did the front of us. When our backside got too cool, we would turn around and warm it just enough, then turn toward the fire once more. When it was dark we would lie down and watch the stars sparkle. Sometimes if we stared long enough at one star it would appear to move. Often on the other side of the lake, another fire would be set. We could hear voices and wonder what they were doing or what they were talking about. Maybe they were drinking, or, maybe they were necking.

Usually we'd end up talking about skinning dipping. Should we or shouldn't we. We'd complain that it was too cold to get wet. Maybe the fire would light us and people could see our nakedness. No, it's too dark and anyone on the other side of the lake wouldn't be able to see much. Should we, shouldn't we. And finally, we'd move away from the light of our bonfire, remove our pyjamas and run into the lake shrieking in delight (that would have surely drawn attention to us). The water by that hour was cold, but so was our skin so the water felt warm compared to what it felt like when we got out. We'd run to the fireside, dry off quickly, put on our pyjamas and climb into our make-shift bed, teeth chattering until we warmed up.

These nights on the beach weren't for sleeping. We'd talk endlessly, as we watched the world above move across the black star lit sky. These were enchanting times, raising all kinds of questions about our universe. Eventually we'd succumb to our bodies need to sleep, only to wake with the birds; our blankets heavy with dew, as we breathed in the chilly early morning mountain air. Eventually nature called and we'd be forced from the warmth of our bedding and head home long enough to eat and prepare for another day on the beach.

When Labor Day and the start of a new school year were close, I'd sit on the beach drawing in all the beauty and memories of a great summer now gone. The trees had started to turn, reflecting their golden colors on the still waters. I'd take one more swim, then another, and another, not wanting to let summer die.

In the winter, I'd meet the neighborhood kids of my age on the beach and we'd skate the frozen lake. Sometimes we'd dare each other to see who could get the closest to the break water where the paddle boat piloted its way to the main lake. The closer we got to open water, the more the ice groaned and crackled. Intimidated, we'd turn back. No one ever made it to open water.

At home in the old shed, I found a pair of skis. They were ancient. The metal harnesses were rusted and the wood faded and worn. I'd never skied before so this was an opportunity to learn. I placed my snow boots into the ski harnesses, tightened the frayed leather straps and without poles headed to the orchard. I struggled to the top of the open area, often sliding back farther than I moved forward. When I finally reached the top, I pointed the skis downhill, held my breath and began sliding. I had no idea how to turn the skis, so if I was heading for a tree,

I just fell to my side in the soft snow. Then I'd climb back to the top and head down again and again until, exhausted, I headed home.

I felt a freedom I had not experienced in a long time. I was happy. This was the best time in my young life. As an adult I taught myself to ski with proper equipment.

Mom was friends with old, white haired, Mr. Irvine who lived across the road. His frame was tall and slim with broad shoulders and his skin wrinkled by the weather and age. His eyes radiated a gentle nature. His log cabin looked like the ones you pass by on the mountain highways that were once trapper's homes. The wood was black from age. Vines covered the porch roof and cascaded down toward the ground. His front and only door was obviously for a much shorter person so Mr. Irvine would have to stoop to enter. Mom visited him often, enjoying discussions on worldly matters. Frequently, various family members would visit Mr. Irvine and he in turn would often invite mom.

When Mom returned from one of these visits she asked me: "would you like to go with Mr. Irvine's family and be their live-in babysitter? "They would care for you, send you to school and then to College and all you have to do is look after their two children." I thought about it for a very short time. I knew they were very religious and in my young naive mind, that meant going to church and wearing hats and gloves. I wondered if mom and dad were trying to get rid of me. Maybe with me gone, money would go that much farther. Even so, I said: "I don't want to go" and that was the end of it. Of course my reasoning may not have had anything to do with reality. It was just the way I felt at the time.

How my life could have been different had I put aside my doubts and fears. To have gone to college! I could have avoided future abuses that were only months away. But why would my parents consider sending their eldest daughter away with strangers for the next five or more years?

The following summer mom's parents and her youngest brother and sister came to live with us. I don't remember how we all had beds to sleep in, but somehow we managed. They left the following spring and we were once again just the six of us.

Chapter Ten

Other than the year when mom came home from the sanitorium, I remember being sad during my childhood. As a little girl, I lived in an area where there were no small children to play with, so I created an imaginary friend and my own form of play. As I matured into my early teens, anxiety had become a part of me. I told my mother that I'd be listening to the teacher and realize I was grasping my loose-leaf binder so tight that my knuckles turned white. This anxiety, this sadness, kept me aloof.

Oh I had people I played with on the beach, but I never learned to have strong friendships with anyone. The only time I recall sharing something in common with people my age, was in junior high as a successful athlete. I was good at whatever sport I played and enjoyed the camaraderie of belonging to a team. But that wasn't enough. I desired the 'in' group, which included boys. Because I wasn't invited to join, I walked behind them, as if I was a part of the group.

Sports helped a lot, but it didn't take away the sadness I felt when I was alone and that seemed to be most times.

I use to look out the window of our home and ponder over the idea of breaking the law so I would go to prison and get out of this house. What could I do that would be a definite prison term without hurting myself or others? I don't know why I had these strong and very real feelings of desperation, but I needed to get away from this family.

I didn't like school, hadn't since grade three. Learning was always a struggle except for sports and art. I had trouble reading. I knew the words, but I just couldn't join the words to create meaningful sentences in my head, or, retain anything of what I had read. It was all a blur in my mind. In class, when we were told to read a short story to ourselves, I thought more about how much faster everyone else read then remembering what I read. When the teacher said to stop and talk about the article, I pretended I had read it and hoped she wouldn't call on me to make a contribution to the discussion.

I never read a book cover to cover, even for book reports. I would find a book that had a cover leaf that gave a precise of the story. I wrote it out in my own words and handed that in as my book report. I once got clumsy and put in a word I didn't know, a direct quote from the precise. The English teacher, Mr. Mac, dropped his glasses down on his nose, looked at me over the top of the lenses and asked: "what is an epic trek?" I was dumbfounded. I had no idea. I told him my mother helped me with the report. Mr. Mac said nothing.

When summer was coming to an end and I was expected to enter grade then, I decided I didn't want to return to school. There was no point in spending the next three years in high school. I wasn't a good student and I hated school.

Dad told me if I wasn't going back to school, then I had to find a permanent job. I told dad I wanted to join the army and be a military policewoman. He tried to discourage me because, he said: "nobody likes the military police. I would be alone and hated. I didn't care. That's what I wanted to do. I needed dad to go with me to the recruiter in case he had to sign a permission form. The officer said I was too young and even with dad's permission, I couldn't join. Disheartened and frustrated we left the office.

I had to begin the search for a job. I put my name in at the local telephone company, but they told me I had to be sixteen and that was months away. With no other decent prospects, I returned to school and entered grade ten a month into the school year.

I don't remember how I met Wally, but we became close very quickly. He was twenty-one years old, had a thick head of black hair, a bit taller than I, slightly overweight and he had a car. Wally often worked the graveyard shift. That meant we had the days to ourselves when I wasn't in school.

He spent a lot of time at our house and often took his before-night-shift nap in my parent's bed. It was during one of these naps that he called me into the bedroom. I was unaware of what would happen next. I just knew I loved how he made me feel.

With my mother only steps away in the living room, I lost my virginity at the age of fifteen. After the first time, he had me whenever we were alone.

One day, Wally and I had decided to go to the midnight movie at the drive-in. After supper, Mom told me that I needed to have a nap before we went, while Wally and mom did the dishes. So I went to my room, which was on the other side of the kitchen wall and laid down, feeling quite like a child.

As mom and Wally talked, I heard my name mentioned. He was telling mom that he planned to marry me and that we'd go on our honeymoon somewhere nice. Then I really felt like a child. We had never talked about marriage. And here he was talking with my mother about it!

In short time it was clear that our relationship was coming to an end. His sister told me he was seeing someone else. I started to challenge him. Why wasn't he calling me as often? Did he have another girlfriend? We would argue, or at least I'd listen to him rant. During our last time together he threatened to tell everyone that I was a prostitute if I said anything about our relationship. I'd never heard that term but something told me this was not good.

Dad came home with a man who was staying at the hotel, all excited. I don't know how old he was, but I recall he seemed younger than dad, but his face was weathered, unkempt and his clothes were well worn. I thought perhaps he was destitute and needed a meal. Instead, he was heading into the mountain wilderness to work a gold claim he established and needed a partner to bring their treasures back to the city. He said it was a sure thing and dad agreed to go with him.

Mom invited the man to stay for dinner. When we were finished, he asked me to show him our mountain. We chatted along the trail until we came to a meadow with tall grass, decaying fallen trees and outcrops of granite. I wanted to know more about him and this exciting adventure for him and dad.

We sat down on the soft grass that was bent over from standing on it. A gentle breeze rustled the trees and the air was filled with the smell of autumn. He spoke of an accident he'd had when he fell off a cliff and landed, straddling a rock, ending his ability to have children. I wondered why he was telling me something so personal. But I also felt sympathetic and wondered how anyone could endure such pain or even live.

He put his arm around my shoulder, drew me close and began kissing me on the lips, like Shorty and Wally did. I gave into him. I thought it was my role to please men.

Besides, he was bigger and stronger and we were far from anyone that might see or hear me. When he was finished, we walked down the mountain together and into my house like this was a normal occurrence. I wonder now, when he told me about his accident, was he telling me it was okay to have sex because I wouldn't get pregnant? I was fifteen! How would I know about these things? The next day dad and this man left for the mountain wilderness.

When their expected day of return came and went, mom became worried. She asked me if I thought there might be a reason this man wouldn't want to come back. I knew what she was referring to. How did she suspect or know? And if she did suspect, why didn't she find out what had happened on the mountain when he took me for his own pleasure, before they left on this trip? Fortunately for me, the "monthly curse" had not begun, so there was no danger of pregnancy, although that would not have entered my mind because I didn't make the connection between sex and pregnancy.

Dad finally did return, without the man. He had abandoned dad overnight at a campsite leaving dad to find his way out of the mountains with no supplies and little knowledge of his location. Nothing more was said. I sensed not only was dad in shock that this man had left him up there, but perhaps he was embarrassed for being taken in by a perfect stranger.

Chapter Eleven

I felt sixteen would never come. I could then apply to the telephone company and make really good money. I could find my own place to live, drive a car and buy things with my own money. So many good things about being sixteen.

There was a young people's dance at the community hall. I told a few fellow students that I was going to be sixteen in a few weeks. "Why don't you have a party", said someone. "Yeh", said someone else. "Yeh?" I asked. I went home and told mom and dad that I wanted to have a birthday party.

I invited everyone from my class and those on the school bus. Ten said they'd come. On the day of my birthday dad brought home donuts, pop and a birthday cake and mom and dad took my siblings to the drive-in theatre. I was full of excitement. The last time I had a birthday party was four years previous. I arranged the kitchen chairs in the living room for extra seating, got my records out for the music, spread the food on the kitchen table, dressed in something special and waited.

It was 7 o'clock and no one had arrived. 7:30, still no one. I phoned my neighbor up the hill and her dad said she couldn't come. I phoned another and he said he was babysitting. "But you said you'd come!" "Sorry, I can't now".

When my family came home about nine, I was alone in the living room. The food was on the kitchen table untouched. I don't know why no one showed up. Maybe I didn't plan well enough. But you would think that out of the ten, some would have come. This was an important birthday in my life. So much of my life was about being sixteen, at least that's the way it felt. I was distraught. I felt so alone and unwanted. Mom and dad were shocked when I told them no one came to my birthday party. They hugged me as I cried. Later we all had pop and donuts. We lit the candles on the cake, I made a wish, blew them out, ate a slice and I went to bed early. To this day, when I plan something, I wonder if anyone will come.

I purchased my first car with eighty dollars I had managed to save from a part time waitress job. The car was old, but it was mine and

I was proud of it. A car would give me independence. I would no longer have to take the bus or wait for a ride to go to town. I wrote my learner's permit and dad began teaching me how to drive. He would be 'helping' me again in his special way of teaching. He took me to the gravel pit up the road for our house. We went in circles while he told me how to shift gears, harping at me the whole time. I felt I was back in the kitchen learning my right from my left. I began crying. Dad drove us home. When I was familiar with shifting gears, I drove on the highway, then in town. When I felt confident driving, I went for my test. I failed miserably. I didn't practice enough. I gave up learning to drive. I adjusted to the disappointment and looked at what I did have. I was earning my own money and we lived in a great neighborhood close to a lake.

Shortly after the biggest purchase in my life, dad crashed his car. Mom asked me if they could use mine and they'd pay me the eighty dollars later. Later never came.

Now that I was sixteen, I made an application at the telephone company and waited for the phone to ring. After a few weeks the recruiter hadn't called. I complained to my folks that I was never going to get a job with them. Dad said I had to keep going back until they finally hired me. So I did, and on one of those visits, they told me to come back on Monday to begin training. That was electrifying news. I had a real job at union wages. The training was only part time so my income was small, but it was enough to rent a room in a boarding house in the city.

My new residence was in a Victorian rooming house in the city. It wasn't the most handsome house on the block, but the price was right. I rented a small bedroom in the back of the house on the second floor with a two burner hot plate, a cupboard for my groceries, a double bed, a dresser and a wardrobe. A little box hung outside on the windowsill where I could store butter and milk. The shared bathroom was just down the hall and fridge privileges were downstairs in the landlady's apartment. All for twenty-five dollars a month, laundry included. I didn't have a toaster, so I used my Girl Guide survival knife, slipped the knife into the side of the bread and hung it over the flames. Later, I bought a used toaster at a second hand store for two dollars.

There were two other rented rooms upstairs. The one in the front of the house was bigger and cost thirty-five dollars a month. It had a closet sized kitchen with a sink, a two burner hot plate and a counter. The bedroom was big enough to include a table and chairs. Eventually I would move into that room when I worked full time. I was on my own and proud. An exciting future full of prospects lay ahead. I bought things I was never able to do because I didn't have any money. One of the first things, after buying food, was a six pack of cola. This is what people did, according to the movies. I felt like part of the world I wanted to be in.

Socializing was limited. I didn't know many people in town and I was younger than most of the staff at the telephone office. Eventually, I became friends with Lidia, one of the operators. She invited me to her home where I met her husband Tony. They were four or five years older than I, so, their lifestyle was new to me. It meant drinking, staying up late or all night and driving out onto the secondary highways to undetermined destinations and partying.

Chapter Twelve

I loved window shopping. When I wasn't working, I wandered down the streets admiring the wares in the shop windows. Sometimes my image would be captured in the reflection of a store window. I was tall and slim, modestly shaped, brown thick hair with blonde highlights bleached by the sun. I had the natural look, no make-up, shoulder length hair and serviceable clothes; nothing special or trendy. My face was youthful and soft, with blue eyes probably being the highlight of my looks. I had always felt a bit homely and clumsy. In fact, dad nicknamed me "tangle foot" because I walked into doorways and caught the corner of furniture or stumbled on the sidewalks.

It was on one of these window shopping walks when my life dramatically changed. It was a perfect summer day. Puffy white clouds lazily crossed the sun's rays creating a dim shadow over the city, then the clouds would move on and the sun would beam down once more. The aroma of food in nearby restaurants and the sounds of traffic filled the warm summer air. People moved slowly making their way to shop, work or just enjoy this carefree day.

As I passed a parked car, I noticed the man in the driver's seat was an acquaintance. His friend sat in the passenger's seat. I stopped to say hello and as I bent over to look through the car window, my purse tipped upside down and the contents scattered onto the ground. I dropped to my knees to gather the items when the passenger in the car stepped out to help. He was of slight build, good looking, well dressed and had a pleasant smile. I was embarrassed; thinking that private part of me was exposed to the whole world. I stuffed the scattered items into my purse as quickly as he handed them to me.

I was so nervous I couldn't meet his eyes. I felt like I was watching someone else going through this situation. He said his name was Monty. "Would you like to go for a coke or something?" he asked.

While sipping on a cherry coke at the café and the three of us puffing away on cigarettes, he told me he was twenty-one and he had recently left the Air Force and was presently unemployed and living with his mother up the hill. I was still recovering from the spilled purse and realizing that a mature man was actually interested in me. This was just like in the movies. Boy meets girl due to an incident and they fall in love.

I relied often on the perceived similarities of my life and that of situations in movies. If it happened in the movies, then that is likely the way life would be. I didn't have much more to go on. I was young and naive. I had no concept of who I was or where I was going in life. I was making it up as I went along with no goals in sight, not even marriage or children.

I liked Monty. He was polite and attentive. After a few dates driving around with his friend and stopping for a coke in the local café, I met his mother. Mrs. C. was a jolly sort who made anyone feel at home in her little two bedroom house up the hill. When Monty was very young, his father died from miner's lung disease. Marie, his sister, was a few years older than Monty and was already married with her own family. Later I would discover that all three were alcoholics.

I was drawn into his life, absorbing his likes and dislikes, his attitude, interests and making them my own. Because he'd been in the Air Force, I became interested in flight and weather conditions. But he never responded to my comments on the subject. In my naivety, I thought he'd be impressed with my interest in something he had done, not knowing that all he did was drink, get reprimanded by his superiors and do only what was absolutely required of him. He never sat in a cockpit, let alone pilot a plane.

His life quickly became my life and any interests I may have had faded. As they say in the movies, "they became one". I thought that was the goal for a couple. I had begun to live a life that would not be my own. I would create a new identity shaped by his influence. I would have no ideas of my own, no interests other than his and no future that I could have without his permission. I thought this was the way it was supposed to be. After all, he was older and more educated, so he must know how to live.

In the evening he and his friend would pick me up to drive around the city and at some point stop for a cherry coke and maybe a donut. I don't recall him ever asking me what I liked to do. I probably wouldn't have known anyway. I was following his lead. When I look back at this part of my life, I was being groomed, set up for abuse and I, in my child-like mind, was part of that set up because I allowed it.

Usually Monty and I sat in the back seat of his friend's car. It was there that he first kissed me. I was in heaven. I was out with a man and even though he didn't own a car, he had a friend who did. I was now like a lot of other girls . . . a boyfriend and a car to cruise the streets. I had loved Wally, who also had a car, but Monty was more exciting and he wasn't just after my body.

One evening, when I was working, I picked up a call from an irate woman and realized it was Mrs. C. "Get me Marie!" she screamed. I connected her to her daughter and listened to the conversation without revealing that I could. She was frantic: "He took a shovel to me." "He was going to kill me".

I couldn't believe my ears. How could Monty do something like that? He was a nice guy. But he could. There was a precedent to Monty's angry behaviour. He had told me before this incident how he hated cats. Once he said, while smiling, and with great bravado, he found a nuisance cat on his porch. Circling his hand over his head, he animated what he did to this unfortunate feline. He picked it up by the tail and swung it high over his head and flung it out to the streets.

I should have seen these actions as a warning. Abusers begin with abusive behavior toward animals then it becomes displayed in their treatment of vulnerable people. But, I thought, he would never hurt me. He loved me. In a moment of self-righteous bravado I told myself I couldn't marry him until he stopped doing things like that. Was I expecting some magic wand to transform him from an abuser to a respectful human being?

I was so young and naive. In the eyes of the law, Wally molested me. And when he threatened to tell people I was a prostitute if I told anyone what he had done to me that was part of the abuse by control. I didn't realize at the time, that Wally, Shorty, Dad and his mining friend had become part of the process to groom me for further abuses. And without the skills to set boundaries, I was a prime target.

These late nights, partying and cruising the highways was taking its toll on my inexperienced young body. I was staying up all night, and then going to work at seven in the morning and throwing up in the bathroom at work. I didn't understand what was wrong with me. I went to a doctor who said I had to quit work . . . I didn't tell him I had an active lifestyle. And why would he suspect anything? I was only sixteen. The doctor signed a letter that said I had to quit work due to stress. I turned in my resignation at work and gave notice to vacate my room at the rooming house. I moved back to mom and dad's and collected unemployment insurance.

Mom wanted to go back to work for the extra badly needed income and I was on unemployment insurance. She spoke with our hairdresser, Lisa, who offered to apprentice both of us. This was something I hadn't considered. When I was younger I toyed with the idea of becoming a chemist, an astronaut or, a military police officer. Later in life I thought of being a horticulturist or a groundwater geologist, but hairdressing was far from any of those. As it turned out I loved it and I had a flare for the craft. We worked during the day on customers under Lisa's supervision and a few evenings a week we had an educational session. I was doing something that was fun and stimulating for my creative abilities. My life was on another path and it felt right.

I was so attracted to Monty, I couldn't think of ever not being with him. I breathed his air. My body ached when we were apart. I paced around my room until he came to my house or phoned. When he didn't call, I took it as sign he was through with me. I would run into the hills and sit among the trees crying. When he called later I said nothing. I was just so happy to hear his voice.

Often my dates with Monty extended beyond midnight, spending most of it in the back seat of the car allowing Monty to touch me intimately. One morning my mother's only response was: "you were kind of late last night weren't you". I was sixteen and out with a man of twenty-one! The age difference was enormous. I was still a kid with a mind that thought like a child. I was not aware of my lack of emotional maturity and all the feelings and responsibilities about intimate relationships. I was developing a pattern with men. I believed my role in an intimate relationship was to please a man, so I did whatever they wanted me to do. They didn't love me. They didn't care about me. But Monty cared.

My brother used to play with a few boys in the neighborhood, but one day one of the boys disappeared. Mom discovered that he had tuberculosis and was taken to a sanitorium for treatment. It wasn't long after that Mathew, who was six at the time, was infected and diagnosed with tuberculosis of the lungs. The doctor said he needed to be in a drier climate where there was a tuberculosis sanitorium for children. Mom and dad found a place and moved. I stayed behind to finish my apprenticeship and live at my hairdresser's home in the city.

But I had Lady, my black and white beagle cross, who had walked with me through so many trials in my short life. She was a loyal and constant companion. I came home from the hair salon to find her gone. I was distraught. "Where's Lady?" I asked. Mom, obviously trying to keep me calm said: "I sold her to a family in a town nearby". I was dismayed, in tears. How could she do this to me? Not to even let me say good-bye. Throughout my life I wondered how Lady fared. Or, maybe mom lied and had her euthanized but was afraid to tell me the truth. I resigned myself to never seeing Lady again and moved on with my life, but never forgave my parents for what they did to Lady and me.

They all left and I was on my own. Monty and I continued dating. I didn't know much about the ramifications of having sex. Monty never mentioned anything about 'protection'. That never occurred to me. I had not even heard of the idea.

Dad found a job bartending. They rented the largest part of an old beaten down two story house that was divided into apartments. They hadn't been living there long when mom wrote that she was sick again and may have to have surgery. I needed to help the family. My job, once again, was to take care of my siblings and my father.

I left Monty and my apprenticeship, packed my few belongings and caught the train. As it turned out, mom wasn't as ill as she thought and really didn't need my help. But I stayed there anyway.

I missed Monty beyond reason, writing several times a week because that's what you do when you miss the person you love . . . just as it was in the movies. I begged him to move here because he would find a job more easily. Eventually he agreed and was on his way. Mom put a bed in the room upstairs and he would eat with us.

Dad convinced his employer to hire Monty and he would train him. A few months later I was in the doctor's office hearing him tell me I was pregnant. The possibility of pregnancy hadn't been a part of my consciousness. I'm not even sure I understood how a baby was conceived. In school all we knew about reproduction was how birds and bees did it. Monty's response was: "well I guess we should get married then". In resignation, I quietly replied: "yeh", remembering his propensity to violence. I was scared. I had no plans for my life. I was going with the flow, living day to day, unable to see my future. And now life was drastically changing, evolving and out of my control. I felt lost and scared. Incapable of finding my way. But I had Monty who would take care of me. I moved through life as if I was unconscious with no awareness of anything but what was expected of me. And what were my parents going to say?

At home I put an anti-nausea remedy given to me by the doctor on the table in front of mom. I asked: "do you know what these are for?" She nodded and asked: "are you?" "Yes".

That night mom told dad. I thought he'd be angry but when they were heading to bed, he said: "goodnight grandma". He never said anything to me. Nothing was said by anyone, nothing. Arrangements were made for a simple marriage service at a church.

Chapter Thirteen

We were new to the city to have made any friends. That begged the question, "who would be our witnesses". Monty asked a regular at the bar to be his best man and I asked the woman who lived in the two room suite in the back of the house to be my maid of honor.

About a week after the decision to marry, Monty and dad came home after being out together for a few hours. Dad left us alone while Monty pulled from his pocket a small box and in it was an engagement ring. Something I hadn't expected. It was a small gold band with a tiny diamond in the center. I thought it was the most beautiful ring I had ever seen.

A week or so later, we held a miserable engagement party at the house in my parents tiny six by nine living room with plastic curtains and an old rug and sofa. The attendees were people dad and Monty worked with at the bar, who likely knew I was pregnant. They were all strangers to me. I sat on the sidelines listening to adult conversation, alone and filled with shame for my pregnancy.

The room Monty used to sleep in upstairs had a small kitchen attached to it. This would be our apartment. We would use the bed Monty had been sleeping in and somehow we acquired a used sofa, a kitchen table with two chairs. This was exciting. Our first home. Together we painted the walls, washed the old worn-out linoleum floor and cleaned the kitchen.

Mom and I went to the Salvation Army clothing store for a wedding outfit. Even though we were looking for an appropriate suit or dress, I gravitated to the wedding dresses not thinking I could afford one. I just wanted to look, to dream of what could be. One stood out. I looked at mom. We delicately stroked the lace. It was calf length with a lace bodice and netting over a satin gathered skirt. I guess I must have had that dreamy look on my face because mom agreed to buy it. It cost $ 35 including the veil. At that time, to me that cheap used dress was beautiful.

The next day we bought a small bouquet of artificial flowers for me and a smaller spray for my maid of honor. Real flowers were too expensive. Mom and dad had barely enough money to live, let alone pay for a wedding. They did their best. I was aware of the distinction between my wedding plans and those I'd seen in the movies, but I was resigned to the poor lifestyle we were facing because we were in love and I was getting married!

The day of the wedding everyone was dressed in their finest. Mom was in a form fitting bodice with a circular skirt and small hat, dad in a dark suit jacket and grey pants that looked like they'd been around a long time and no longer fit well. My two sisters wore pretty dresses with a flower in their hair. And my brother wore an outfit similar to his daddy.

Monty stayed overnight at his best man's house so we wouldn't see each other until we walked down the aisle, as was the custom. Alone upstairs in our new apartment, I slipped into my wedding dress, filled my bra with tissue to give me some form to my upper body, stepped into my new flat white shoes that would keep me from being taller than Monty, set the veil on my head, picked up my silk flowered bouquet and went downstairs.

The family had already left and there was nothing for me to do but wait for dad to return and take me to the church. I waited. I paced the floor. No one phoned to see if I was on my way. I was feeling left out, forgotten. Surely someone would realize the bride wasn't present at the church. Daje vu my sixteenth birthday party. The hour came and went and still no one had arrived to transport me to my wedding. Just as I was about to cry, I looked out the window and in a flurry dad was running up the stairs: "no one told me to come back for you!"

On August 16, 1958, Monty, with a childish drunken grin on his face and I, walked arm in arm down the aisle in the hollow silence of the chapel. No music, no alter flowers. In the pews were my family, dad's parents and a few bar people. The ceremony was brief, like our engagement. When the minister said: "you may kiss the bride", Monty tried to find the parting in the veil and in his drunkenness stumbled, swore and awkwardly lifted the veil.

Pictures were taken, followed by a ride to someone's rumpus room for the reception. Mom had set up plates of cheese and crackers on a table with a small but lovely wedding cake in the centre. Mom and dad did the best they could with their limited funds. But it didn't help me to get over the feeling that I was a stranger in someone else's pathetic wedding. I didn't know most of the people. They were all adults. I couldn't get the courage to talk to anyone. What would I say? I was a typical teenager who would rather escape than have to socialize with adults. I had such mixed emotions. I was uncomfortable, but I was also happy to be married to Monty.

People sat around the room like manikins, total strangers, probably there for the free beer which flowed freely. I drank a glass of port because I was told I was expected to have something to drink and I didn't like beer. Someone toasted the 'happy couple', followed by the gift opening. We had gone through the process from engagement to wedding ceremony as expected, as tradition dictates, as by route. I struggled to see this as my dream wedding, but it lacked the luster I saw in the movies. The feelings and the tone of the wedding was without the promise and excitement of new beginnings.

We left shortly after for our honeymoon. I couldn't get out of there fast enough. We returned to our apartment and changed, got into a borrowed car and drove to a motel on the outskirts of the city for two nights. A part of me was sad and yet, I was in love with this man and he loved me. We were husband and wife now with a baby on the way. I was only seventeen with the maturity of a thirteen year old.

In the privacy of our room we toasted with a glass of cheap champagne, not that Monty needed anymore booze. The next day we took a drive into the country. When we returned Monty was bored and we drove into the city to drink more beer with his drinking buddies and a visit with my parents.

I look at our wedding photos now and I am astonished to see that this child in the photo, in the white cheesy Salvation Army wedding dress was me. Innocence and ignorance encased my demeanor. I looked like I was playing dress up. But this time, this child was also having a child. And the man she married was an alcoholic, angry, disrespectful, a wife batterer and child abuser. I was lost in this maze of my life. I didn't know how to cook and certainly didn't know the responsibility of a wife and mother or to myself. I would learn the hard way.

Chapter Fourteen

By now I was having morning sickness. The only bathroom in the house was on the main floor. This meant I had to rush down the stairs to bend my head in the toilet before I would vomit. It was touch and go most of the time, but fortunately I was young and able to move fast. I threw up every morning for months and when that was over, I had heartburn for the remainder of my pregnancy.

Because my mother feared I'd fall while rushing down the stairs to the bathroom to vomit, they all moved to another house not far away so Monty and I could rent the two rooms downstairs that were once their kitchen and living room. For us, their "living room" became our bedroom. The back apartment was still held by the couple with a baby. The rest of the house was going to be rented to someone else.

Monty had been laid off five months after we were married, so we lived off his unemployment insurance. Our grocery shopping consisted of a maximum of $5 worth of food at any one time. To save money we stayed in bed in the morning so we didn't have to have breakfast. Entertainment had to be created by us which was mainly playing cards and visiting with our neighbors who were also on low incomes. People Monty knew from the bar had loaned me two maternity outfits. After two months I was tired of them, but there was no money to buy anything new.

During the eighth and ninth month, I was heavy and very uncomfortable. Pressure on my bladder caused me to get up through the night to go to the bathroom. Our bed was against the wall on one side and Monty insisted on sleeping on the outside so I had to climb over him in my bulk, wetting myself in the process. There was no reasoning with him.

Someone had loaned us a baby crib that we placed in the small space under the archway between our kitchen and bedroom. I went about preparing the baby's bed like I had done with my dolls; soft sheets and a blanket with a stuffed toy in one corner. I was so eager to have this baby and play house that I made the crib up months before my due date.

The few baby clothes we had were second hand or items mom bought for us. We had the basics, nighties, under shirts and cloth diapers.

On February 27, 1959, Vern was born. It was a long but easy labor. I didn't have classes like the young mothers have now, so I didn't know what to expect and how to deal with it. My solution was to follow the contractions. I would feel them coming, notice the pressure and hardness of my belly, and then feel it subside. No big deal. I did this over and over again. I couldn't understand what made the other women in labor scream so loudly. Occasionally, I walked the hallway for exercise.

The worst was the humiliation of the nurses and my doctor coming in frequently to examine me, consulting with one another in front of me like I wasn't there. In due time, I was wheeled into the cold sterile delivery room with all the scary instruments and equipment. This felt more like surgery than delivering a soft, warm baby. The nurses went about preparing me. Then they turned on the huge blinding light overhead. Was this an inquisition? What was I, who had just turned eighteen a week ago, doing having a baby? Then we all waited and waited. I felt so exposed, so vulnerable and embarrassed. Eventually I had to do the hard pushing. The doctor asked me if I wanted to see my baby being born. I was horrified. Why would I want to see that? It was bad enough so many others were watching, but to be involved in that seemed disgusting. I abruptly said NO.

Vern was born and as quickly as he came into this world he was whisked away and I didn't see him until after Monty had visited me. He had seen the baby before I had. Monty cried when he came into the room repeating a few times that we had a son. Vern was beautiful he said. Later when the nurse brought Vern in for the first time I was able to see he had a mop of dark hair, a long body and everything was perfectly intact. He smelled delightful, sweet and innocent. And he was beautiful.

A week later we brought our son home and I embarked on the life of being a mother. I had helped mom with the babies and thought I knew enough, but I still had no idea what was expected of me. I bought Dr. Spock's baby book. When dad saw it he said: "you don't need that do you?" I suppose he was implying that I already had adequate experience, but it seemed like an order, a disappointment in me. I threw the book away.

I went about my duties as the situation required. Waking when Vern did, feeding, changing and bathing him. But I also held him, sang nursery songs I'd heard mom sing years ago and looked at him in amazement and wonder of this tiny human being. So perfect, so innocent, so trusting.

I was bathing him in the ancient rusty kitchen sink and doing what I thought was right, making it up as I bumbled along. Without warning the Victorian Order of Nurses (VON) knocked on my door. Their initial visit consisted of surveying what I was already doing and giving me information on how best to look after my newborn. They told me I could not under any circumstances bath him in the kitchen sink, so on their second and last visit, they brought me a donated baby tub and a few other essential items. They were very helpful, but I felt invaded by these women. Like a typical teenager I knew everything.

I breast fed him, because the doctor said I should, for his first six weeks but stopped abruptly when I felt aroused while feeding him. I had no idea this could happen and it disgusted and frightened me.

The initial pleasures of having our first child were eclipsed by the beatings. Monty had hit me the first three months after we were married, then he stopped for the remainder of my pregnancy and the first month after delivery.

The beatings were getting worse, more frequent and I didn't want to take it any longer. I was miserable and afraid all the time. Where had Monty gone? Where was this kind, caring, gentle man I fell in love with? I know now, he had a fire in him from his own abuse and family life that created a rage he could not understand or stop.

After one of the beatings, I left Monty. Dad came and helped me move what I needed to their house. Only hours later, Monty came to the door, drunk and asked to see me. We went on the front porch and he pleaded with me to return, crying and full of remorse. Looking back, he was scared of losing his version of a family. I gave into his tears, leaving Vern with mom and dad for the night. We picked up Vern and our things the next day.

When that honeymoon was over, Monty began hitting me again. Over the next eleven years, the cycle of wife battering raged. After a beating he would apologize, we would behave as if we were on our honeymoon and the love between us was wonderful, then tension would rise, I would feel the tension but did not understand what it meant until many years later. The tension would end with a beating, and then he would promise never to do it again. Most times he claimed he didn't remember what he had done to me. The cycle would begin again . . . honeymoon, tension, abuse, honeymoon.

Each time, I'd think it was my fault. I needed to be a better wife and mother. I believed everything he said. I was: a bitch, whore, slut, good-for-nothing. There was no end to the repulsive words that he spat at me. He didn't care that our baby was in the room or within hearing distance. His words became ingrained in me, a part of who I was and was reinforced by physical abuse. Each time he beat me, my self-worth lessened. I began to believe I was of no value to him, our child or anyone else. I would attempt to get out of this man's abusive clutches and save myself a few more times before the final flight.

Shortly after the first time I left and returned to Monty, we moved to an old rental house. It had two bedrooms, living room, kitchen and bathroom. It was perfect for our young family. The living room carpet was dirty, so we got a bucket of water and soap and scrubbed the carpet with a brush. I decorated as best I could with the little money we had.

A year later I was pregnant once more. After enduring the humiliation of labor at the hospital for Vern's birth, I vowed I would wait until the last minute before going to the hospital. On August 28, 1960, Lynn was born. Her delivery was quick and easy. She was tiny, sweet and lovely. Shortly after I brought her home, she was sleeping longer hours than normal and when I tried to feed her from the bottle, she had trouble suckling and kept regurgitating what she managed to swallow. I thought she was just having difficulties learning how to suckle. She began crying often and for long periods . . . sharp cries. She was in pain. I thought colic and tried the usual home remedies, but nothing worked. A week had gone by. She wouldn't take in any food; she just cried. I called my mother and she consulted with her mother and we decided to take the baby to the doctor's office. He examined her and said she must be taken immediately to the hospital.

I was sure Lynn was going to die. Mom told my grandmother, who then flew in to say good-bye to Lynn and support me in my loss. Together we went to the hospital. This was the first time I saw my baby since she went into the hospital. I never visited her nor did Monty. For some reason I didn't think I was allowed.

When I looked into the nursery, I saw this tiny body comforted by a loving nurse. Lynn was eagerly feeding. Her pale blonde hair had been shaven where they inserted an intravenous needle. Her color was good, she wasn't crying and she was eating. I began to cry. I was shocked when the nurse asked me if I'd like to feed her. I thought only nurses could handle the babies when they were in the hospital. I gently took her into my arms, her warm soft sweet smelling body blended into mine. She was going to be okay and I could take her home soon. Lynn was now on a soya based formula. She continued to thrive and was a normal little baby. They kept Lynn there for a few weeks until she was hydrated and feeding properly. She had gastroenteritis.

Chapter Fifteen

Monty was working at a sleazy bar and came home late and usually drunk. On one occasion, he was so drunk he passed out in the car. I went to his side and slapped his face to try to waken him. Wrong thing to do.

Like turning on a light, he began attacking me. He threw me to the ground along the path to the house. I was terrified, but relieved that the babysitter was there so Monty would stop abusing me. I drove the sitter home, dreading how Monty would be when I returned. As soon as I entered the house he attacked. He threw me onto the living room floor. He began hitting me with a closed fist; his arms flailing over my head and crashing onto me. He looked like a freak with foam spitting from his mouth. I wanted him to stop, but I was physically weaker than him. My only resource was to pretend to black out. I collapsed on the floor. He was shocked. He gathered me into his arms, rocking back and forth, repeating over and over again: "no, no". I lay limp in his arms for a short time and pretended to regain consciousness. He helped me to my feet and we went to bed. The next morning my eye was swollen and black and my jaw hurt. He moved around the house quietly until he went to work. My jaw never fully recovered and clicks often.

The next time I went to see my doctor, I told him of the beatings and his solution was to wait for Monty to come home drunk, tie him to the bed and beat him. And what do you suppose he'd do the next day or the next time he got drunk? I hate to think of the consequences.

The second time I left Monty, I was intent on divorcing him. I found a job as a waitress in a downtown restaurant and resided in a rooming house. My plan was to send my son and newborn baby girl to my mother's in the north until I had a home for the three of us.

Meanwhile, Gary, a handsome young patron of the café, flirted with me. Soon we were dating. I felt alive, connected to the world. No longer afraid. I told Monty of my plans for the children. He wasn't happy and said nothing.

I was at work when I received a phone call from Social Services. The woman told me that if I sent the children to my mother, even for a short time, they would remove them from her home and return them to their father. I had no choice but to return to him if I wanted to be with the children.

The cost to me was more and frequent physical, sexual and psychological abuse. I was trapped with no hope of a better life. In my mind I had to downplay the impact of the abuse. I became depressed, frustrated, miserable, alone and afraid again. I quit the café and became a stay at home mom and wife. During my following frequent visits to doctors, for some reason, I never revealed my true story. I was prescribed anti-depressants as the solution.

Soon after I moved back Gary called to ask me out and I accepted. I knew this was wrong, but I needed a break. He was someone interested in me, he liked me, and he was attentive. We dated a few times going to nice restaurants where we looked at each other and we talked; something that never happened in my married life with Monty.

Meanwhile, the number of beatings escalated and became more violent than the last. I could no longer endure the fear and pain. I didn't want to die; I just needed to escape, even if it was for a little while. Monty wouldn't be home for hours. I took a handful of my anti-depressants and entered a world of numbness, unable to care about anything. I lay on the sofa barely able to lift my head. The children played quietly, almost as if they sensed my condition.

I didn't understand at the time, but I had shut down emotionally long ago. I was a prisoner with no chance of escape. Enjoying life was impossible. I was emotionally bankrupt. I had nothing to offer my children or anyone else including myself. I just knew I had to flee or I would die, either by my own hands or by Monty's.

Gary called and said he was moving. I was crushed. He was my only break from this wretched life. He asked me to join him. I was apprehensive and exhilarated, all at the same time. I was going to break out, run and be free of this caustic miserable man who had no regard for me.

When Monty was working, I packed a suitcase and arranged for a sitter. I left with Gary for what I thought was forever. I would have someone who loved and cared for me; someone who wouldn't hurt me.

The children would be fine, I told myself. They didn't need me. I knew deep down that I was a useless mother, just as Monty had told me many times. A number of researchers have said that when a person is told they are no good often enough, they begin to believe they aren't worthy of anyone's love and are incapable of giving love. The children always had food, clean clothes and play time. But anything more was beyond what I could offer. I was void of feeling or giving love. What I had with the men in my life was the idea of love, just like in the movies. I was not motivated to improve my life. Why should I, I was no good? I was beaten down figuratively and physically. I had to escape this prison called Monty's family. Gary would provide a safe and peaceful home. He would be attentive as he had already been and he would protect me. As I walked out the door saying good-bye to the children, I saw Vern watching me . . . his sad eyes following me. That image sealed in my mind forever.

Shortly after we moved, Gary left me. I moved into the YWCA and found a job in a lady's wear store downtown.

I was twenty but looked of legal age and could go to the bars. I was promiscuous. It was like I was experiencing the teen life I never really had. I was suddenly released from bondage enjoying life. I was seeking love and safety, someone to rescue me. Of course I never found it . . . certainly not in bars.

On my own for several months I decided to seek a divorce. I found a lawyer who would set in motion the paper work for a divorce. I saw Monty for the first time in a year, in court. I stood in the witness box and admitted to everyone in the court room that I had committed adultery. I had to. This was the only way I could secure a divorce. The divorce was granted and I left the court house.

Outside Monty followed me. He asked me to join him for a drink. He talked about the children and how they needed their mother. After a few more drinks I was mellowing. I was feeling sad and lonely for the children. We talked about repairing our relationship. I was more confident that I could make it work. I told him I now knew how to make a man happy, thinking that I had had enough relationships with men that gave me experience on how a wife should take care of her husband. How I believed that without any real new knowledge is beyond me. And why was providing better sex the answer to our problems? I still believed that a woman is only present to please and perform for a man. But I told Monty his job as a bartender was not healthy for our relationship, that perhaps he could find something else. He found a job with a bakery close to where I lived. Monty and I returned to his place and packed a rental truck and with Vern and Lynn sitting between us, we moved.

The children and I were getting re-acquainted. We played hide and seek and wrestled on the floor and I tucked them into bed at night. But for Monty and I the honeymoon was over in short time. He didn't like the children and me playing. "Quiet down, you're too noisy". So we stopped our play time.

I continued to work at the store but now had two children to take to the babysitters. I found a sitter in a newspaper ad. I had never met these people, but I was relieved that their fee was affordable. How Monty and I could even contemplate leaving our children with people we didn't know is still a puzzle. Monty offered no opinion on the matter so I took the children to their new sitter. When I look back on this situation, I realize this babysitter wasn't the best choice. Every day I dropped the kids off, they would cry. They didn't appear to be abused, but perhaps they were mentally and emotionally. I didn't have that kind of awareness and so they continued to be unhappy with their babysitter.

Monty used the only car we owned so that meant I had to bus the children to the sitters, catch the bus to work, and then do the reverse at the end of the day. Many times with Lynn in my arms and holding Vern by the hand, we had to run for the bus. Missing it would mean a thirty minute wait for the next one.

Soon it was apparent that Monty was allergic to the flour dust and returned to bartending.

My back began to hurt. I was in agony crying all the way on the bus and often at work when no one was watching. The store manager needed to cut back on staff and because of my condition, he laid me off.

I returned to my former life of housewife and mother; stuck at home and waiting on the whims of my husband to take his "old lady" out for dinner. When our food arrived we would eat in silence. He read the newspaper while I watched. Not working also meant I could lie down to relieve the back pain.

I needed to do something with my time or I would be hopelessly depressed. Across from our basement apartment was a church. I began attending services and eventually bible study. The minister was a compassionate and kind person who let me talk about my feelings many times during our stay in that house. His presence across the street gave me a sense of safety.

I began sketching and painting. I arranged the living room furniture so the sofa was on an angle in the corner creating a small work space with a table and a chair. There my art supplies would be protected from the children. I could watch them and work on my art at the same time.

I didn't have my own money to buy many supplies so I used the cardboard pieces that came with Monty's shirts from the dry cleaners as my canvasses. If I ran out of those, I'd use any flat surface I could find. One charcoal sketch was on a pull down blind; an elephant being attacked by a lion. It's one of my pieces that family members remember as one of their favorites. I was like a machine, churning out dozens of sketches and paintings for several months. My subjects were pictures in the newspaper and magazines. My father somehow ended up with them and much later I discovered they had been destroyed.

The lack of my own money made me dependent on Monty. I couldn't do anything outside the house, including taking the children to the doctor, without asking Monty for money. It was his form of control over me. I was returning from an appointment with my one year old and a newborn in my arms. I deposited the bus fare and sat down in the nearest seat. The driver called back so everyone on the bus could hear that I didn't deposit the full amount. I told him I only had the exact change so he must be mistaken, or perhaps I dropped a nickel in the snow when I was boarding. He argued with me, but there was nothing I could do. I couldn't walk home in the cold winter day and I guess he realized that and said nothing more. I was so humiliated.

My back condition worsened. Hot sharp pains shot down the back of my left leg. The surgeon wanted to operate. Then, I discovered I was pregnant and that halted the planned surgery. The surgeon told me to go to bed until the baby was born and walk only when necessary. With two small children I couldn't possibly follow the doctor's instructions, so I phoned dad and asked him if Betty could come to help me. She was still in high school, but the teacher agreed to let her out of school as long as she did the homework given to her. She was a great help to me. She cooked the meals, cleaned the house and took care of the children while I lay on the sofa all day. I think Betty stayed with us for a month. When she ran out of homework she needed to return home.

My day consisted of lying on the sofa during the day watching TV for the remainder of my pregnancy. Lynn was about three years old, Vern was four. Lynn would climb onto the sofa very carefully and plant herself in the bend of my knees as I lay on my side. She would chatter away in her baby talk and play with her toys. Vern usually played on the floor in front of the sofa where I could touch him from time to time. They were good kids and gave me no trouble.

Six months later I went into labor. It was May 24, 1963. While Monty slept, I sat up most of the night playing solitaire and tolerating the sciatic pain until I knew it was time. When I woke him and told him to take me to the hospital, he got up nonchalantly, dressed and waited for me in the car. He dropped me off at the hospital emergency entrance and to the shock of the nurse, went back home to bed and work later that morning.

Les was reluctant to come into this world, but eventually I heard him wail. The procedure for delivering babies had not changed since I delivered Vern. They whisked Les away as soon as he was viable. I didn't see him until the next morning. When Monty came to visit the next evening I asked him if he'd seen our son and he said in a casual gesture that he had not. I was hurt. How could he not want to see our son? He was behaving as if this was only one of so many that it wasn't anything special, just another baby. Days later Monty picked us up and we went home.

I was in so much pain tending to Les I could barely sit or stand more than five minutes. Sitting in the easy chair feeding him was extremely painful. I couldn't feed him in bed because I would disturb Monty. I made a larger hole in the nipple of his bottles so he'd eat faster. I had no idea this would cause him distress. But it did. He cried often because his belly was cramping.

After about two weeks, I called the doctor and told him I couldn't take the pain any longer and needed the surgery. Marie, Monty's sister, flew in to take the baby to care for him in her home until I was well. Lynn went to live with my mother and Vern stayed with Monty's cousin while he worked. Marie soon discovered Les had continuous belly aches. She noticed the enlarged baby bottle nipples and replaced them with new ones. He recovered and thrived.

Mom would call me from time to time and report how Lynn was doing. I cried when she told me she thought Lynn had a hearing problem. I cried out of guilt. I had struck Lynn often on the side of the head. Perhaps I thought, I had damaged her ear. But Lynn's problem wasn't a damaged ear; she was unloved and full of fear from the violence in our home. She didn't respond when spoken to because she was afraid. When she spoke her voice was soft and barely audible.

In the hospital I was in traction for three weeks waiting for a neurosurgeon to examine me. The pain was unforgiving. When I walked the hallways for exercise I dragged my left leg and could barely put any pressure on it to walk. The doctor doped me up and ordered massage to relax my muscles.

Dad and his parents came to visit. As soon as I saw dad, I grabbed him, cried and held him close. I was terrified. I was going to have surgery and could come out of it paralyzed.

Finally the neurosurgeon examined me and the surgery was ordered in a few days. The operation went well and two weeks, after recovering from a discectomy between the fourth and fifth lumbar, I went home. The doctor had been reluctant to release me because I needed more healing, but I also needed to get home to my children.

My first night home Monty demanded sex. I was still very sore but that didn't matter. When we got up the next day, there was blood on the sheets from where my incision had opened slightly. Fortunately it wasn't serious. We left for a vacation within the week to pick up our nine week old son.

Chapter Sixteen

We enjoyed our holiday back in the mountains so much we decided to move back. Before we left, Monty had the promise of a bartending job on our return and we found a house to rent not far from Monty's family. The excitement of the move was the only relief I had from the beatings. Monty was distracted. I was relieved.

Once we were settled, I approached the telephone company for a position. I started off as an operator, was promoted to supervisor and in short time I had another promotion to district traffic clerk. I became active in the union and held a few of the executive positions.

When I discovered I could submit articles to the in-house newspaper, I set out to find something of interest that was relative to the company. I submitted a number of articles and each time I won an award for the top story. My prize was only $5, but that wasn't important, it was the recognition of my work and obvious talent.

Up to this point, we could only afford to rent a home. Now we had a better chance of buying one. We found a house and with a loan for the down payment through my employer's loan plan, we bought our first house; two small bedrooms, one on either side of the bathroom off the hall; a kitchen and living room plus a full basement.

The decorating would be whatever furnishings we had at the time. No theme and no plan, but functional, neat and tidy. The three children would share the smaller bedroom. The two boys in bunk beds and our daughter slept in a twin bed across from them. There was little room to play unless they used their beds to spread their toys on or they played in the living room. The house was adequate. The master bedroom was just the right size for our double bed, a dresser and two night stands. I had taken it upon myself to make it as pretty as I knew how. My color selection was in the trendy purple hues. I felt it was picture perfect, just like in the magazines and movies. It even looked safe. But over the months the 'safe' room developed flaws and gained invisible dark memories . . . memories that would almost destroy me.

Shortly after we bought our house, I quit work. I liked working because it was a distraction from what was happening at home. It meant having my own money and being with adults. In time, I couldn't do my job and take the beatings and tension at home. I was getting depressed again, lacked energy and enthusiasm.

There were times when Monty was in my face screaming obscenities, I would strike him first, just to get the beating over with. I was in a catacomb of fear. Any solutions I had to our problems were met with a dead end and anything I did I was not good enough. There was no escape.

Most nights, Monty came home about three in the morning. I'd get up, make him a lunch and watch him eat while he read the paper. Then we'd climb into bed, he'd turn his back to me and pass out. I would struggle to sleep. And like most nights, the house was quiet. But there were the other nights . . . .

Chapter Seventeen

The startling, yet anticipated sound of the key slipping into the lock woke me. With lightning speed, a pain burst through my body creating a muscle spasm in my gut; the moisture in my mouth evaporated. My body became paralyzed with fear, like a deer in the headlights. Adrenaline pounded through my body, my heart raced, breathing became difficult, thinking impossible; instinctually I curled up making myself as small as I could. This was all too familiar.

I felt no power, no control of what would happen next. I could hear him falling against the wall in the hallway as he staggered toward our bedroom. The door opened with exploding force. He stood there leaning against its frame. He stumbled toward the bed and tore the bedding from me. Obscene words stormed from of his mouth spelling degradation and humiliation. I coiled even more. I was terrified. All this happened in lightning speed. There was no time to run even if my body would move.

The first blow weighted heavy across my hip. His forceful hands clamped onto my shoulders and I was flung about. The world began spinning, I couldn't focus. Monty was not a big man, but the rage that came from somewhere deep inside him was released by alcohol, driving his powerful fist down onto my face and for a split second, a flash of light pierced my head and then black.

When light came, I was wrenched from the bed and propelled down the hall. The world was a blur. He charged through the children's door, dragging me, then pushing me and I collided with the floor between the children's beds. Somewhere in this room were my children, but my world at that moment was only the shadow of this man raging in the darkness. Glinting images, like a photograph, a second in life, shrouded in a haze with no perimeters, told me the children were sitting up, motionless. I held my arms over my face and head, and waited for the next blow. Another blow and the children disappeared. All I saw next was an aura of terror and shock enveloping their tiny innocent faces. He shrieked words to belittle me. I'm a terrible mother, a slut and a whore. His shoe pierced my side.

In a huff he reeled and stumbled heavily toward the living room leaving me on the floor, frozen in time. There was no before or after this incident. I was in this moment with no other kind of world beyond my body. I tried to breath but my lungs wouldn't expand. My mind wanted me to move, but I was physically paralyzed where he threw me.

I heard him collapse onto the sofa. Carefully I raised my body, weak from the trauma, bent over in fear. I heard the muffled sounds of children crying. But in my struggle to survive, I didn't make the connection that the crying was coming from my children, who had just been terrorized.

My only concern was to survive that night. I knew I had to get out of their room so their world would be calm. I needed to return to bed. The hallway to the master bedroom was short, but I had to pass the doorway to the living room. As I crept along I tried to keep myself as small as possible so he wouldn't notice me. I saw his face was pressed against the arm of the sofa, his cheeks pleated under the weight of his head and saliva draining from his mouth, his eyes were closed. My greatest fear was that he would open them, see me and attack again. I focused on the bedroom door as I slunk along the hall. I inched my battered body into bed, pulled the covers over me and placed my head on the pillow. My head was vibrating as if electricity was running through my brain. I had no awareness of my body. I didn't know if it hurt or if it was numb. It was like it didn't exist. I lay awake, afraid to close my eyes. Exhausted, I finally drifted into a troubled sleep. In a flash, I heard him moving in the living room, instantly my heart began to race; my body went rigid. My breathing went shallow. If I could have held my breath I might not exist. None of this was a conscious effort. I was reacting to the fear of what could and would likely happen. He slithered into bed beside me. With swift determined anger, he grabbed my hips pulling them close to him and he raped me. When he was finished, he slumped onto his side and passed out. I wanted to cry but I was afraid I might waken him and he would attack yet again.

The alarm startled me from my fitful sleep, like it does any normal morning. He turned over. His face was calm, smooth like an innocent child as his body rose and fell in rhythm while he slept. Reality struck my body as I began moving. It was heavy, stiff and sore and my eye throbbed. I quietly hobbled into the bathroom. The mirror revealed the night's terror. My eye was swollen and had already begun to turn dark. I got the children breakfast and later I took them outside. Their play was solemn and restrained. No one said anything about last night.

The fresh morning air stabbed at my battered face. The harsh sun stung my eyes. When I returned to the kitchen, he was gone. The house was quiet. I left the children outside and I moved about my normal daily routine of wiping walls, washing floors and vacuuming carpets in an attempt to create the perfect home and wondering what I did wrong this time. And how can I be better.

In the afternoon, Monty returned home bearing gifts; a bouquet of flowers with an invitation to dine out. He was sorry he said, and it wouldn't happen again. He hadn't remembered much, but he was sorry. His head hung and I could hear the muffled sounds of guarded crying. Were these tears of remorse or manipulation?

I took him in my arms anyway and told him I loved him. He gently kissed my swollen eye. I didn't want to risk his retaliation if I didn't acquiesce to his offering. We began once more, like we had many times; all was forgotten in the bliss of yet another honeymoon. I had the expectation that our lives together would be what I thought was normal. I simply had to work toward being the perfect wife and mother. Only then, would I satisfy him. Only then would the beatings stop.

Pleasing him was short lived. The anxiety I felt lying beside him remembering those familiar feelings was there for a reason. It was a warning; an instinctive primal message from my body that my life was once again in danger; like our primitive ancestors who could feel the presence of a predator before sight or smell that would reveal intent to steal their lives.

Monty had just returned from a two hour drive out of town with his brother-in-law, Ted. They went there often, leaving early on a Sunday morning and returning late afternoon. I found out years later that they would spend most of the day in a bar drinking and flirting with women. Once they found someone willing, they'd move on to a motel to have sex. Was it guilt that led him to beat me? Perhaps it was disrespect for all women; that we were all whores.

This time he was sober, or at least as sober as an alcoholic can be. This time it was broad daylight. He started yelling at me, faulting me for everything that was wrong, and then the power of his fist came down on me. But this time it hit where there would be no visible signs. This time he pushed my face into a pillow on the sofa until I could barely breathe. When he finally released his pressure, I ran into the kitchen, and called the police. As Monty lunged toward me, I raised the receiver and brought it crashing down on his head. I used every bit of strength I had in me. The thud on his head reverberated up to my shoulder like the bouncing of a fallen tree as it hit the ground. My intention was to knock him out, then the police would come and take him away and I would not live in fear any longer. To my shock, this didn't happen. Monty clutched his head, staggered backward and came at me with full force. At that instant, the doorbell rang.

I could see the shadow of two police officers through the door window. They entered the living room but stayed close to the door. Monty had resigned himself to the sofa slouching with his head bowed and playing with his hands. Still filled with fear, I don't remember telling them why I called. One of the officers asked me: "did Monty assault you?" In my ignorance, I thought he was asking if Monty had used a gun or knife against me so my response was: "no". The officers left.

Now, I had called the police, they believed they had no reason to take action and I was left with this man who had tried to kill me. I silently went about preparing dinner leaving Monty sleeping on the sofa.

The beatings and berating's didn't end. My body often ached from his blows, my jaw was hit so many times it was clicking when I chewed and twice he gave me a black eye that was so swollen I couldn't see out of it for days. Each time he got drunk he would hit me again and again. I thought, if he only stopped drinking, I would be safe. But his problem was more complex. Drunk or sober, he beat me.

Following each beating, I worked even harder to make the house, the children and me perfect. I continued to wash the floors, wipe the walls and dust daily. I manicured the lawn. When Monty brought his drinking buddies home, I was the perfect entertainer, serving them drinks and snacks. The children had to be perfect. They couldn't make a lot of noise in their play; they couldn't ask for anything, they would get what they needed and no more. The children stopped laughing. When Monty came home at two in the morning, I'd get up and make him bacon and eggs and watch him eat while he read the newspaper. There was nothing that was out of order.

    My only escape was into myself. Contact with family members was limited to the odd letter between mother and me. My only connection to the outside world was spending coffee time with a neighbor my age. But we never talked about the abuse. I discovered years later, she was also being abused.

    I had to pretend life was good and follow Monty's instructions. I loathed me. My five foot seven, one hundred and twenty pound figure was no longer attractive to him or me. I was useless, a whore, a bad mother, a terrible wife and human being. I could do nothing right. My mind was easily manipulated by anyone who wanted to dominate me. As Margaret Robison writes in her book: The Long Journey Home: *"How do you live when you can't believe what your own mind tells you? You find someone else's mind to believe in."* p198.

    I was anesthetized by the exhaustion of being in survival mode. I was emotionally unconscious and bankrupt. I watched television for hours on end, escaping into the black box. I thought constantly of suicide to get out of this prison and to stop the pain.

    My shoulders drooped, I rarely smiled and I felt fatigued. My mind was without coherent thoughts. I could not understand who I was and how I was going to survive. Depression took over and I became a robot wandering aimlessly through the days.

    The effects of trauma on victims are well described in Peter Levine's book: "In An Unspoken Voice". He described my life perfectly: *"you feel that you are in a state of helpless resignation and lack the energy to fuel your life and move forward. This collapse, defeat and loss of the will to live are at the very core of deep trauma."* P 49

    I had tried everything I could think of to make our lives better until I realized I needed outside help. My doctor referred me to a psychiatrist. His diagnosis was paranoid schizophrenia. Relieved by the diagnosis, I was able to put a label on what was happening to me. Without question

I believed that I was mentally ill. I questioned every thought I had. If I was crazy then whatever I was thinking was the crazy part of me and my thoughts were not to be trusted.

After a few visits, the psychiatrist suggested I have electro shock therapy. I would be in the hospital for a month and receive seven treatments, but I'd feel better in the end, he told me. I don't remember much about my stay in the hospital. I did paint-by numbers picture, even though I was an accomplished artist, weaved a tray and attended exercise classes. I don't recall any therapy sessions with the doctor. I was allowed to wash my hair in one of the maintenance rooms. I found a razor blade, lifted it and placed it in my bedside table drawer. When the doctor came on his rounds, I chose to give it to him. He said nothing and nothing happened over that matter.

I returned home with a prescription that he said would continue to balance the chemistry in my brain. I felt like a stranger when I got home. Not quite there and not knowing where I belonged. I did get better, for a short time.

The beatings began again shortly after I was home from the hospital. It was the same all over again. With no hope of escape, even for a few hours a day, I was slipping into that familiar world of emotional unconsciousness. I was feeling trapped and isolating myself from the outside world.

It became obvious to me that my brain chemistry wasn't the problem. Monty and his beatings were. I stopped taking the pills. I needed to get a break from the house and meet people. I asked Monty if I could go back to school to learn to be a secretary. He responded: "no you'll get too independent then". At least he was honest.

During the last time Monty would ever beat me, an image flashed through my mind. I was going to grab the butcher knife and stab him. In that same breath, I thought of the children. Their father would be dead and their mother in prison. I couldn't let that happen.

I told Monty we needed to talk. We went for a drive without the children and I explained that I needed a break from him. He replied: "Oh no not again". Soon I noticed the car inching toward the shoulder of the highway. I could see beyond the edge of the road a sudden steep drop hundreds of feet down. I became stiff, trying to press the imaginary brake on the passenger side, my heart began racing and I was holding my breath. Then he said something that sent chills through me: "I guess if we both die, my sister will raise our kids". He brought the car back to the lane and we proceeded home. My body remained frozen. What was going to happen when we got home?

The next day, courage and strength came from somewhere deep inside. It was clear to me that the next beating could mean my life. I began making phone calls and filling out employment applications. Within a few days I had two job offers and I had found a two bedroom furnished apartment in an old two story house across from the children's school. Now that both were secured, I told Monty I was leaving. He said: "take the girl and leave the boys". I was shocked. He had no thoughts on how this would impact the children by being separated. Were they just pieces of furniture to him that we divided? Fearing his fury, I did as I was told. I couldn't afford to make this departure any more difficult and risk another beating that may end up in the death of one of us.

I sat the children down that afternoon when Monty was at work and told them Lynn and I would be moving to an apartment close to the school. The boys could visit us any time. I made clear to them; at least I hope I did, that this wasn't their fault. They sat bent over on the sofa, sad, looking confused and on the verge of tears. Anything else I told them is a blur. This was 1969; Vern was ten, Lynn nine and Les six. The next day I moved personal effects for Lynn and I; selecting only necessary items from the house for our use. I don't remember, but I think the children were in school when I moved out. I was fleeing. I was scared. I was relieved and excited. I was sad and felt the weight of guilt for leaving my boys behind.

I was an incompetent mother and unable to do anything right. I tried myself, found myself guilty of abandoning my boys and created my own prison without parole. I was convinced no one would want to know me. For the next forty-four years, guilt became my shadow, my memory, always there following me. I eventually became that shadow, hollow, with unfathomable depths of darkness, an eclipse of myself, unable to feel or enjoy the sensation of touch. It was my answer to being invisible. I was a contradiction, wanting to be invisible, but wanting to be acknowledged and loved. If I stayed invisible, I could move about in society and not be detected and abused. I would just exist. But I craved love and acceptance. This feeling, this awareness, became baggage, weighing me down by some invisible force that prevented me from feeling light and free of any burdens.

Chapter Eighteen

Lynn and I settled into our apartment. It wasn't much, but I didn't have to deal with Monty any longer. At least that's what I thought. He began dropping in unannounced and drunk, telling me how I should be living. Finally, one evening when he staggered up my stairs I called the police. When they arrived, Monty's demeanor changed in the face of these powerful men. He stopped bothering me.

The boys came over as often as they wanted. Les loved to show me his lunch bucket and all the great foods his Aunt had provided. I took my children on hikes, walks and sometimes just had a meal together.

On one visit they told me the firemen had to break down the door at their house. Apparently Monty had tried to commit suicide. I went to the house to talk with Monty and suggested I move back into the house and he move out. But he would have nothing to do with that idea and I left.

There were many times, when I walked the hill to my apartment, I'd pass Monty's car parked outside a bar. The boys were always in the car waiting, unhappy and sometimes quarreling. I wanted to take them from the car and disappear. But I was afraid of the repercussions. I knew first hand, Monty's wrath. Monty could do nothing without booze. When we took the children on vacations he'd have to stop for a beer at every roadside pub. When we went camping, the provisions always included one or two boxes of beer and when he ran out, he'd go to the nearest liquor store or bar to replenish his supply.

I needed to break our legal ties and gain custody of my children. I tried again, but I had to prove that Monty had committed adultery or abused me. The adultery I couldn't prove, but I thought I had a case with abuse. I gave a lawyer a retainer and he contacted my doctor to be a witness. The doctor said he couldn't because he never saw evidence of physical abuse. I guess I never went to him when I had a black eye or bruises on my body. Perhaps I only went to the doctor when I was depressed. I can't remember.

In short time a court date was set. While waiting for court to begin, my lawyer came to me and said this case was going to be tougher than he expected and I'd have to give him more money, right then and there. I didn't have that kind of money with me or in the bank, so the case was dropped. I should have reported the lawyer to the Law Society, but I was too broken to have any fight left in me. I had to carry on.

I didn't know what a "normal" life was or what to expect, but I was on a path of self-discovery. The movies and TV were my mentors. I wanted to create the kind of life I saw in the movies and on TV because their lives seemed so much better than what I had. The more I could become like them, the more "normal" my life would be. I prepared a table that was closer to the elegance I saw in the movies; a table cloth and napkins with an attractive wine glass. Because all the actors drank orange juice in the morning, I did. When I was older and found I enjoyed wine, I had a glass with dinner; because that's the way it was in the movies. I continued to work toward the "new me", but everything I was doing was external. I didn't think about digging deep into my psyche. Now I was away from Monty, I would have a 'normal' life. But, there was no time to change me. I was constantly distracted from one drama after another.

I knew Lynn wasn't happy. I had this distorted idea that just because I was feeling free and relieved, Lynn would also. Perhaps if I made our new home cozy and pretty we could both enjoy our lives. My apartment extended out onto a back porch that had been neglected and filled with junk. I threw out the junk, painted the porch with fresh clean colors and bought a few outdoor chairs. I rearranged the furniture in the apartment and made the place attractive.

One day, I packed a lunch and towels and we headed down the hill to the beach. Holding Lynn's tiny hand, I began skipping and singing, swinging her little arm, but she didn't join in, not even a a smile. After that I stopped trying. I had no understanding of what to do with children. I had expectations on her as I would of an adult. If she didn't embrace my new found happiness, then I didn't know what to do. How wrong of me to expect her to feel as I did. I had disrupted her life as she knew it. I had taken her from her brothers and father. I never thought to ask her how she felt.

I now know the harm brought to my children while living in a house of violence. A child in an angry home doesn't have to see or hear the violence; it impacts them even if they're in another room, when they're sleeping or even when they are in their mother's womb. Their young innocent minds and bodies absorb the tension before the beatings. Their bodies feel every blow and wonder when they will be beaten. My children didn't have to hear the words their father screeched; they felt them. They could not articulate their feelings; they acted them. When I think back on how they behaved, they may well have been emotionally shut down. I'm certain Lynn was. Most times they were quiet, shy, obedient. They didn't have that sparkle in their eyes.

Recent studies on how violence affects children states that: *". . . (a child) being in an environment of anger and abuse has an impact on children in many ways. It affects their brain development. That in turn affects every aspect of their development: physical, mental, emotional and spiritual. It increases children's level of anxiety and fear; it affects their ability to learn to connect with other people"*. The impact on them affects how they see the world and how they react to it. *"They become fearful and anxious. They may believe the world is a dangerous place . . . they may become aggressive . . . or passive/ overly obedient thinking they cannot change any part of their lives . . . lose energy and hope, disconnect from the real world . . . they may have trouble learning because so much of their brain is busy dealing with the stress of an abusive environment . . . (there is) a great risk of growing up to be abusive to others, to be abused, or both . . . and if children continue to be exposed to violence and abuse, the trauma will continue to affect their brains and development . . . Brain scans show that children in abusive environments use much of their brain to watch out for danger. Less of their brain is available for healthy growth and development . . . it affects their physical, emotional and mental development, their ability to form healthy relationships . . . (the violence affects) them even when the child is not consciously aware of the violence in the home . . . they may feel anxious or panicky, have an increased heart rate . . . they may be watchful and attentive all the time, as though on 'red alert'. Because their brains are distracted by fear, the children may find it hard to concentrate or pay attention, difficult sleeping, difficulty learning"*. Alberta Children's Services Prevention of Family Violence and Bullying booklet. Alberta Children Services.

Researchers now may have evidence that the fetus can be affected by negative emotions and a violent environment for the mother.

"We know that infants are often directly involved in violent domestic incidents. They are held as a shield by the mother, hit by thrown objects, or intentionally threatened or hurt to terrify the mother. Even when they are apparently lying passively in their cots, infants are exquisitely sensitive to their surroundings and especially to the emotional signals given out by their caregivers, including the caregiver's depressed, anxious, fearful or angry mood.

At birth, a baby's brain is 25% of its adult weight, increasing to 66% by the end of the first year due to the 'brain growth spurt' which occurs between the seventh prenatal month and the child's first birthday. The developing brain is most vulnerable to the impact of traumatic experiences during this time. New research on brain development suggests that exposure to extreme trauma will change the organisation of the brain, resulting in difficulties in dealing with stresses later in life." Perry, B D, 1997, 'Incubated in terror: neurodevelopmental factors in the "Cycle of Violence"', in J D Osofsky, ed., *Children in a Violent Society*, Guilford Publications, NewYork *www.community.nsw.gov.au/docswr/_assets/main/.../dv_paper.pdf*

My children absorbed the idea that women were subservient, that it was okay to abuse them. I saw this in Vern and Lynn. When Vern had a serious relationship, he told me he was so angry with his girlfriend that he sat her down hard on a chair. They married but were divorced in short time. When Lynn had her first serious relationship, the man who supposedly loved her began hitting her. Fortunately she left him a lot sooner than I had.

Les' life was negatively affected in the beginning, but later developed differently. When he was a toddler, he whined most of the time. I didn't understand that this was how he demonstrated his feelings about the tension in the home. When he later played hockey and was billeted out to various homes, he had an opportunity to see how loving families behaved. When I saw him years after I left, he was different than the other two children. He seemed calmer.

I hold myself responsible for the things I did to my children and the things I did not do for them. They deserved better. In my fear and frustration I lashed out on them; slapping them in the face, screaming at them, spanking them, not talking to them, threatening them with the wooden spoon and probably used it on them, however I don't remember. My thinking was so distorted. I seemed to think that if I told them once not to do something, they should remember and behave. I feared that if they damaged something in their play, I would get a beating. But of course, early life is an experiment on how to behave and how far a child can push. I didn't understand that. I didn't protect them from their father's abuse, especially when he would tickle the boy's genitals. They would giggle and squirm to get away from him, but he kept after them until I pleaded with him to stop. Other times he strapped them with his belt.

Chapter Nineteen

My new job was not difficult and I was grateful for the union wages and benefits. The customer records were not up to date so I had to put in long hours, along with my supervisor, Vince. He was six feet tall, thin red hair that was turning white, a bit stocky, but a strong physique. The bonus for working those extra hours was overtime pay. After my regular hours, I walked home for supper with Lynn, and then returned back to work for another two or three hours. This meant Lynn was alone for extended periods. I'm sure she was lonely and was definitely neglected.

Soon my relationship with my supervisor extended to dating and then to love. Red flags were popping up frequently, warning me about Vince, but I did not see them or perhaps I did not want to. I had not noticed that Vince drank heavily. All my life, people around me drank every day and were often drunk or with a hangover. This was normal behaviour and lifestyle.

One late night, when Lynn and I were sleeping, there was a commotion on the ground floor apartment below me. Vince told me the next day that he had tried to climb into the window downstairs, thinking it was my place and almost got caught! He was probably drunk. I laughed it off feeling flattered.

I was in awe of people with high intellect and education, so when Vince told me he was a self-taught accountant; I assumed he was intelligent, worldly, and knowledgeable. I was willing to believe anything he said. He talked like he was intelligent, at least better than me. I thought: "so what do I know, he has grade twelve, he's a self-taught accountant and held many jobs in accounting; anything he says must be right." And Monty? He had grade twelve and was in the Air Force getting that additional training. He must know more than me. Later I would find out how wrong I was. I may not have had a higher education at the time, but I had life experience, a burgeoning creative talent, well organized and I was practical.

Vince was divorced and had a son and daughter, both around the same ages as Vern and Lynn. His daughter lived with his ex-wife, back east. His son lived at a mountain country boarding school just outside the city so Vince and he could visit often. What I did not know was that Vince had abducted his son and shortly after we had started dating, he ended up in jail until his ex-wife came and picked up her son. This was the first of a number of incidents that would show me that Vince acted as though he was above the law, including not submitting his income taxes. This person I was in love with constantly withheld important information from me. His character flaws would all be disclosed to me over the eleven years we were together. Between the drunken dates, the problem over his son and trying to break into the downstairs apartment, I should have known this was not a relationship I needed or should desire. In my desperation to be loved and protected, I ignored or were not conscious of the signs or denied that they were important, just as I had with Monty's heavy drinking and violence toward his mother. Being in love and being told I was loved, was like a drug to me. It made my head spin and my heart race. And, the bigger and stronger the man, the more I desired him. I thought I would be safe with someone powerful. My only thoughts were about him and how to please him. There was no rational thought, no consideration for possible consequences.

After Vince's son left, Vince wanted to move east where he once lived and be closer to his children. He asked me to go with him. In the latter part of 1969, we gave our notice at work and prepared to move. I can only imagine what my boys were feeling when I told them. They probably had no idea they would not see me for a very long time and I was oblivious to their pain. I can still see their sad, confused faces on our last few hours together. Nor, did I consider how Lynn was feeling. She had already lost the family and home she once knew. Now I was taking her from her lifelong friends. Kids do not have much say in these big decisions. But they often bear the brunt of them. I, on the other hand, was excited. I was getting out of this town and away from Monty and I was in a loving relationship. This was a chance at a new beginning. But who was this person I trusted? I had only known Vince for two or three months. I was unaware he was an alcoholic. Later I would learn he was also: dishonest, irresponsible, manipulative and demeaning to me.

We packed our things and sent them ahead by train, loaded Lynn and her kitten into my newly purchased Volkswagen bug and headed east. When we arrived we moved into an apartment. Without unpacking even the bedding, Vince wanted to visit his friends. I didn't understand why this was necessary at that moment, but I wanted to be with him, so we left Lynn all alone in this strange city and apartment with the job of unpacking her things and putting them away. I deserted her. How I could have done that is beyond any sensibility.

Vince and his friends were political activists, taking part in the anti-war movement, the New Democractic Party and the emerging Women's Liberation Movement. I knew nothing of these things. Political activism was Vince's life and I felt that if I wanted to be with him, I would have to be a part of his activities. I could not imagine branching out on my own and thinking for myself. I had this attitude I would go down any path directed by someone else and see where it led me. I did not understand that success in self-discovery requires my input, my participation and control of where I was going. I made decisions recklessly. I did not think about: options, consequences and dangers. I was like an innocent child being led by a trusting caregiver. I wanted to be with Vince and because I had not considered that I could do something on my own, I was unaware that my life was about to drastically change. I still didn't understand the need to learn about boundaries and healthy decisions so I could protect myself.

This was the time when the women's liberation movement was at its infancy. I began going to meetings, learning how women, including myself, have been second class citizens with very few rights. We needed to make the government aware that we wanted to be equal to men in job opportunities, wages, in the courts and educational institutions. Eventually our demands would include the right to control our bodies, the right to available legal safe abortions and supporting Dr. Henry Morgentaler, the man who defied the law and opened the first safe abortion clinic in Canada.

As my experience in the women's movement increased, I relied on Vince's perspective less and less. I grew into a new me, with my own thoughts and opinions. As I evolved I began standing up for myself. This caused conflict between us. I became strong and independent.

This was quite common during that period. There were many divorces and break-ups because the woman in the relationship: wanted more say, more time to herself, had her own ideas and wanted a different lifestyle. However, Vince continued to support and encourage me despite our differences. I am grateful to him.

I became a voice for change in women's pursuits. I was not only breaking new ground for women, but for myself, discovering our power and skills. I was becoming liberated from the old beliefs that women were submissive, inferior and on this earth to please and obey men. I began to see the influence I could make on society and discovered I had untapped skills while experiencing a huge learning curve. Public speaking, being assertive and actually having beliefs was empowering. I organized meetings, spoke out at public gatherings, conferences and made presentations to government bodies on behalf of the Women's Liberation Movement. This was now my role in life and a challenge to who I had been. I was excited, renewed and alive. In my old life, I was uncomfortable if people listened to me. I would lose my train of thought. I overcame that problem because I had something worthy to say and I learned to speak eloquently.

I worked at a desk job for an oil company during the day and attended meetings several evenings a week. Often circulated leaflets to the general public on the streets, passing on our message or informing people of a meeting we had organized. Occasionally, weekends were spent demonstrating on the steps of Parliament Hill.

When we went out of town, Lynn would reluctantly come along. It wasn't much of a life for her. At home she passed the time watching television or being in her room, quiet and sad. I didn't know what to do with her to help her be happy. Until I was seven, I was an only child. I played by myself most of the time. It was normal to me.

But I think Lynn was sad for other reasons. When we were together I don't think I behaved in a loving manner. I didn't do things with her, or even have a conversation with her. I was afraid to help her with her homework assignments because I didn't think I knew enough to be of any help. I took a "modern mathematics" course and did well in it, but even then I felt my knowledge was inadequate. What did I know about helping a child deal with a new lifestyle? Again I treated her like an adult expecting her to find her way just as I had. She was alone and had to create her own life as best she could. I wrote to the boys and they responded, but I didn't write as often as I should. I really didn't know what to put in the letters. They wouldn't be interested in women's liberation, but that was my life.

They sent me their school photos and I'm not sure, but I think I sent them birthday and Christmas cards. I don't remember if I sent them gifts. We were living on very low incomes so I probably did not have money for gifts.

I soon learned how irresponsible Vince was. Early one morning when it was still dark outside, someone knocked on our door. The stranger asked for my car keys in a demanding voice. Shocked I asked why. He told me we had missed two payments on the car and he was repossessing. I had given Vince the money to make those payments and he obviously used the money for his own purposes. I was embarrassed and angry. He apologized but he acted like a kid caught with his hand in the cookie jar. This didn't mean a whole lot to him. Just that he got caught in his deceit.

Vince, in the early days of our relationship, had asked me why I did not go to university. I had never considered that possibility. It was an enticing thought, but I soon abandoned the idea and went about my daily routine of working and dating Vince.

We decided to move to a smaller community. Once settled we developed friends with others of the same interests. One of the people in our political circle was a professor. I talked with him about the possibilities of applying to the local university as a mature student without a high school diploma. He told me to take a grade twelve English course during the summer. A passing grade would look good on the application, he told me.

This meant I had to quit my day job at the oil company because the course was five full days a week. I probably would have lost that job anyway because my job as the credit clerk was to phone customers who were in arrears and find ways of getting money out of them. I believed every sad story they gave me and consequently wasn't getting the money they owed the company.

I chose the grade twelve English summer course being offered at the local high school. The University approved my passing grade and my application to attend University.

In the fall semester of 1970 I enrolled in five courses of the General Arts Diploma program, which qualified me as a full time student, a prerequisite for the student loan. Vince supported us until university began and my application for a student loan and grant and been approved. It was enough to survive with one dependent.

Considering I never liked school or did well, the prospects of returning to school was unnerving. All I could see was a B.A. next to my name after three years of post-secondary education. This would mean I would be perceived as intelligent by everyone around me, or so I thought. How to get that B.A. was not part of my thinking. I didn't know what to expect and how much my mind would be challenged.

Lectures were difficult and I struggled. Absorbing the contents of the lectures and learning to take notes was foreign to me. I did what was asked of me, but I just couldn't do the work to the satisfaction of myself or the professors. Reading and comprehension were part of my problems. My language skills were inadequate. A tutorial leader once asked me if English was my second language. My marks were not good, but they were enough to enrol the following year along with Vince who decided to quit work and seek a university degree in economics. We were going to live totally on student loans and grants. I was hoping he would be able to help me in the classes we both took. But that was not my reality. He did not help me. Vince of course excelled. His marks were high, he became the student Ombudsman and a political activist on campus, far surpassing my abilities. When he ran out of student grant money he was able to find sources. He knew how to get grants and bursaries that I did not even know existed. And he never shared that money or how I could apply for the grants.

Despite taking additional seminars in the development of good study habits and speed reading, I just couldn't learn the material. I was overwhelmed by all that was expected of me. I sequestered myself in the library to study, hoping the environment of so much knowledge would, through osmosis, help me understand what I was trying to learn. After about an hour my heavy eyes began to close and I drifted off into another world, and then abruptly return to reality. At that point I had to give up and go home. I went to the campus doctor about this problem and he gave me a prescription for uppers. "Uppers" were not part of my awareness nor did I know they could have side effects. The jitters were uncomfortable, so I stopped taking them. Besides they did not solve my problem.

Finally I realized university was too advanced for my poor educational background and abilities. I dropped out at the end of the first semester of my second year. I felt defeated and stupid, like I had all through my school years.

The entire one and a half years in university was not a lost cause. I had absorbed more than I realized. There was life outside of my world. I was exposed to a culture of thought, ideas, processing challenges, reflection and new perspectives. I learned about life other than my own. My eyes were opening. Psychology was fascinating. Geology was intriguing.

It was a challenge to go to university for the first time and to organize a women's group. But I did it. I learned along the way, just not academically.

I had developed in other areas I never thought possible. My shy, meek, in-the-background personality shifted, developed and flourished. I became the motivator and spokeswoman for the women's liberation movement in our small community of 100,000 souls. I pushed aside my reservations of inadequacy and "did it anyway".

I had learned to love the prospect of learning. I could not return to my former self. I vowed I would find a way to get a better education and decided college was a good possibility. The teaching methods and subjects were different. The programs were geared to gain a career rather than accumulate academic standings that might end up in a career. To be successful this time, I had to better prepare myself.

I worked for about a year as a receptionist and took English classes in the evening at the college. The first course, I received a 2.5 out of 4 mark, which was average. When the second course ended in May of 1973, I had moved my mark a full point . . . and I was enjoying going to school and studying.

It was during this period that for the first time in my thirty-two years, I read a book, cover to cover and remembered what I had read. The book was "Lost Horizon". I followed that with the daunting account of Russian life in "And Quiet Flows the Don". I took that book everywhere I went and stole moments where I could read a chapter. When I was finished I felt I had lost a friend. I had learned to read and wanted more of that pleasure.

In September 1973, I enrolled in the local college in the Radio and TV Productions two year certificate program. I quit work just before College courses began, and, with a small income tax refund, I purchased an airline ticket to visit the boys.

To cut my expenses, I asked my former employer/hairdresser if I could stay at her home. She was more than happy to help me.

The boys were so much bigger than the last time I saw them. They were a bit reserved, but I think they enjoyed themselves. I certainly did. I rented a boat for the afternoon and for a while, I piloted the boat, then Vern wanted to take over, but the longer he was at the wheel, the more reckless he became, scaring Les, so I told Vern he either had to slow down or I would pilot the boat. Much to his chagrin, he slowed down. Later we had lunch. We didn't have much time together because I had only enough money for my expenses and a little left over for entertainment with them, but at least I had some time with them.

Lynn still wasn't happy, had no friends and was lonely. She spoke so softly I had to ask her to repeat herself many times. She found ways to entertain herself, but her activity didn't change her demeanor. Seeing her this way was painful. I didn't understand her problem and I didn't put the effort into finding ways to help her. I didn't show her the love she so desperately needed.

Eventually, I asked her if she'd like to live with her dad and brothers. She said yes. I phoned Monty and in short time she was packed. I said good-bye to her at the airport, knowing I probably wouldn't see her for a long time.

I couldn't seem to keep anything going smoothly and didn't understand why or how to make the necessary changes.

Back at school, I felt a bit more secure after developing my English skills. I withdrew from the women's movement. It was consuming too much of my time and energy. I couldn't afford to jeopardize my future to make a decent wage. I excelled in College. I was on the dean's honor roll for the duration of the two year program. Instructors commended me on my work and as a result I received one of their bursaries. I had gained respect from students in the program, self-respect, confidence and I had a view of my future.

My relationship with Vince was disintegrating. His drinking was getting worse and I became suspicious that he might be having an affair and he was, as I later discovered. Not just one, but many. We had our happy times where we enjoyed our mutual interests: dancing, the movies, dining out and skiing. I remained optimistic and dedicated to keeping our relationship. When his final divorce papers came I asked him to marry me. I ignored the red flags and went into romance mode, thinking that marriage would change everything. He said "Yes" like he was agreeing to go for coffee.

When I phoned Lynn to tell her I was marrying Vince, she pleaded with me to send her a plane ticket. I really wanted her to come, but I had a choice: her plane ticket or my wedding. There wasn't enough money for both. When I told her, I could hear the disappointment in her voice.

I made my own wedding dress from a floor length housecoat pattern and altered the design slightly using soft pink brocade trimmed with lace and attaching a sheer pink chiffon hood. I carried a bouquet of silk flowers. On October 13, 1973 on the thirteen hour on the thirteenth floor of the University, (that should have been an omen in itself), Vince and I married.

The wedding was so much more than my marriage to Monty. I was proud of the lovely dress I made. Vince completed the fairy tale image I had, wearing a black rented tux. We stood at the back of the room facing an array of elegant white silk flowers in pedestal vases, an alter adorned with more white silk flowers and ivy and a table under the alter where the pages of our vows lay between two tall white candles in silver holders. All designed by friends in the drama department. Together we walked down the aisle before a group of sixty friends and family. We spoke vows composed by ourselves before a Unitarian minister who was also one of our university professors. We exchanged identical bands made from costume jewellery metal, because we didn't have the money to buy gold bands. My friend Sherry was my maid of honor and Vince's best man was a long-time friend.

When I think back on how Vince looked, I realize he was withdrawn, had a scowl on his face and probably drunk. A close friend of his, a psychiatrist, remarked on Vince's heavy drinking. But I refused to recognize the seriousness of his behaviour. I was in motion and the momentum carried me into this fantasy of a romantic ceremony and wedded bliss.

We prepared a buffet of finger food with the help of my mother and bought a modest amount of wine. During the reception, Vince table hopped with a bottle or two of wine in hand. When those were gone, he found more. He was about to take the last of three bottles of champagne (wedding gifts) to another table when I stopped him. He could hardly keep his eyes open he was so drunk. I was disappointed. The gifts we received came mostly from students who had little money but we had impacted their lives and I guess they wanted to show their gratitude.

This was an exciting moment in time for me. Our mutual interests were what I focused on. I put aside our differences, his dishonesty and adultery and how he manipulated me so that my decisions were actually his decisions. I loved this man and I was not going to listen to the voice coming from my gut that said this marriage was a bad idea. I only saw a bright future for us. I was gaining more independence, thanks to the women's movement and I was excelling in college and now I was married to someone who never raised a hand to me.

When the celebration was over, Vince's family cleaned the hall before returning to their home town. We had talked about spending a few nights in a larger city for our honeymoon, but when we got back to our place, Vince said he was too tired (too drunk) so we did not go. I was disappointed but I accepted the decision. Now, I thought, our relationship was solid. We were married and made a commitment to one another to be faithful and all that until the day we died. Hah!

Shortly after we married, Vince went out of town for a week to a political convention. I was on my own in the apartment and enjoying my time alone. I went downstairs and picked up the mail. Stuffed into our mail box was a small package. I couldn't imagine what it was or from whom as there was no return address. I took it upstairs, sat down and opened it. Shock and terror engulfed me. It was a dead mouse! Who would do such a thing? This was followed by a number of phone calls with silence on the other end or threats to my life and to get out of town. And more hate mail. Our wedding picture had been in the newspaper and the sender of this hate mail clipped it out and sent it to me with Vince's head cut off, an axe in my hand with blood dripping from it. I was terrified and on edge until Vince returned home. The last straw was when we came home after school and found someone had broken into our apartment, stole items, turned the typewriter on its back and a number of books were placed on the floor. However, this looked more like a staged break and enter. Whoever did this could have broken the typewriter, could have damaged the books but they hadn't.

Now I was really concerned. Our home had been invaded. The offender was getting too close. Vince phoned the police. They came, walked around, interviewed us and left saying they would look into it. Days went by and we heard nothing from the police. We assumed their lack of commitment to finding the person was because we were political activists. Vince said he was going to get a gun. The investigator told him he likely wouldn't get a permit and left. Nothing was ever done and there were no further incidents.

Sometime in 1974, Lynn returned to me. I decorated her room with feminine things to make her feel welcome and to let her know I was happy she was back. But I hadn't changed where she was concerned. I had little time for her. I was consumed with Vince's activities. He was often missing in action. He'd come home either drunk or didn't come home at all until the next morning. I was becoming miserable and resentful. He was staying out more and more, telling me one lie after the other on where he'd been and with whom and what he was doing.

The last time Vince would deceive me was the time I woke about three in the morning wondering where he was this time. I had my suspicions, so I left the apartment and walked a few blocks to the house of a woman I knew from University. Our van was parked in her driveway. The door to her house was gaping open. I knocked on the screen door. No answer. I called to Vince. No answer. I returned home. Ten minutes later, he walked through the door looking sheepish.

The next day he admitted he'd been seeing this woman. But he also told me something that cut through me like a knife. He said: "if I don't leave, I may rape Lynn". I told him he should leave. I was shocked and devastated. He stayed, I think for about a week until he found a place to live. Lynn was abandoned even more by me in my grief. We barely spoke. She was sad all the time and I was crying.

Vern phoned and said he wanted to come and live with us. I agreed. When he was settled, I went with him to register in the local high school. Vern wasn't happy that he didn't have spending money so he decided to quit school and get a job. I let him. If I had counselled him and gave him direction, he could have finished grade twelve and had his high school diploma. But again, I treated him like an adult and let him make his own decisions. He found a job and we were all adjusting to living in small quarters.

On completion of my program at the college, I approached a radio producer to be a freelance broadcast journalist. As a freelancer I would present an idea to a producer and if accepted, I would do the research, tape interviews, put all that together with an introductory script and hand it in ready for airing. I had to purchase a reel to reel recorder, a microphone and a cassette recorder. It also meant we would have to move closer to my work. This was a huge investment for me at the time and a trust in myself that I could produce quality work. This was something I had to do for me and for my children. When I look back on this decision and my situation, I am in awe of my courage and strength to take on such a challenge. I never considered what might go wrong, only that I had to do this.

I found a two bedroom apartment close to the downtown core. With the help of a reluctant Vince who let me know by his behaviour that helping us was an imposition, we loaded a rental truck and moved toward the next chapter in our lives.

Our new home was in an old building that needed a lot of TLC. I had no money or abilities to make the place more livable, but we managed with what we had. I slept in the living room and the kids had their own rooms. Vern looked for a job and Lynn enrolled in high school. I think the experience in a large city was very frightening for her. The student population was large and she knew no one and I again, didn't help her adjust. Vince found a job at a gas station and bought a used bike for his transportation.

My first project for the station was in the winery business. The approach was to discover the steps involved in producing a fine wine. I had a great time. I was going to like this business. I handed in my finished product. It wasn't usable. I felt defeated. The producer assured me, rejection on the first item was quite normal and not to give up. He guided me through the next assignment, which ultimately aired. I am grateful for his support and trust. I was on my way. I had a lot to learn as a freelance broadcast journalist. I had many frustrating moments preparing an item for airing. A finished two to three minute item required several hours of editing the taped interviews. Eventually I became quite proficient and was able to earn enough to pay our living expenses.

The responsibility of two children and beginning a new career provided a number of difficult challenges. Vern and Lynn were fighting, not just verbally but physically. I wasn't doing much for either of them. I began to think there was something wrong with me that I could not successfully create a calm and happy environment for my family. I became depressed. I remember riding my bike past the psychiatric hospital and thinking I should talk to someone. I had been feeling overwhelmed by my situation. But, I didn't go in because I was afraid that if I appeared to be incapable of looking after my children, social services would take them away and put them in foster care. I couldn't allow that to happen.

As our lives together deteriorated, Vern decided to return to his dad's house. Shortly after, Lynn followed. Life without Lynn and Vern was difficult. I felt like a part of me didn't belong anywhere. I felt guilty for not being capable of coping and being a good mother. I was a failure again. A dark cloud hung over me, but I pushed on. I had to be successful in my new career and wanted to do more than survive in life.

To cope, I shut down any emotions I had and I put aside my guilt for the loss of my children. I didn't allow anyone to get close to me for fear of being hurt or discovering my incompetence as a mother. I thought of my children every day but to be able to do anything, I couldn't allow myself to be pulled down by guilt and the sense of loss. I created a new life for me as a single woman. I found a junior one bedroom apartment closer to work.

I found a psychiatrist and began therapy trying to come to terms with my behaviour and feelings. I told him that I had been in the psychiatric ward in a hospital in the west and had seven electro shock therapy treatments. He took down the particulars and contacted the hospital for the diagnosis and treatment records. When he read them to me, he said: "there's no way you are a paranoid schizophrenic". I was shocked and relieved. After such a diagnosis and my experience in the psych ward, I mistrusted my sanity. Anytime I had difficulty, I believed it was because I was schizophrenic. Then I wondered what my children's father told them about me. Did they think I was crazy and not to be trusted, perhaps even feared?

Chapter Twenty

My new career developed and my work was valued. I created taped items and sold them to producers one after the other. I had an article printed in a children's magazine and co-wrote a front page article for one of the major newspapers on the Black Out that affected eastern Canada and the U.S. I wasn't making a lot of money, but I could take care of myself. I was surviving. Most important, I enjoyed my work.

I functioned well, most of the time. The children crept into my mind, but I would push those thoughts and feelings away because there was nothing I could do to change the way things were. I didn't have the money to visit or phone them and writing letters was difficult. I didn't know what to write that would be of interest to them. I should have at least sent them a note, but I don't think I did. When I dwelled on my failings, the pain and guilt was too much for me to handle. That is when something quite bizarre happened.

Often I rode my bike to the shopping mall to window shop. It was only three blocks from my apartment, but if I bought something then I could put the items in my basket. I secured my bike to the stand outside the Mall's main entrance, where I normally leave it and entered.

I casually meandered through a department store, drifting from one display to the other. When I checked my watch I realized I needed to find my bike and go to the bank before it closed. *As I passed a display of irons I stopped to take a look and suddenly, day je vu. This moment had happened before. I wasn't alarmed. I had experienced day je vu many times in the past. I moved away from the section and passed through the perfume area getting deeper and deeper among the counters of bottled perfume. The deeper I went, the stronger the aromas penetrated my nostrils, burning like a hot iron. I became anxious. My body felt like it was going to seize. My throat began to close. I knew I had to get out, and fast. I became confused. I needed to find a door, but all I saw were windows, counters and people. I was panic stricken. My world was out of focus. The items in the store were a blur. People were mulling around, but they were like silhouettes of themselves, illuminated by a strong light coming from the windows. They were closing in on me. I felt very small. Nothing was familiar. Then I began to ask myself: Where am I? Where's the* door? I need to get out! I tried to be calm and asked myself what door did I enter? I couldn't remember. The anxiety increased. I must find any door and get out! I was sure that if I headed for the windows and the light, I'd find a door, eventually. As I maneuvered my way between counters, I saw a door. I decided I'd take any door, just so long as I got out of the building. I stepped outside and looked up and down the street. Nothing was familiar. I must get my bike! I must get home! Fortunately the door I exited was where my bike was. It was as if my body knew where to go, but my mind wasn't connecting. I remembered I had to go to the bank. How or why I could do that kind of thinking is beyond my understanding. I walked my bike up the incline toward the bank. What day was it? What year? What city? Those thoughts replayed in my mind, over and over. I kept looking up and down the street trying to figure out where I was. Anxiety intensified and my brain felt like it wasn't attached to my body; that I didn't exist. Rational thought had no bearing. I was certain no one could see me because I didn't know where I was. I was in a strange city. Like a programmed robot, I entered the bank and went to the teller. I don't know what transactions I made, but I did what I had intended to do, I guess. I even spoke to the cashier but don't recall what I said or her response. Anxiety was rising. I needed to know where I was and the date. Outside I checked the newspaper at an outdoor stand to determine what city I was in and the date. A sigh of relief. My head was beginning to ache. Home. I had to get home. I didn't know how far or where it was, but I had to make it. At home I'd be safe. I'd make sense of this. I crossed busy intersections unaware of the traffic or dangers, as if letting my bike lead the way. I don't know if I followed the lights or the crowds crossing with the lights. My head was pounding with excruciating pain. I could barely keep my eyes opened because the sun was too bright. I entered my apartment unable to make sense of my behavior and experience.

 I phoned a friend who was a nurse. A friend of hers, who was also a nurse, was visiting. I told them what I was experiencing as best I could. She asked me to go to her place. I told her I didn't think I could manage that. So they came over. For the rest of the evening, these feelings of displacement and fear rose like waves. Pain distorted my face and tears drained from me uncontrollably. Then I'd calm down and hold my aching head until another wave rose. They asked me if I had taken any drugs or smoked grass. But I had done neither and never have. As time passed, they asked if there was someone else that could come over and stay the night. They called Andrew, my friend and colleague. While he was making supper the aroma set off another wave sending me once more into panic and tears. I gasped from the pain and had to be reminded to breath. What was wrong with me? Why wouldn't this stop? I don't know how long this lasted. I don't recall eating or going to bed. When I woke the next day, the symptoms were gone and I was exhausted. Each time I shared this incident with a doctor or a friend, I cried. I was afraid I was going crazy.

The doctor ordered an EEG. The results only indicated, he said, a rare form of epilepsy. A competent psychiatrist many years later, drew a much clearer picture of this episode. She told me when doctors don't know what has happened in the brain they call it epilepsy. What had happened to me was actually dissociation, a symptom of Post Traumatic Stress Disorder. The smell of the perfume was a trigger to a flashback. I didn't know, at them time, the connection with perfume or smells. I would realize later, when I wrote this book.

I discovered that Vince had moved to an apartment building directly across from me. We began talking, but my heart wasn't in developing anything intimate with him. I had trust issues, but movies and dinners were okay.

I was enjoying my freelance work, but it was a feast or famine existence attempting to come up with ideas, sell them and produce them for air. I wanted a full time job with benefits. I applied for a permanent position with the company's morning show in one of their northern stations.

I was so excited when I heard I won the position that all the saliva in my mouth evaporated. I could barely talk as I ran from office to office announcing my success. On air hosting would be a change from interviews on the tape and living in the north added to the challenge. The company would pay my moving expenses. All I had to do was pack a few personal items in a suitcase and catch a plane. The staff gave me a good-bye/good luck dinner and an original painting of a polar bear, appropriate decoration for my new location.

I lived in a hotel for six weeks waiting for the moving truck to arrive. Living in a hotel sounds exciting, but after six weeks I was getting bored with eating in restaurants all the time, and my manager was pressuring me to move out of the hotel. But where would I go if I had no furniture or ways to make meals? I don't know what he expected me to do. I had no power over the moving company. When I was told the truck would be arriving within a week, I found an apartment. When it arrived they unloaded immediately. It was like Christmas unpacking all my things. There was one problem: my typewriter had a crack in it rendering it useless. I complained. They gave me a small cheque for damages. I signed the release papers, but only too soon. When I took my bike for a ride I discovered the front wheel was bent. When I complained the second time, they told me I had signed the release papers and they weren't going to do anything for me. I found out later that the truck had been in an accident! I was angry, but I knew a fight would just create hard feelings and in a small town that isn't always a good thing.

Vince and I stayed in touch by writing letters and occasionally phoning. It was nice to have someone I knew to talk with and share my experiences. I wrote to the children to let them know where I was and my new address.

The station work was quite different from what I had been doing. I tried to remember everything I'd learned about on air broadcasting from College but after three months on the job my manager and I realized this was not for me. My abilities to be spontaneous on the air and to challenge political figures on topics important to the area were lacking. I was better producing, taping interviews and selling them. I contacted the producer at my old job and asked if they would be interested in my work once more. They didn't hesitate to accept me back.

During one of our phone conversations, Vince and I decided to live together when I moved back. Bad idea! He hadn't stopped drinking and continued to be dishonest and unfaithful.

Within the first few weeks back, Vince and I went to a social gathering. I couldn't understand my feelings. I felt the chaos in the room was closing in on me. I had trouble breathing, I was dizzy and near tears. Vince convinced me to leave and drive home. He'd get a ride with someone. Why didn't he take me home? I don't know how I managed in the traffic. The whole drive was a blur. Once home, I rested and decided it was too soon for me to be in a crowd or socializing. I rested.

For five years, I worked on contract as story producer for a few shows. My abilities were acknowledged and my contract renewed several times. When John Diefenbaker, one of Canada's prime ministers died, I approached the executive producer to create a show using interviews with people who knew Mr. Diefenbaker. The production went well. I co-produced and showed a new side of my abilities. My colleagues were impressed.

Vince had an offer to work in a small city close by as the sales manager for a water treatment company, so we moved. The plan was that I'd commute between the two cities. I'd stay at my mother's from Monday to Wednesday, commute for an overnight stay with Vince and return to work Thursday and Friday, commuting back home for the weekend.

On moving day Vince and two young fellows we hired, loaded the truck and drove to our new home. My job was to stay behind and clean up, then follow with our two cats. When I arrived the three men were sitting on the floor among all the books unloaded from the boxes, drinking beer. I was shocked and really annoyed. What's the point in unloading the books if the bookshelves aren't put together? And why not empty the kitchen things from the boxes and put them away. The whole two hours they had before I arrived was emptying the boxes of books and bottles of beer! I should have turned around and gone back. But I didn't and I paid dearly.

I began having migraines that started shortly after we moved. I thought I would go crazy. I couldn't concentrate at work. My whole existence was up in the morning with pain, travel in pain, work with pain and go to bed with pain. Vince didn't care. He had had experiences with migraines, but mine weren't important to him. He couldn't tolerate anything that would invade his desires. My world began spinning out of control, again. When I was home for the weekend, I'd clean house and do the laundry . . . . his laundry! And clean the messes he had made while I was living at my mother's! And he let me! What was I thinking? When my contract came to an end I was unemployed and living with Vince.

Vince was too busy with his life to include me. I went into therapy. It was a group at the day centre in the local hospital. After a few days, I decided it was time to tell the group about myself. At my next one-on-one session with the psychologist, he told me he and the staff noticed that when I was telling my story, I was flat, no emotion and they were concerned. I didn't realize it at the time, but this was just another example of how much I had shut down.

I had to find work. I applied and was invited to the interview in another province. When I returned, Vince told me he wasn't willing to move for my job. He was concerned that this next position would be a repeat of my northern experience, and then we'd both be out of work. He was so self-centered. He was okay with moving for the sake of a job for him, but not for me. I didn't get the position, so I agreed to work with Vince as his assistant.

After eight months of migraines, they faded away until I was pain free. I think part of the problem was that I was surrounded by negative people. My mother had nothing positive to say, and Vince was a self-centered man whose only goals were: to be the best salesman for the company and to find his next drink and girlfriend. I was relieved of the pain of migraines but I had another obstacle ahead . . . leaving Vince. But that would take more humiliation, deception, manipulation and finally a threat to my life.

Christmas was coming and I went about decorating the house and buying gifts. Mom would be over to celebrate with us. Vince was in his own world, but he did notice gifts under the tree. He was angry that we were going to exchange gifts. He didn't like to celebrating Christmas. Neither of us were Christians, but I liked the music, the decorations, the food and gift giving. His way was to drink to oblivion. In a huff Christmas Eve, he went to one of the cheap stores and bought gifts that I wouldn't have given to charity. It was obvious he bought them under duress, like a child who is told to do something he didn't want to do, so he did the minimum.

He wasn't doing well at his job. He was being a maverick in a company that had only one leader and that was the president. Often the two clashed. Vince's employment with the company was coming to an end. He began searching and received a job offer in another province.

In the midst of a blizzard he drove off with our things in a rental truck. I followed with our two cats by air. Once we were settled, I decided I would go back to school to develop a trade. I approached

Employment Services and was granted schooling in the esthetics program. I would have to wait for three months for the next semester.

After a short period it was clear Vince's job wasn't going to work out. He began searching for something else. He found an opportunity to be partners with someone at another water treatment company in another area of the province. Again we moved. But I kept my commitment to go to school.

When we were settled, we went for a meeting with the prospective business partner. Vince told me to wait outside the office while he talked to the owner of the store. When he emerged hours later, I was told I would work for free as a receptionist and my free labor would be our contribution toward the partnership! I was astonished and angry. How could he have done such a deceitful thing? He knew that I was planning to go back to school. How could he donate my labor without consulting me? I guess he had known long ago, he could have his way with me. Through his persuasive methods, he convinced me this would be a good thing for both of us. Yeh? Only a good thing for him.

The only concession I'd asked; was that he must not attempt to teach me how to do accounting. It was something I just couldn't understand no matter how many different ways it was taught. I told him, just show me what has to be done and I will learn by example. He agreed, but he didn't keep his word. A month after we began working in the business, he sat me down and began his lecture on the basics of accounting. I felt beaten, ignored, invisible.

He also made many attempts to humiliate me in front of people. If I did something at work that was not to his liking, he'd stand in the middle of the office, in front of the staff, yelling about my incompetence.

He continued to take advantage of me, deceive me and was unfaithful. It got to the point where one day I was so angry with him I began screaming and throwing things. He just never listened to me. I felt lost and alone. After my outburst, nothing changed between us.

Meanwhile, Les and his friend came to stay with us when he was playing in a hockey tournament. I didn't have a great deal to offer him for comfort as we didn't have much furniture; however, the landlord had left a set of bunk beds in the finished basement. It was good to see

Les and have him around. But the visit was too short. He and his friend left to return home a few days later.

I knew Vince was having an affair. Our marriage was doomed. During one of our arguments he told me I made him so angry he wanted to kill me! Whether he meant it or not didn't matter. That was the word and the feeling that set me in motion to get out of the relationship.

I began making plans to leave. When Vince discovered I was searching for work in another town, he confronted me. He tried to manipulate me, telling me I wouldn't be able to survive on my own because I couldn't do anything. I was so shocked and hurt by his words and attitude. After all that I had accomplished, and all that I had given him, he would say those things.

I contacted Employment Services and they said I could begin the Esthetics program beginning in November. I called someone I knew and asked her if I could stay for the duration of my schooling. She agreed.

At the house, the rent and utilities were in my name. My concern was that Vince wouldn't pay them and I'd be stuck with bills I wasn't responsible for. I gave notice of vacating the house and from our mutual savings; I paid the rent and the utilities for the next month and ordered the utility companies to cancel the service when that credit was exhausted. I kept half of the remaining savings which was less than $500. Vince and I said good-bye, hugged and I was on my way to yet another new beginning.

Chapter Twenty-One

The same study problems were still with me. My solution was to rise very early and study when my brain was fresh, create a study group and focus on getting through the program. Graduation day was one of the highlights of my life. I held the highest marks in the class and received a school pin to commemorate my success. And, there was more to celebrate.

After the graduation ceremony, I rushed to an interview at a full service high end salon. At the end of the interview I was told I had the job. To begin with, I'd do manicures, and then I'd move on to the other treatments. Hardly able to swallow for the lack of saliva and excitement, I ran to the bar where my class was celebrating. I was floating. I was an honor student, I had a confirmed job and it was my fortieth birthday, February 20, 1981. I could barely sit still at the bar. I received cards and gifts from my fellow classmates and we all toasted to ourselves for a job well done in school.

I was determined to be the best I could be in this field. I took post graduate courses in advanced make-up applications, massage therapy and many weekend seminars on new techniques.

I was at a trade show when I overheard a woman say she was looking for someone to move to her salon in the north. I had loved the adventure of the north and was excited to hear I might be able to return.

I started up a conversation with her and made an agreement that I would go there for the next long weekend in September to see if we could work well together. To my surprise, when I arrived, she had booked twelve massages for my first day, and similar the next day! Normally, I only booked five in an eight hour shift.

When I left, the owner paid for my flight and I had over $300 in tips and an arrangement that I would move there in a month's time. I was exhausted but exhilarated at the prospects of making a good living as soon as I started working.

I found a small one bedroom house to rent within walking distance of the salon. It didn't take long to develop a group of friends, as is the northern way. We had one thing in common; we wanted to get the full experience of the north. Cross country skiing, holidays, dinners, and birthdays were all done together. We wanted to make sure no one was lonely. It was a great time. We all experienced the beauty and wonder of this untainted incredible part of Canada.

I also enjoyed having a group of friends for the first time in my adult life. It was a tremendous boost to my self-esteem. I felt there would always be someone I could count on. My birthday was days away. I was to meet a few people for dinner at a specified restaurant. When I arrived, there were two notes of apologies that they couldn't attend. Others just didn't show up. I had my birthday dinner alone and hurt. De je vu of my sixteenth birthday.

I had gained experience very quickly in this busy salon, but the owner, who wasn't an esthetician, and I didn't agree on treatment procedures. I wanted more autonomy in making decisions. I decided I would have to find a job in the south or begin my own practice.

I stayed until early spring and left for the south to be a nanny to a five year old girl and a housekeeper to the single mother. It was a job I would do until I could build up my savings and open my own business. At the end of summer, the woman was laid off and I had to find another way of making a living.

Chapter Twenty-Two

I don't remember how it all began, but Monty and I had lengthy discussions on the phone a few. All three of our children were living at his house and perhaps that's why we began talking. A few years after I left him and the boys, he had a skiing accident. The damage to his body left him a quadriplegic with minimal strength and movement in his arms and hands. He told me he had caregivers to look after him and if I moved there, he would let them go and I would get paid by the government to look after him and he had a spare bedroom for me. It seemed like a safe arrangement. He couldn't beat me anymore and I would see my children on a daily basis and hopefully re-establish a relationship with them.

I moved into his house occupying the upstairs bedroom. It was quite an adjustment but so good to see the kids all together. Well, he was wrong or he lied. The government wouldn't pay me to look after him. He had to keep the existing caregivers or pay for private ones out of his own pocket.

The problems between Monty and I hadn't gone away. He was miserable to deal with and constantly reminding people that they could walk and he couldn't. He had a sharp tongue and a vindictive cruel mind. The end came when he accused me of being dishonest and stealing grocery money. I left and moved to a temporary place with the help of social services.

I was still on unemployment insurance payments and discovered that the federal government, through the Unemployment Insurance division, had a 'make work' program where I could create a job for myself. This was an opportunity to start my own business while being financially supported by UI. I put together a proposal where I would hire two others and we'd offer our services to homebound people. I'd provide hand and foot care; the other two would do odd jobs around the client's homes: change light bulbs, house cleaning and minor repairs. It worked really well and I had a small clientele in a very short time.

At nights and weekends I rented space in a local salon to build up another kind of clientele who would want facials and massages as well as the hand and foot care. On March the eighth, the program came to an end and I was entirely on my own with no government safety net. I had a clientele in the salon and home service to seniors. The other two people I worked with would have to find their own jobs.

An old school mate of mine owned a business in town and a few rental properties. One of them was a very old empty house that probably should have been condemned, about five blocks from the salon. I asked him if I could rent the upstairs apartment for $150 a month plus utilities. He agreed. I had a one bedroom apartment with a dining room, living room, bathroom and kitchen. Off the kitchen was a door to a very small landing over the roof of the porch below. I painted walls and floors to sanitize the place and cleaned the kitchen and bathroom. My efforts paid off. It was still an old beat up place, but my apartment looked bright, clean and cozy.

My first problem was furniture. I didn't have any. I had left it with Vince. I knew he was in a city close by so I called him and told him I wanted my things. My hairdresser friends and I drove to his house with a van. When we arrived Vince had all my things on the front lawn. I went inside his apartment and noticed he had "forgotten" a few items, including a small organ and books. I thought how dishonest he still is, but I didn't find it worthwhile to challenge him. We loaded up the van and moved my things into my new home.

Eventually, with very basic tools and no experience, I made the landing on the roof more spacious. I included a two sided three foot wall with a shelf for privacy. When I acquired a puppy, I added a small fence around the landing where she could stay during the day while I was at work.

Frenchy was adorable. Her fur was pitch black and slightly curly. Everything about her was miniature: her paws, no bigger than my thumb; her little ears that disappeared in the darkness of her fur and her tail was the size of a small pencil that wagged vigorously when I went home for lunch and at the end of the day.

About a year later I opened my own business in esthetics and massage on the second floor of a commercial building on the main street. This was new territory for me. I'd never run a business before, but I did have experience in bookkeeping, budgeting, organization and

I had common sense. I didn't allow the 'what ifs' to enter my mind. I knew what I wanted and I went about creating it.

In the beginning I rented one room. I didn't have a large amount of start-up money so I built most of my own furniture, painted the walls and installed carpet myself. Eventually over the years I took over three adjoining rooms.

I was introducing the skin care business to the area and needed to bring awareness to my services to the community. I approached the local newspaper and asked if I could write a column once a week at no charge. They agreed and I did that for the next five years with a loyal following. As my business grew I expanded by providing services to smaller communities in the surrounding area. My journalism skills were developing so, I wrote an article for one of the professional magazines in the world-wide esthetics community. To my amazement it was published.

To further my exposure and support a community that had helped me become successful, I joined the Chamber of Commerce and became an active participant. My commitment to support my community brought me to the attention of the local mayor at that time. He invited me to join the Economic Development Commission. Our challenge was to find ways to bring more people and industry to the city. I volunteered to find someone to put a video together that would be shown at trade fairs. It was a good video and showed the city at its best.

The Economic Development Commission chairperson asked for volunteers to sit on the airport committee. The first person to volunteer asked that I be selected to join him. Obviously my name and credibility was high. With my business, the home service to my senior clientele and my community activities, I was busy. I was making a comfortable living, saw my children often, and I had a group of friends for social occasions.

My skills as an esthetician grew until I felt competent enough to compete at conferences. My hairdresser friends had already competed many times, but now I wanted to be part of that experience. To ensure success my friends and I created a team that would enter into esthetic and hair competitions; three hairdressers and myself. They groomed the hair and created costumes and I designed and applied the make-up and nail art. In the many times we entered, my work received top marks. I entered a fantasy make-up competition and with Les, Walter and Jane doing the hair and clothes. I won the top BC prize. Next I entered a nail art competition in Spokane taking the top prize for Washington. I had a full clientele with a waiting list and confidence in my abilities. I was feeling success at its best.

Modelling seemed to be an avenue that helped me with my self-esteem. I never had any official training, but a situation presented itself when a former sorority member, Linda, asked me to be in her fashion show of vintage clothing and hats. It was great fun modelling the gorgeous clothes. My body was slender and well proportioned. I knew how to walk in high heels and I had a pleasant smile. I was feeling beautiful for the first time in my life.

My children had moved out of their dad's house to their own apartments. Les was out of town playing hockey, going to university and living in billeted homes. I'd see him the odd time in the summer when he returned. Lynn and I visited a little and both she and Vern came to my clinic for services. Our relationships were tenuous. I felt I had to prove myself. I was clumsy and didn't do a good job of being a mother. I alienated Vern with insensitive behavior. I felt Lynn was holding me at a distance. I tried, but like Vern told me so often . . . I tried too hard. I'm not sure what that really meant but I did the best I knew how.

One winter Lynn had to have knee surgery. I agreed to drive her to the hospital but that day I had a difficult decision to make. Vern came to me. I could see he was in great emotional pain. He was depressed and didn't want to live. He had been in that state before. I was concerned for his safety. I had a choice to make: I leave him and hope he wouldn't kill himself, or drive Lynn to the hospital. I chose to stay with Vern and talk with him until he had calmed down.

As soon as I could get away, I drove to the hospital and was by Lynn's side when she came out of the recovery room. It was hard to see her in pain. I wanted to do more for her but I was limited to stroking her hair and wiping her face with a cool washcloth.

Vern and his girlfriend decided to get married. I didn't have any money to help with the costs so I was feeling like I was on the side lines. It didn't help that I was running low on energy and couldn't help in the preparations. I don't remember why I was so tired but I managed to hold the rehearsal dinner at my place. I was embarrassed at the house I lived in, but I think my apartment showed well once my guests got through the broken down stairwell.

The wedding was beautiful and I was impressed with my children. Both my sons looked like men now and were quite capable in front of the microphone and Lynn had grown into a lovely woman.

Chapter Twenty-Three

Then I met Norman. I was assisting a ballroom dance instructor once a week and Norman and his partner were two of the students. After I helped Norman with a few steps he returned to his date for the remainder of the class, while I moved on to the next couple.

The next day Norman phoned. Would I join him for brunch? I was surprised. I assumed his dance partner was also his intimate partner. He told me they were just friends. I learned later in our relationship that this wasn't quite true, she was a love interest and when he started dating me, he dumped her.

During a pleasant conversation over brunch I told Norman a little of myself, the involvement in my community and that I had a financially sound business. I owned a mobile home on the lake and drove a new car. My life was good.

Norman told me he had recently graduated with a degree in psychology. His practice was limited and he was working from his home as he built a clientele. He was handsome, blue eyes, of average build, soft white hair that made him appear older than his years, a little shorter than myself and five years older. He seemed to be an intelligent kind man. He was at times child-like but I took that as his form of humour. He had been married twice and was in the process of divorcing his second wife. The marriage had not ended well and he was in the midst of a settlement in court that at times got him upset. I was supportive and let him vent.

His ex-wife and I shared the same first name. Whenever Norman was about to say my name he'd begin with a deep breath of frustration. He asked me to change my name. I didn't like my name at the time either, so with the same recklessness in decision making, I was willing. One evening we spent about an hour coming up with the name Tina, or something like that.

Changing who I was became part of his behavior, whether it was conscious or not, he would eventually damage my sense of self drastically. After my name change, that really didn't take effect, he began whittling away who I was and how I felt about myself. My compromises in his favour, would drive me down to one of my lowest levels of living. I wasn't even aware it was happening.

The gradual destruction, along with my willingness to let it happen, began with something that didn't feel all that important at the time, but there would be more incidents that followed. Each time became more intense, more cruel and debilitating.

I had season's tickets to live theatre out of town and still had two more shows to attend. Norman was not happy and said I shouldn't be going on my own. But I did. The next show I felt the pressure. I was attracted to Norman and wanted to please him. At the time it didn't seem to be important, so I didn't go. But of course it was. Live theatre was part of my life and I turned away from something I loved. Again, I was not respecting myself.

Norman had the knowledge and skills to know how to manipulate for his own purposes and he used them on me until I didn't know who I was any longer.

We were sitting at his dining room table just finishing our meal, when he brought his chair around, sat facing me directly and stared into my eyes without a word. I felt uncomfortable, but at the same time flattered. It felt like he wanted to be close to me, to get to know me, look into my soul. I didn't realize this was a technique to unsettle me. To claim me. I stayed in my chair, frozen, unable to move. I ignored the inner voice that said: "walk away!"

At the end of one of our dates, he walked me to my car and said: "I don't want you to leave", implying that he wanted me to go to bed with him. I was flattered. This was just like in the movies! After two failed intimate relationships I was still struggling to experience how love developed and felt, and I was using life in the movies as a guide.

I liked our relationship as it was. I could go home and be myself and date him when it was convenient. But I didn't listen to my needs or my instincts. It wasn't long after we began dating that I moved into his house and rented out my much loved home on the beach. I was now his. I no longer had a home of my own to run back to if I needed to flee.

I began feeling trapped. He knew every move I made, where I went and when I would arrive home. When I was leaving for work, he'd ask me what time I'd be home. If I was late, I'd get the silent treatment that could go on for days. I was feeling suffocated and anxious. I walked lightly so as not to trigger a fight or risk possible abuse.

He had told me once, when he was angry with his previous wife, that he threw an axe at her. How did I not see that as a warning? Again, I believed he wouldn't do that to me, just as I had with Monty's violent acts. She must have deserved it, I told myself! Oh how anti-woman could I get for the sake of love from a man.

If I was working on my business journals, he'd get upset that I was working on them longer than necessary. He had begun finding fault with everything about me and he wasn't going to stop until I was completely the way he wanted me. I know now that would not be possible. Perfection is never possible. He would never end bullying and manipulating me.

My hair was the next issue. At the time, I had shoulder length hair that was permed. As we passed each other in the bedroom on evening, he flipped one side of my hair and said "is this all yours?" in a tone that told me he didn't like it. I let the perm grow out and cut my hair short to his liking.

The next incident was over an outfit I'd bought. It was just before some social event and when I reached for it in the closet he said: "you're not going out with me in that outfit". I chose something else. Life with him would be too difficult if I were to say no.

Norman didn't have to hit me. His words and attitude were enough intimidation. I didn't want to challenge him for fear of more silent treatments, a beating or losing him. It didn't matter that he was changing me. Staying with him was most important. We just had to work out our differences. The only thing was . . . I was the one doing the work and making the changes. I believed he was more educated than I and a psychologist, so he must know what is best for me. I had this attitude that whatever a man asked of me, I would go along to find out where it would take me. I still hadn't learned how to set boundaries that would protect me from abuse or the threat of death.

He had unique ways to criticize me that often took me by surprise. He scoffed at my home on the beach; he chuckled at the concerns I had with my business; he wanted to party Friday nights. I didn't want to stay up late because I had to work Saturdays. Eventually I changed my opening days to accommodate him, losing valuable clients. He then had me from Friday evening until Monday morning.

Then he wanted me to quit my business and get a "real" job. A realtor he said. But he wasn't rational. If I had done that, I wouldn't be available Friday nights or weekends because I'd be showing houses.

He didn't like that I was constantly going to meetings. I quit the Chamber, the Economic Development Commission and the Airport committee. I confined my business to the city.

He then convinced me that I should destroy things that represented my history: my wedding band that I had remade into a lovely ring; the vinyl record that once belonged to my children. It had their childish "art" work all over it. When they were young we use to play it at Christmas time because it was a story by Bing Crosby about a little boy who wanted an axe and a buck skinned jacket for Christmas. The kids loved it. But I threw it away. Photos, any memorabilia of my previous life were destroyed. I wish now I still had those things, especially the children's record.

He was isolating me and I didn't even notice or care. He was all about controlling me. He was jealous of my high profile position in the community and my successful business. He had none of that.

I couldn't believe he would ever harm me in any way and I didn't see, or perhaps not want to see, that what he was doing to me was a form of injury that would have long lasting effect.

I began feeling vulnerable, afraid I was going to make a mistake. I became short tempered, getting angry at the slightest thing, maybe I dropped something at work and had to re-sanitize the item, or at home, I'd be drying dishes and drop cutlery. Anything could set me off. I wanted to throw things that impeded my serenity. I saw simple, normal, daily incidents as overriding what I wanted to accomplish. I needed to crush and destroy.

Norman was away at a seminar for a week. I was alone in his house. I had just finished eating when I had this sudden, compelling urge to throw something and see it smash into a million pieces. I had a dish in my hand. I threw it to the floor, then another and another. When I ran out of dishes, I grabbed my wine glasses, the ones my kids had given me. I threw them one at a time, feeling the pleasure of seeing the tiny pieces scatter across the ceramic floor and the noise. That was important. To hear them smash. I felt such release. When I was done, I was exhausted. I had broken a whole set of my six piece setting and six wine glasses.

Then reality set in and I realized what I had done. Some of the ceramic tiles were chipped or cracked and some of the broken pieces of dishes and glasses had bounced off the floor scratching and chipping the cupboards. The dishes and glasses were mine, but not the house!

I cleaned up the mess and wondered how I was going to explain to Norman my behaviour and the damage. I fixed the cupboards with wood filler and paint, but the ceramic tiles would stay as they were. He wasn't impressed but he didn't say much.

Did Monty feel as I did when I broke all those dishes? Did he feel the rage building and needed a release? But, he didn't break dishes, he broke me. I became shattered pieces of myself. I was left with scars that couldn't be fixed. Norman expected sex every night, no exceptions. If I turned away from him he was angry and stopped talking to me for days. To keep harmony between us, I gave in and pleased him without any satisfaction for myself.

When I developed a cold that kept me up through the night coughing, I would leave the bed and go downstairs to lie on the sofa so I wouldn't disturb him. My coughing kept me awake for hours, but finally I would drift off to sleep only to be abruptly awakened by his call to come to bed. He did that every night while I was sick. Between coughing and him waking me, I got very little sleep during those two weeks. He didn't seem to think he was doing anything wrong and therefore never apologized for waking me.

Norman needed a full time job. His clientele was too small to make enough money. (I wonder why?) He told me he could look outside of our city, but what about me, he asked. Immediately, without consideration for my world, I said I could take my skills anywhere and if he found a job elsewhere, I would go with him. What a fool I was! I had worked hard to gain status in the community and to establish a strong clientele. I was respected and my opinions and contributions were appreciated.

I was planning a trip to Malaysia. I had the money in the bank and contacts there. All I had to do was set a date and buy my airfare. But I turned my back on the trip of a lifetime.

Norman did find a job and we moved. To qualify, he had to be licensed, so his services would be accepted by health benefit programs and give expert testimony in the courts. He would then be legitimate in his field. He was required to intern in the psychiatric unit at a hospital in another province for one year, then pass the North America licensing exam. This would be a year when his life was work and study. He didn't consult me about this decision to put our lives on hold for twelve months and I didn't open the discussion.

It was a heavy load. He worked all day at the hospital, and then came home to study volumes of material. I told him I would assume the domestic responsibilities for the next year so he'd have time to study. Every waking moment was spent around Norman's schedule. When we went on a vacation, he took his study material with him and I amused myself. I was okay with that. By this time I had a job my career was going well. When he passed the exam, he would be on his way to success and we would have a healthy income and life. This was for our future, I told myself.

When we first moved, I was out of work and I had little money. Ordinarily we split the costs of utilities and other household expenses. So I asked him if he could carry the financial load until I found work. He didn't like that idea but gave in. In short time, I found a job in a local salon, and we resumed the sharing of domestic expenses. However, he was earning a lot more than I, so I suggested he pay a greater share of our expenses. He reluctantly gave in to that idea.

When his studying was over and he passed the exam, we went to Europe for a holiday. Days before we left, I had dental surgery and was on antibiotics. Very quickly I developed cystitis, often a side effect of those drugs. I was feeling miserable and in pain. I told Norman, but he didn't seem to care. I didn't speak the language well enough to explain my symptoms to a doctor and I couldn't find over the counter drugs for the problem, so I struggled with the symptoms which made it difficult to enjoy myself and be with the others.

During the last week in Europe, Norman gave me the silent treatment for something I did or didn't do. He was impossible to deal with when he was that way. He wouldn't talk. I had no idea what he expected of me. My solution was to leave him to work out his feelings. He was upset with that as well, claiming I was inattentive to his needs.

Meanwhile I was still in pain and feeling quite ill. On our way home we stopped in London for a few days. I found a chemist who gave me enough pills to relieve my symptoms until I got home.

We did the usual touring of London, including a search for information about my distant relatives. According to my grandfather, the family held a prestigious position in early British society. A family crest was on display in one of the historic buildings in London and I wanted to find it and gather information on the family.

We went to the curator of the museum who was quite familiar with the family name. He photo copied pages for me from an old dusty book from the early nineteenth century. When we got home I placed the papers in my filing cabinet that contained other legal documents, including divorce papers from Vince. When I left Norman, I discovered he had stolen the museum copies and my divorce paper. How childish. How typical. Jealousy and one up-man-ship were his issues. He couldn't handle anyone he knew that was more important and successful than he was.

Norman continued to control me. I was expected to be home right after work. There was no time to visit with someone, shop and just relax. If I was late, even if I called to let him know, I'd get the silent treatment. He wanted me to watch a movie that showed some particular psychological drama that intrigued him. I knew the story and didn't care to watch it again. It was about a woman who was stoned to death for some societal sin. I knew it would upset me and refused to watch it. He yelled at me, taunted me and finally grabbed two kitchen chairs, shoved me into one of them in front of the television and forced me to sit beside him and watch the movie from start to finish.

I was frozen in time, unable to move, afraid to move and afraid to express my feelings. When the movie ended, I quietly removed myself from the room while he extolled the virtues of the film. I felt abused, invisible and all the other symptoms I'd experienced when I was beaten by Monty or manipulated and berated by Vince.

I think now, Norman had a mean streak that ran deep and his behaviour was child-like. I heard a number of women say their husband was like a child. But this was different. Norman did what he pleased no matter who it hurt. When he didn't like something I said, he would mimic me, distorting his face and looking juvenile. On one of many odd incidents, I was outside cleaning the yard. I had raked the debris from around the base of a tree and was making a pile on the lawn. He came outside, picked up a rake and began putting all the debris back into the areas I had just cleaned up.

He broke client confidence several times. When we were out shopping or socially, he would point out a client. Then he'd tell me their issues. He had one older client who was being accused of molesting his granddaughter. Norman laughingly said that he really liked the guy, without saying anything of the man's immorality. What psychologist would say something like that? Child molesters are smooth and perhaps even likeable. That's how they lure children.

Another time he told me about a male client who would tell his wife as they were going to sleep, that he wanted to talk with her about something in the morning. Norman saw this as another form of abuse based. Shortly after he told me about this man, we were in bed and about to roll over and go to sleep when he told me the same thing: "I need to talk to you about something in the morning". That was cruel and sinister. Of course it prevented me from having a decent sleep that night, worrying about what he wanted to say and thinking I had done something wrong. And in the morning, he didn't have anything to say. One evening over dinner he was talking about a personality test he had just studied. We got talking about it and I was keen to hear what it would reveal. He asked me if I'd like to do it. I said yes, but only on the condition that no one, including him, would see what I had entered on the test. Secretly, I decided I would lie on the test, just in case. I didn't want to reveal anything about myself that he didn't already know.

When I had finished I left it on the table for a moment. When I returned, he had evaluated it and gave me the results. I was furious. I had his word he wouldn't do that. He gave me a smug smile and said he needed to learn how to give the test. I never did tell him I'd lied. That was my secret. Now I wish that I had, just to see the look on his face. But of course that would have been asking for trouble. This incident and the comment before bed made me feel I was his personal experimental laboratory.

I began to feel depressed. My doctor gave me a prescription for an anti-depressant. When Norman discovered the pills, he was angry and wouldn't talk to me for days.

I went to his colleague for therapy. I came to understand that I was giving away too much. I told Norman and he became enraged, accusing me of being the taker. Again, I got the silent treatment for days. I spent many nights awake, unable to even feel sleepy. I'd get up in the cold winter night, turn the furnace on and lay close to the television to keep the volume down. He'd wake and turn the furnace down and go back to bed.

I was sinking deeper and deeper into the abyss of depression. This was all too familiar. Norman never accepted any responsibility for anything that went wrong for us. He never said he was sorry and he let the blame rest on me for whatever happened that wasn't good for him or us.

Norman couldn't let go of the idea that I believed I was giving away too much of myself. He started an argument that I refused to engage in. The veins in his neck enlarged, his face was red and his body ridged, screaming at me only inches from my face.

He left the room. When I heard him going down the stairs to the basement, I went into the living room and turned on the television in an attempt to calm myself. I didn't realize he had climbed the stairs and was in the kitchen. Suddenly something whizzed by my head and landed in the wall creating a dent in the plaster. The crystal glass fell to the floor. Then another. I crouched down on the sofa to avoid the third and fourth glasses. My dog, was terrified and shaking as she pressed against my body. I buried my head behind the sofa pillows until I heard him leave the room. He had gone back downstairs and was foraging in the basement. I knew he had a hand gun down there somewhere. I had never seen it but he had told me he had one. I became concerned for my life.

In my night clothes I grabbed my car keys and coat, and in my slippers fled the house. I didn't know where to go. If I went to a safe house I would have to put Frenchy in a kennel and that would be cruel to her and it wasn't what I wanted for myself. I needed her. She was the only thing that gave me warmth and love. I took a chance and went to my therapist's house. She took me in and showed me to her only empty space, a cold and frosty room in the basement that contained a bed and table. She gave me an Ativan and Frenchy and I curled up together and I drifted off to sleep. At least I was safe, or so I thought.

The next day I had a full schedule at work but I needed my clothes and toiletries. I called the police and they met me in front of the house to give me support and protection if there was a need. When I tried to open the screen door, it was locked for the first time since we lived there. The police phoned Norman and he unlatched the door and the police accompanied me into the house. I saw that the dent in the wall was already repaired with a fresh coat of dry wall mud. I heard him ask the police: "is this really necessary". The police replied: "the woman feels it is". I wish now that I had shown the police the damage to the wall.

Over the next few weeks, I lived at my therapist's house in the cold drafty room where ice collected around the window and a cold draft blew in from under the icy patio door. My boxes of things were piled high leaving very little space to move. My mother came and stayed in a motel close by for a few days.

Shortly after I moved in, my therapist said she had spoken with Norman and he wasn't aiming the glasses at me; as if implying that I was overreacting; that this wasn't abuse. Immediately I felt stabbed in the gut. My therapist talked with Norman, my abuser, about the incident without my permission! Now I wasn't safe in that house either. I should have reported her, but I had enough on my plate as it was. I had to get out of this miserable place. It wasn't safe or healthy.

When I left Monty and Vince, I never felt desperate. I knew I was leaving and in a very short time I had a place to live and a job or school. I took control of my life. But with Norman, I didn't see the violence coming. I was destitute. I fled with no plans. I saw myself living in my car or in one of those apartments that were occupied by the 'down and out', which I believed I was.

Chapter Twenty-Four

I found a basement suite in a good location near a dog run and moved. I talked with Norman over the phone and made arrangements to remove the rest of my things and sell some of them to him, mainly because he had abused them and I no longer wanted to have damaged goods. It was enough that I was damaged.

I stayed in that suite for a year going about my routine like a robot, a very familiar state of being. I spent every day, trying to think of a way to kill myself without it being messy or painful, and guaranteed to work. Nothing mattered any longer. I wasn't a good person, I couldn't keep a relationship with anyone, I had nothing to offer, my children were no longer a part of my life, I couldn't trust anyone and I was alone. What was the point in living? This time it wasn't that I just wanted to end the pain. I wanted to die.

It was February and my fiftieth birthday was approaching. While I was giving a client a pedicure, she asked me what I was going to do to celebrate. I told her nothing. She said: "if I had to borrow the money, I'd do something special for those fifty years". That was like a light bulb illuminating the room. Of course. I could do that. What a great idea.

Because I had no friends, I decided to invite special clients who were loyal to me. I had a goal. I had something to look forward to, to plan and prepare. I felt alive. I made arrangements with a local English pub that I was inviting twelve guests and I would pay for their dinner. I sent out invitations with a request to dress like a tacky tourist and meet me at the pub. As each client entered the pub in their tacky tourist costume, all heads in the pub turned and we all laughed and clapped. In the middle of February, we all sat around in our sunglasses, colorful shirts and sun hats.

What I hadn't expected were gifts and beautiful cards. The most memorable gift was a journal with an inscription inside: "may this book be filled with happy thoughts and happy memories". I had each guest write something in it. I was touched by everything they wrote. They had given me a boost of enthusiasm for life.

I hadn't made arrangements for a birthday cake, but was pleasantly surprised when the pub gave me one complete with candles. It was a perfect birthday party. The next day at work, birthday cards poured in with such tenderness and encouraging words of hope and love. I felt really special. This experience gave me a new look at life. I did have people who cared and my clinic was financially sound. I decided it was time to buy a house.

I had sold my home on the beach and that gave me the funds to make an offer of $25,000 on a little one bedroom. It was a beaten up old house that was once a drug dealer's pad. The five hundred and ninety square foot house was on a narrow twenty-five foot wide lot, on a well treed street close to an even better dog run and within walking distance to downtown. I secured a mortgage of $20,000 with very little effort. This was an exciting time. I felt renewed. I had my own house, on my own lot and a backyard for my dog to freely move around.

In December 1991, I took possession of this shabby little house. Every day, working with clients was followed by four or five hours in the evenings plus the weekends, renovating and decorating my new home. I did all the renovations myself except the rewiring and plumbing.

To better understand how to do some of the things I wanted to do on the house, I rode my bike in the housing developments and observed how the carpenters built the frames, how the wiring was placed in the walls, how the insulation and siding were installed. My greatest challenge in building was the inability to envision a structure in three dimensions. Often I'd have to tear my project apart and begin again. My attitude was: "if a man can do it so can I", and "I'll figure out how to lift heavy things". And I did.

I wanted the house to be liveable by Christmas, and it was. I had a finished bedroom and living room. The kitchen and bathroom would be done during the remainder of the winter. I was breaking new ground for myself. Designing the décor was easy compared to renovating. I re-created carpentry by trial and error (since I had no formal training). It was hard work, but I didn't mind. This was my house! I could do anything I wanted. That was a sense of freedom I had not experienced before.

My mother came to stay for the Christmas holidays and we managed somehow to put a fine turkey dinner together in my broken down kitchen.

When work on the house was finished, I found a store front property a block away from the house and moved my clinic. This was perfect. I could walk to work and walk home for lunch.

In the spring I worked on new skills: I built a fence to protect my dog and built a covered deck eight by sixteen feet. I wanted a beautiful garden of flowers, shrubs, trees and a vegetable patch. I'd never had any of those things. I researched the gardening books, purchased subscriptions to a number of gardening magazines and created a spectacular garden that was a show stopper to anyone passing by or visiting.

In time, I realized it would be cheaper if I moved my business into my home. But I lacked the space. I had already paid off the mortgage so it wasn't difficult to take a loan against the house for an addition.

I hired a contractor to build a two story addition on the back of the house. Upstairs would be my bedroom; the main floor would be my living room with a gas fireplace to heat the entire addition.

At this point in my life I had done enough renovating that I was capable of monitoring the contractors work. Sometimes his mistakes were glaring, other times not as evident. Like the time he had just finished pouring the cement for the foundation. When I came home I noticed it was not as wide as the house and it was short two feet of what I had asked for. The next time I noticed some of the floor joist weren't lining up evenly and one side of the frame was shorter than the other. When he was supposedly finished, all the screws to hold the closet door in place were on the floor and the banister was too high. With each discovered error, I called the inspector who made the contractor correct the problems. In the end the inspector added a few more problems to the list. I stood my ground and I was proud I had the courage to do so. I know longer trusted the contractor. I didn't want anything to go wrong with the roof so I hired a roofer and asked the contractor to reduce my bill by the estimated cost of the roof. He didn't like the idea, but conceded.

In my new living room I faux painted the feature wall, giving it an old rustic look, another new skill that drew a number of impressive remarks by clients, and I painted the rest of the walls and trim myself.

I'm Still Here

As soon as the addition was finished, I quickly moved my furniture into it and proceeded to do the renovations in the old living room in the front of the house, which would eventually be my clinic. I built a partition to create two treatment rooms. One room was for facials and massage and the other for manicures and pedicures. It was perfect.

I wanted a side board for the dining room. I shopped for one in all the stores and what I did like was out of my price range. I loved working with wood, so I built it myself. With that success under my belt, I took a basic carpentry course and built an oak chest that I still have today.

When I began the addition project, the covered deck I had built had to come down, so after the addition was completed, rebuilt the covered deck and made it deeper. Now it was twelve feet deep and sixteen wide providing me with an outdoor living room. From there I could look out onto my colorful garden complete with a pond. I put a twin size mattress in one of the corners of the deck and covered it with a throw and a number of pillows. I added a television with a stand, an easy chair, and a small table and chairs to dine on. I basically lived and slept out there from about April to October for several years. It was my personal park and luxury hotel. I felt safe and secure with a six foot fence surrounding the back yard.

Life was good. Most of my activities, I did alone. I went on vacations travelling to many locations in the world, bought new furniture, built what I couldn't find, dined at restaurants often, went to conferences and workshops to improve and update my skills, bought things and clothes when I wanted and added to my RRSPs. For my birthdays I went to a neighboring city for a fine dining experience, live theatre and shopping.

I kept to myself and rarely did anything with another person and that was okay. To avoid looking conspicuously alone in restaurants, I learned I was more comfortable taking a book or magazine with me.

One bright sunny summer day I passed a colleague on the street. He and a partner set up a tour company to take people on holiday tours to various cities in Europe. Often he would take professionals as well, to teach or entertain the residents of the cities in the tour. He asked me if I would like to teach a two week basic facials course in one of the cities on the tour. Immediately I said yes. I had never taught before but this was a chance in a lifetime. I had a slight case of trepidation, but also very excited.

I had sixty-five students broken into two classes. One class in the morning and the other in the afternoon. Rather than written exams, I gave daily verbal quizzes. This gave me an opportunity to see how well they were absorbing the material. Most students were doing very well.

I was treated to the ballet, a local concert, a huge open market and the opportunity to see many wonderful sites. My students were very unhappy when our time together was ending. They held a lunch for me and presented me with many gifts. I was touched by their generosity and love. I could not help but cry. Hugs and more tears later, I left and returned to my hotel room to pack.

Back home, I thought of my children. How were they doing? Where were they? The community gossip grapevine told me snippets about my children. I only knew that Lynn had a baby, Les was married and owned a business and Vern was wandering from job to job. They were on my mind every day. I was reminded of them by the sight of someone who resembled one of them or their birthday, my birthday, and other family occasions. I feared for Vern. The last time I saw him, he was drinking heavily. I had images of him drunk and living on the streets. I lived with the guilt of abandoning my children and loathing myself for my actions.

I went through periods of depression, therapy, medications. Sometimes I would get relief, but most times, the underlying feeling was sadness for all my losses. I didn't make friends because I was afraid they would ask me if I had children and was I going to visit them for Christmas. My work kept me from being totally isolated from the world.

I had many things to be thankful for. I had created what I had with my own hands and was respected for my skills in my clinic and in creating a beautiful home and garden. I had become accustomed to celebrating special occasions on my own. Each Christmas I made my special breakfast of mimosas, crepes stuffed with fruit and topped with whipped cream, and coffee.

One year I had the idea to pretend Santa had found me. A few months before Christmas I began shopping for things I liked. I wrapped them in Christmas wrapping paper and put them in the closet and away from sight. When I put up the tree, all those 'gifts' came out of the closet and placed under the tree. I even had things for Frenchy. Christmas morning I sat by the tree with a mimosa and watched her sniff out her gifts of treats and toys. Then I'd open mine while she nibbled on her find.

Despite my efforts to feel happy, what I was doing wasn't enough. Something was missing. Something kept me from being at peace. My mind became focused on unwanted feelings. Other times, I'd be going about my regular routine and without warning I had images in my mind that were difficult to put into words. Images too violent and gruesome to describe. Where was all this coming from?

I was riding my bicycle downtown on my way home when a very sudden, strong sense of impending doom hit me in the gut as if life was drawn from me. I held my breath, my body stiffened. I was frightened. That same feeling haunted me for days. Several days later, my world changed. *I felt closed in, afraid, my breathing was shallow, I was confused. I couldn't figure out where I was or what to do.*

I recall contacting a friend who drove me to the hospital. I was cuffed to monitor my blood pressure and my finger was clamped to measure my pulse. I couldn't focus visually or mentally. The doctor came, asked questions, checked my vitals and gave me an Ativan. While he was gone, a wave of this feeling returned, overwhelming me. I told my friend it was happening again. She called for help and another Ativan was given. Through my fog, I heard the doctor say he thought it might be an anxiety attack. I felt so helpless, vulnerable, lost. Was I finally losing my mind?

Somehow I got home, maybe my friend drove me. I don't remember. I was resting in the living room trying to cope with what had happened when the doorbell rang. A delivery man was there with a prescription. I called the pharmacist and asked her what this was about. She said I had dropped the prescription off and left. I didn't remember doing any of that. The pills were for anxiety.

I recovered only to experience a similar episode months later, preceded by the feelings of impending doom days before. This time it was worse. I was sitting in my favorite café close to my home, when it came like a wave washing over me. The room seemed to be floating. I felt like I had just been parachuted into a foreign land. I had a dreadful feeling the world was not right for me. I stopped eating and sat looking around the room unable to focus on any one thing or the owner. My head was spinning. The café owner asked: "are you alright Elizabeth?" I looked at him, not quite understanding, yet knowing that he knew something was wrong with me. I told him I needed to find my friend, Marion, who worked at a clinic across from the hospital, which was only four blocks away. Something was wrong with me. I was scared. I felt like I would collapse any time. But I had to stay strong long enough to find my friend. I would be safe with her. I opened the door letting it close behind me. I stood there on the sidewalk in front of the café dazed. Which direction do I walk? How far is it? Do I stay on the same street all the way? I opened the door and asked the café owner to point me in the right direction, and then he told me he would phone ahead and tell Marion that I was on my way.

I walked up the hill hoping I would see a familiar landmark. I felt like I was stepping into a foggy street and couldn't see ahead of me. I was like a migrating animal, not conscious of where I was going, only knowing I had to get there and trusting that my body would carry me. I did my best to tell Marion what was happening to me. She phoned hospital emergency and told them I was on my way. With her directions, I walked across the street and into the emergency unit door.

Recently I asked Marion what she remembered about that episode. She said that when I arrived at her office, I was scared, shaking and crying. My breathing was rapid and short and my pupils were dilated. My eyes, she said, darted around like I thought someone was going to pounce on me.

I lay on the stretcher, exhausted. The nurse cuffed my arm for blood pressure and clamped my finger for pulse. As I waited I guess I drifted off to sleep. In my dream state I could feel someone gently stroking my leg. I woke to the sight of a woman in a navy uniform. The doctor came and asked me questions and checked my heart. When I seemed to be lucid he sent me home. I would understand what had happened to me in a few years.

Chapter Twenty-Five

Frenchy died in 1999 at the age of fifteen, having developed three kinds of cancer. I had promised her and myself, I would not let her live in hopeless pain and I would be by her side when she died. That dreadful evening she went into a convulsion. At that point I knew it was time. The next day I went to the veterinarian for a tranquilizer. I returned home and put the pill in her favorite food, fed her a handful of treats and waited for our ride. We got into my friend's car, I placed her pillow on my lap and invited her to sit with me. She pressed her body against me, shaking all the way to the clinic. Uncontrollable tears streamed down my face.

I watched as the vet placed the needle in her leg for the tranquiller and waited as her body no longer resisted and she dropped to her side. Then the vet pushed the fatal drug into the tube. I held her head in my arm as she slowly succumbed. Gradually her breathing slowed down until finally her chest stopped rising and falling. The night before I had a nightmare; she was still alive when the vet was putting her body into the incinerator. I couldn't bear the thought she might still be alive when I left her there. When the vet said she was gone, he let me listen with the stethoscope so I was certain she was dead. The vet left us alone so I could say good-bye.

I lifted her limp body into my arms and her head flopped backward. There was no resistance in her. She was gone taking a part of me with her. Her body was still there, but she was gone. I cried all the way home clinging to her pillow and continued to grieve for days. I was devastated. She was my love, my life. She had gone through years of torment and drama with me.

On top of the sadness I carried, I dove into a well of dark endless depression. The only living thing I could count on was dead. Through Frenchy, I had discovered what love felt like, what it meant to be loved and to love. I couldn't do anything but think of how much she had meant to me and what a hole she left in my heart. I felt she had taken a part of my soul with her. I would have done anything to keep her safe and loved. Is this what I could have felt with my children if I had not had so much trauma in my life?

She would never know what gift she had given me. It was the gift of knowing real honest love. I never felt it with my children. Never knew what it meant to love them; never understood that all the kindness I gave my dog was something I lacked for my children or myself.

She had been my constant and loyal companion. She gave me love, five beautiful puppies and I paid respect to her love by letting her go before her cancer pain took hold and made her life unbearable.

My grief ran deep and was immobilizing me. I needed relief, if for nothing else but to continue working and making a living. The doctor gave me anti-depressants that caused me to sleep endless hours. One day during my lunch break, I lay down on the sofa for a short nap only to be woken from a drug induced sleep by a client.

Chapter Twenty-Six

I was on my own again. Very soon I was dating two men at the same time. There was Fred, who worked up north and visited periodically when he came out and Frank, a local insurance salesman. When Fred was up north working, I'd see Frank. When Fred was in town I dated only him. There was nothing serious with either one. Dinner and dancing was our connection; an activity I enjoyed with both of them.

I soon discovered these relationships weren't satisfying. When Fred came to town, he just showed up and expected me to go out with him. I felt like I was a date of convenience and not important enough to call ahead. Dating Frank was completely different. He belonged to some strange 'therapy' type group and insisted I join. I didn't like the sounds of this organization so I continued to say no. When I told someone in the 'real therapy' world about this, I was told to avoid them like the plague. The pressure to join was becoming a problem. I decided neither one of them was worth the hassle. After a few months I said good-bye to both men.

The year was 1991 and it was the last time I dated anyone. I had decided I didn't make good choices when it came to men. I was better off without them and that has proven to be the best decision for me. Having men in my life was a huge distraction from my endeavors to understand who I was. I always gave too much and my efforts were not reciprocated. I also discovered I could sense when a man was weak or vulnerable. I would be mean to him, short and argumentative, bossy and unrelenting. I didn't like myself when I was with a man and I needed to feel good about me.

One thing was certain. I was not happy. I was depressed and looking for answers. Medications weren't helping and gave me too many uncomfortable side effects. Cognitive therapy always helped on the surface, but I just couldn't get a handle on something that I was sure ran much deeper. I tried the "cure of the day": telling my reflection 'I love you'; daily affirmations; meditation; self-help books; listening to motivational speakers; personality tests; listing all my accomplishments and skills; creating a goals list; group therapy; fun things like psychics; tea leaf readings; auras; Tarot cards. Any one of these 'cures' by themselves didn't work, but together they stimulated thought. I continued to search for answers to my feelings. I decided to try an experience that proved to be painful and cause me more grief.

Two of my clients told me they had their 'faces read' by a psychic. He had come to Canada to tour the larger centres and spread awareness of his technique, that he called psychosomatic therapy. My clients said he was quite accurate on identifying their personalities and issues but he didn't perform 'therapy' on them.

I was intrigued, so I decided to see what he had to say about me. I knew it was like the fun things I had already tried, but sometimes there's something in what these people say that fits and stimulates thought. I was ignoring my instincts instead of making decisions that were good for me. I was letting life happen. In the past when I made decisions that way, I ended up in trouble and this experience proved to have the same outcome.

The appointment was held in a woman's house who owned a business in town. I felt this was safe. She would be there.

The woman met me at the door and just as I was talking to her about something trivial, this funny looking character burst into the room. He wore white casual linen pants and shirt of the middle east influence. His long white hair and ill groomed beard made him look wild. I immediately thought of a spiritual guru standing before me. The image was perfect, if that's what he wanted to portray. He cupped my hands in his and began kissing and stroking them over and over again while muttering something inaudible. I smiled awkwardly at his hostess. This was too weird. My inner voice poked me and said, "run!" Once again, I ignored the red flags.

He invited me into the living room where two dining room chairs were positioned faced to face. I sat in one and he sat in the other. He pulled his chair closer so his knees were between mine. I was a bit uncomfortable in this position but, I thought, it was necessary to be close, so he could read my face. He asked me what I wanted. I told him to tell me what he could see in my face.

Before he spoke he rested his elbows on my thighs, pressing them harder and harder until pain registered. I was in instant acute pain.

Every muscle in my body contracted. Yet, I was unable to move away from him. I instinctively placed my hands on his shoulders and began pushing. His face was only inches away. The harder he pressed, the greater the pain and the less I could move. He was talking to me, but I don't remember what he said. I couldn't concentrate. His hands then moved under my breasts and he again pressed harder and harder until I could barely breathe from the pain. He pressed in other areas of my body but I can't remember where. I was pushing against him, using all the strength I could muster, but he was a great deal stronger. Between gasps for air I asked him to 'stop!' I couldn't say anything more than that. The more I resisted the harder he pressed and the less resistance I had. I could feel my arms getting weaker. I was becoming more and more vulnerable to his wishes. I was terrified. He was not listening to me. When he finally stopped, I began to cry uncontrollably. He told me to hug him, when I did he said "tighter, tighter". I did as I was told and I sobbed.

My upper body and thighs were burning with pain. My head was spinning, the room had no definition. He guided me to the doorway where I paid the hundred dollar fee and made the next appointment. I think I said something about 'needing it because I obviously needed help'. But my memory is clouded at this point. He had claimed me. I was his to do with as he pleased. He had pressed me to the point of submission.

I left the house but I couldn't feel the ground beneath my feet. The world was a blur. I was bewildered and I was afraid. I reached for my bike as a river of tears wet my face. I rode home unaware of my surroundings. The only thing that was important was to get home safely. For the rest of the day, I was in a daze. Nothing mattered. I was a robot doing what was necessary to survive.

The next day when I rose, my shoulders and arms were sore from pushing this self-appointed "therapist" away. I felt like I had worked out in a gym power lifting for too long. I had an appointment with my chiropractor that morning. As I was lying on her treatment bed face down, she walked into the room and greeted me as she usually has: "how are you today". I began to tell her that I was okay, then broke down and sobbed. She gently touched my shoulder and in a soft voice asked me to sit up. I cried even harder. My head hung low as I told her what happened. I was so full of shame I couldn't lift my head. I didn't want her to look into my eyes. I was too vulnerable even with someone I trusted.

She examined the bruises on my body then asked me what I wanted to do. I told her I needed to talk with someone. She called the rape crisis centre, gave me twenty dollars, called a cab and had one of her assistants accompany me to the centre. I was a wreck.

I know the counsellor asked questions, but I don't remember what I said. I cried more than I could talk. She asked me who she could call to come down and support me. She called Jane, who came down right away.

While the counsellor called the police, Jane asked me the man's name and went on the computer to find his web page.

When I was calmer, the counsellor told me the police were in another room and if I was ready, we could go there and they would take my statement. I became painfully aware this was serious. I was about to give evidence to charge Vlad for a crime. I was still in shock, trying to understand how this could have happened to me and attempting to come to grips with the fact that I had been violated. All the while I'm thinking: "this can't be happening, I just want to go to the safety of my home".

The counsellor and I walked together down the hall. I didn't want to go, but I had to. I felt I was about to be violated once more. I don't really remember what the hallway was like or how long it was, but I felt as if my mind took still photographs with each step of this long walk. I went from one click of the camera to the next. My body was shaking. I thought my legs would not hold me upright for much longer. I didn't want to relive what had happened to me again, especially to strangers. I was in shock, scared, vulnerable.

She opened the door. I halted and braced my hands on the door frame. There in this very small room were two very large men (at least that's how they seemed) in dark blue uniforms with guns and all sorts of things hanging from their belts that alarmed me. I stopped breathing and held to the frame of the door. I felt like a deer in the headlights.

The counsellor encouraged me and said that I would be okay, it was the police and I was safe. I wasn't convinced, but I went in and sat down with her close behind me. Both officers identified themselves in a low and soft voice. The older officer said he was going to step out of the room and let the younger officer take my statement. The counsellor wanted to stay, but the officer said they preferred that no one else be in the room. My eyes followed her as she opened the door to leave. Our eyes met. Inside, I was saying: "please don't abandon me". But I couldn't mouth the words. I wasn't sure what would happen next. I wanted to flee.

It was just the two of us in a tiny room with little space between us. I wanted the room to be bigger but had to accept that it wasn't. In a compassionate and soft voice the officer asked me the normal identification questions and then asked me to tell him what happened. He said not to bother about the order of the event, just let it all out. He listened quietly as he wrote my words. I unravelled what had happened to me, crying and sometimes sobbing. I had no way of making sense of what had occurred. I just knew I had been violated and I was in pain physically and emotionally. I couldn't lift my head to look at the officer. I was embarrassed. Why couldn't this officer be a woman? He kept writing. Somehow I knew I was shaking inside uncontrollably even though I was unaware I had a body. It was like the only part of me that was real was my mouth as I spewed out the horror of what had happened to me.

The counsellor stepped into the room and said she was going to join us. The officer didn't object. Her presence was of some comfort. While I was giving my statement, part of me didn't want to admit I had been violated but as I talked, I became aware that what happened was real. As difficult as it was, I needed to tell my story and stop Vlad from hurting others.

When I had nothing left to say, the counsellor took me to her office and let me calm down before Jane drove me home. I am grateful to her for her friendship and support.

My erratic state of mind and body seemed to go on for what felt like weeks. I moved around in a fog. I had trouble speaking, distorting words and often stuttering. I couldn't think of the right words to say or, if I had them in my head, the words wouldn't come out. I napped in a drugged state during the day and slept heavy at night. I was impatient with myself, I couldn't concentrate, couldn't walk straight. It was like I was drunk all the time. I thought I was going crazy or perhaps I had a stroke.

I went back to the rape crisis centre to talk with a counsellor. After a while she asked me what I needed to do. I told her I just felt like curling up in a ball on the floor. She said: "why don't you". I slid from my chair and curled up in a fetal position on the floor. She put a pillow under my head and suddenly like a dam bursting, I cried hard, loud and long. When I finally stopped I looked up, her face was wet with tears. Exhausted and somewhat relieved I went home and rested.

After the police had interviewed me they went to see Vlad for his statement. The two statements went to the Crown prosecutor. I was going for knee surgery the day the police officer in charge called me with the bad news. The Crown decided not to prosecute. The officer said it was probably because it would be Vlad's word against mine and the case would be hard to prove. I was dumbfounded. Did they all think I was lying? I was hurt and felt no one believed me. Traumatized again. I went into surgery troubled and in shock. When I woke from surgery the first thing I did was cry.

After I overcame the shock of the news, I went to the police station and spoke with the officer in charge of sexual abuse cases. She asked me why I wanted Vlad prosecuted. I knew it was too late for me. He had already violated me and I couldn't go to court against him. I said: "So he can't do this to anyone else". She said: "we'll get him". This was of little consolation. No one believed me. To help me live with the Crown's decision I told myself that at least his actions were in the police records. If there was another complaint, the court system would look at him more seriously.

Not long after I received a phone call from the woman who had been doing my year end. She said she could no longer do them because she supported Vlad and knew I was saying bad things about him. I was stunned. It is a sad time, when a woman does not believe another woman about sexual assault.

About the same time, Jane, went to one of Vlad's public sessions to check him out. She said the two women on either side of him in front of the audience wore white billowy dresses and from time to time turned to look at him with a mesmerised grin that made Jane feel sick to her stomach.

The following spring when he was due back in town, I noticed his advertising signs didn't appear anywhere. And the following year was the same. He was still appearing in larger centers, but at least he wouldn't be traumatizing women in my city.

The police gave me a Financial Benefits form to fill out and mail. These forms are handed out to all victims of violent crimes and mailed to a committee who discussed the application. The amounts awarded vary according to the discretion of the panel and their mandate. A few months later I received a cheque in the mail for $1000. Somebody believed me! That helped. It wasn't justice, but, somebody believed me. That is one of the most important things to a victim of a violent crime. There is always that doubt that no one will believe the story and that maybe it wasn't as terrible as I had thought. To be believed, means the abuse happened.

What is it about me that I have gone from one inappropriate relationship or situation to another creating more drama for myself? I kept seeking answers from those less likely to help and usually compounding my problems, whether it was intimate relations with men or weird perpetrators like Vlad. Repeatedly, I was locked in my pain without a friendly voice to sooth me, inside or outside of me.

The answer was in a book I read. Peter A. Levine wrote: "In An Unspoken Voice" on how and why I was getting into relationships that weren't healthy and safe. In my disconnected mind set, when I was struggling to understand my life and who I was, I reached out to *"each new relationship possibility as providing the caring protection that will calm (my) inner anxieties and buoy up (my) fragile sense of self."* In other words: 'looking for love in all the wrong places'. *"Even when one's idealized (fantasy) rescuers become abusive, one seems oblivious to the early signs of that abuse and becomes increasingly ensnared in a damaging liaison precisely because it is so familiar or 'like family'."* p110

He states that the part of the brain that can see the red flags is supressed. All the physical and vocal emotions in the possible relationship are not discernible. There's no ability to know if this person is to be trusted.

As I learned more about myself, I was even more convinced, I would not have another relationship with a man because I could not trust myself in my selection of men to keep me safe. In the past, when a man showed me attention, I grabbed onto him; seeing him as my saviour and protector. I was blinded to physical and emotional red flags; in denial. 'He couldn't possibly hurt me'. 'He loves me'. And, 'a loving person protects'. How could I possibly have a healthy relationship with someone believing as I did? I was in survival mode and seeking someone to save me unaware that the only one that can save me is me.

I also decided it was not safe to have a friendship with a woman. I was too vulnerable to know who I could trust or if I knew how to behave in a sensitive and appropriate manner. I had made far too many social faux pas that hurt or offended others and embarrassed myself in my inept attempt to be accepted by others.

All these years from youth to the present day, I have been in a constant state of alertness to any abuse. My body has been tense and ready to fight or flee. When neither of the actions occurred, the body sent messages to the brain to stay on alert. And according to Levine, if I can't understand where the distress is coming from, I'll continue to look for solutions. Hence the face reader, the psychic, the seeking of people to help me understand and my intimate relationships with men. *"Our minds will stay on overdrive, obsessively searching for causes in the past and dreading the future. We will stay tense and on guard, feeling fear, terror and helplessness because our bodies continue to signal danger to our brains."* p183

And I did just that. With each relationship, whether it was intimate or friendship, I was looking for answers. I was not plugged into the other person and their story. I cut them off and began talking about my issues, my thoughts on a subject. They may have sent signals that they were not feeling heard. In other situations I did not see the danger signals that I could be harmed.

Consequently, I have not recognized any meaningful friendships. I kept people at a distance, afraid to let them into my world. Eventually, if a "friend" or family member showed one slight indiscretion that offended or hurt me, I cut them out of my life with no feelings of regret. To me they were all dangerous.

Only recently have I realized the caring friendship in Marion and Naomi. They have stood by me, listened to me, let me offend them and have never abandoned me for the past twenty-two and thirty-seven years respectively. Obviously they have seen something in me that is worthwhile.

Chapter Twenty-Seven

My siblings and I didn't know much about one another except what we gathered from our mother, who stayed in touch with all of us. By the time I was gone from my parents' home and married with a child, my siblings were still under the age of ten. We didn't have much in common. I had been their babysitter over those ten years and their second mother while mom was in the sanitorium. I usually lived in a different city than the others with long distances between us. My only contact with family was with my mother, but not often.

The first in-depth connection was with Ellen. We talked on the phone often. When I decided to hike the Camino in Spain during the month of July, to celebrate the new millennium, she asked if she could go along. First we took a vacation in Hawaii to see how we would be together. That experience set the stage for our next adventure. We made a commitment to hike the Camino. Ellen and I decided not to begin in the Pyrenees, which was the starting point for most pilgrims, because we would have to go through Pamplona. July 1st was the famous Bull Run and we knew it would be too chaotic and we probably wouldn't find a place to stay. Logrono would be the perfect starting point and cut about two hundred kilometers off the hike. As it was, six hundred kilometers proved to be enough.

Our plan included: arrival in Barcelona, July 1st, spend three nights there to acclimatize and head for Logrono by train where we'd begin this exciting, unforgettable journey. Our destination was Santiago de Compostela on the west coast. We'd stay in Santiago for three nights, fly out to London, and take a train to Liverpool to visit our cousins. We'd be away for a month, the longest either of us had been away from home.

I established a training program beginning January 1, 2000, of gradually walking farther and farther over the next six months. I did the necessary strength building in a gym and researched what we needed to pack for our survival. We knew we had to make, on average, twenty-five kilometers a day. Ellen didn't have access to a gym so she just did a lot more walking.

We made a list of all the things we would pack. Light summer weight clothes would be enough for most days, but we added a warm lightweight jacket for evenings. I found cheap plastic rain suits, just in case.

We chose medium sized backpacks with plenty of pockets for easy access to incidentals along the trail. July is hot in northern Spain, so a sleeping bag liner would be enough cover during the night. We tried on hiking boots but decided they would be too heavy and hot. Instead we bought cross country running shoes which turned out to be perfect. We'd pack sandals for the times when we had reached our daily destination and wanted to cool and relax our feet.

Because I was familiar with proper foot care, I had the best product available to prevent blisters and tired burning feet. We would use a heavy foot cream from Gehwol, specifically for athletes, foot powder and Smart Wool socks. Cotton isn't advisable for long hikes.

I began working out at the YWCA with a trainer who was also a backpacking hiker. I walked on the treadmill and elliptical, building my time from fifteen minutes to an hour each day, five days a week. I started with no backpack, graduated to an empty backpack and added weight with towels and blankets as I built my endurance. When spring arrived, I walked with a full pack outside with my dog going several kilometers a day. I had regular visits with my chiropractor and during the last week before departure, I went three times.

June 30, 2000 was our departure date. We would meet in the airport and took off for London, then transferred to a smaller plane for Barcelona. To avoid waiting at the carousels in Barcelona and guaranteeing our packs would arrive with us, I suggested we take our backpacks as a carry-on. We were excited. I was apprehensive. This trip would be a test to our commitment to finish the hike; our endurance; and our friendship. We had agreed that if during the hike, one of us couldn't continue, we'd both go home.

We continued to talk on the phone about our trip, but one of those calls would change my life, again.

In the spring of 2000 Ellen called to ask if I would consider taking in a puppy who needed special care. She had rescued him from a puppy mill and had nurtured him to reasonable health, but he needed ongoing special attention.

Frenchy had died a year ago and I had decided I didn't want another dog. Instead, I had purchased a canary and that was about all the responsibility I wanted. But she convinced me I was the only person who could care for this unfortunate puppy's needs. He was too needy for a family. He required someone who could give undivided attention and could afford his medical bills.

We had planned to meet in a city half way between her place and mine in May to shop for our trip so we decided this would be the best time for me to pick up this puppy, which would by then, be eleven weeks old and stable.

When I walked into the hotel room, this little black ball of fluff greeted me. He was undersized, weighing in at about five pounds, no undercoat and a bloated hard belly, but he had come a long way from his miserable existence of filth and disease. When Ellen first got him, the veterinarian told her, this pup should be put down. She told him the pup needed a chance and she was prepared to do whatever it took to make him healthy. The veterinarian told her to feed the pup every hour, twenty four hours a day for a week in order to ensure he would live. And she did just that.

When I got Trigo home I took him the next day to a very special veterinarian with a huge heart and gentle manner. He had helped me through the death of Frenchy so I trusted him. He said Trigo had a severe case of parasites. It took three rounds of meds to get rid of them.

I began to identify Trigo by the amount of money he cost me. Trigo was my $1000 pup, then he was my $2000 pup, and the cost kept rising. We were in the pet clinic numerous times for so many problems including surgeries. Trigo became so use to going there that he had stopped shaking while we waited to see the doctor.

By June, Trigo had a full thick body of pitch black soft wavy fur with a white blazer on his chest and a patch of white on his chin looking like a thin goatee. He had a touch of white on his paws as if he'd stepped in a tray of paint long enough to get a little on each paw. I loved his eyes. They had a mischievous glint that told me he was going to be a handful. And he was. It soon became clear he was the alpha dog in this pack. I hired a trainer to help me put Trigo in his place in this pack. Unfortunately I didn't train as well as the dog and Trigo remained the alpha.

In his early months both ears stood straight up, but as he aged, one dropped adding to his distinctive character. His breed was questionable, but I guessed he was a medium sized schnauzer cross. When mature, he weighed in at about thirty pounds and stood just under two feet. He was playful, loved to run free at speeds that only a greyhound or border collie could surpass. His strong ego was evident when he would rest his front paws on the side of a planter near my back porch, with his body erect, overseeing his domain. He had a sense of pride noticeable in his eyes and stature. Trigo had a hearty deep bark that warned anyone who approached that he could mean business until they came up to him and he turned to mush wiggling his body and wagging his abundantly bushy long tail like a fan at full speed.

When I first made the decision to take Trigo, I had not thought of what I would do with him when I was in Spain for a month. Fortunately a wonderful animal lover took him. I had no concerns for Trigo's safety and well-being.

Chapter Twenty-Eight

My dog was in good hands, my training was finished and it had paid off. I had turned fifty-nine in February and felt like I was thirty. I was ready to go.

When we met at the airport, Ellen gave me a baseball cap in red and white with Canada to Spain 2000 embroidered across the face of the cap. I noticed she didn't carry her backpack, she had checked hers in instead of carrying it on the plane. I was concerned and hoped it wouldn't affect us and our plans. When we arrived at the Barcelona airport, Ellen's pack wasn't there. After much investigation we were told it was on another flight that might have been heading for Germany. The airline said they would find it and deliver it within a few days.

Unfortunately, this meant our time in Barcelona was spent looking for outdoor equipment and supplies in case the pack didn't arrive. We didn't get to see much of the sights of this historic city. What we did see were piles of garbage due to a long weekend of celebrations, urine soaked corners on the streets and expensive food. When her pack arrived on the 2nd day we checked out, much to the chagrin of the hotel, and caught the next train to Logrono.

I had taught myself enough Spanish that I wouldn't starve and always have a place to stay. However, on the train, the accents were too strong for me to understand the announcements over the public announcement system. This made us a bit nervous. What if we missed our stop? At one point, I went to the steps of the train to find out where we were. Fortunately I found someone who told me it wasn't time to get off.

"Logrono, next stop" blasted the announcer. I was struck with excitement. We really were beginning this wonderful journey. Dark clouds moved in and just as we stepped off the train, the clouds opened and we were caught in a torrential downpour. We headed for the bano (bathroom) to put on the cheap set of rain pants and jacket.

When we stepped outside, the clouds had moved on and the hot July sun was beaming down. So we removed our rain gear that had already ripped and threw them away. We decided that it was hot enough here that if it rained, we wouldn't be cold and the clothes would dry quickly.

We wandered through the streets trying to get a sense of direction and I guess we looked lost because a man on a bike dressed in racing clothes approached us and asked in broken English if we needed help. He told us to remain where we were and he rode ahead to find the alberque. Shortly he returned and gave us explicit directions and told us the alberque was open and expecting us. This was the first of many kind and comforting acts of kindness we would experience along the Camino.

We knew we were on the right path when we noticed the yellow shell, the icon for the pilgrimage, embedded in the cobble stoned roads. The rain started up again so when we arrived, we were greeted with a towel to dry ourselves. We read and signed an agreement of the rules of the Camino, which included a request for a donation at each night's stay, the equivalent of about three dollars Canadian; filled out our application for our Camino passport that would be stamped at each checkpoint (tapas bar/alberque/refugio) along the trail. This passport would be proof to the Camino authorities in Santiago that we had hiked the Camino, the Way of St. James. I was bound for this adventure not knowing that The Way would change my life and self-image forever.

After dinner at a restaurant close by, we collapsed into our beds snuggled into our liners with our backpacks at our feet and our Canadian passport, money and Camino passport in our money belts around our waist. We never heard about theft, but we were warned not to take chances.

In the morning we got directions, from the kind people at the registration desk, to the trail outside the city, had breakfast and gathered our things to head out. The morning was bright with a clear sky and comfortable temperature. We headed out on a secondary highway to the unknown. At the top of a slight hill just outside of Logrono was a small community. We thought we had already arrived at our next stop where we'd stay the night, but according to our map, we had only walked seven kilometers and had another sixteen or so to go!

Already hot and very tired; we went to a tapas bar for another breakfast with flavors to please the most knowledgeable culinary expert. A tortilla (frittata) of: tuna, egg, corn, potatoes and cheese in a pie crust, a fresh crusty bun, a glass of freshly squeezed Valencia orange juice and espresso. We couldn't conceive of walking any farther so we took a bus, forgetting what we had agreed to at the Alberque in Logrono.

At our next stop we were turned away by a very abrupt monk at the alberque because we had taken a bus part way. He was known to go to the bus stop to see if any pilgrims got off, then he'd make a mental note. We were reminded by an English speaking pilgrim, of the clearly stated agreement we signed that stated that to be entitled to a bed, we had to have walked the distance between alberques or refugios. Those who rode a bike went to the end of the registration line and any other form of transportation meant; wait until 9pm and if there was a bed available we could stay, otherwise, we would have to find a hotel. Instead of risking a night on the street, we booked a room in the only hotel in the town. I felt very pleased with myself because I managed to ask for the room in Spanish. Of course I didn't understand the clerks reply, but understood when she gave us a key.

Each morning we rose with the sun, had breakfast and hit the trail, arriving in the next community about two or three o'clock. We registered, got our passport stamped, found our beds, and headed for a shower. We soon discovered the pilgrims on the trail ahead of us, used up all the hot water for showers. Fortunately it was thirty-five to forty degrees Celsius outside and we were hot, so cold showers weren't so bad. There were times when we really wanted a quiet room with a hot shower, so we stayed in bed and breakfast hotels or hostels. We did that twice along "The Way".

Once refreshed, we dressed in next day's clothes, washed the clothes of the day and went in search of a tapas bar or cafe for lunch. An hour or so later we returned to write in our journals and take a nap. After two hours of sound sleep, we'd go sightseeing (more walking!) and shop for the next day's lunch, and if we found an internet café, we sent emails back home.

By then the sun had set and the restaurants were open for supper. True to European custom, most shops and restaurants closed for a few hours after lunch. By nine o'clock we were in bed and asleep within five minutes.

On about the fifth day it was obvious we had packed more than we needed and the packs were heavy. We approached the head person at the refugio with our problem. He said we could send a package of those excesses to Santiago and pick it up at the main postal station. He offered to put the parcel in the mail himself if we gave him the money to pay for the postage. Any money left over could go to the Camino fund. I removed my day pack and we stuffed it with the excesses which included appropriate clothes to wear in the big cities. With great faith in the process, we gave him the pack, wondering if it would be there when we arrived. Now we had just two sets of clothing. One we wore and the other that was laundered upon arrival of the next refugio. As we approached Galicia where humidity is high, we often hung our laundered clothes on the outside of our packs because they didn't dry during the night.

For eighteen days we walked, rested, ate and slept. We never tired of noticing that every refugio was uphill from the trail. A mean trick for exhausted pilgrims. One of the hostels stayed true to form. It was ninety-eight steps to our room and no elevator. Exhausted, hot and hungry, we had to make one last effort to push ourselves up the hill then the stairs. No justice! It was amazing how that happened. There were minor problems: the snorers, late night talkers and snackers rustling the wrappings in bed. But there were a lot of good things: the lovely people who shared stories and the man who initiated a group of us to share nursery songs from our respective cultures as we walked. We supported one another, exchanged information and helpful hints. Sometimes we walked in groups, other times we were alone, knowing hikers were just ahead or just behind.

We had taken enough Spanish money with us to do for about a week. The rest we'd withdraw from the automatic bank machines. What we didn't know, was that sometimes the ABMs in villages ran out of cash, or if they were inside a bank, the bank was closed at just about any hour. We were shocked, but laughed it off as part of the adventure. Between the two of us we loaned each other money and managed not to starve.

There was one very difficult day near the end of the hike. We had a choice of two roads to the same city. A helpful local told us, one road was the scenic route, the other was shorter. We chose the scenic route which turned out to be over thirty-five kilometers in forty degree Celsius temperatures. It was a hard walk because some of it was on a busy highway and there were times we weren't sure if we were on the trail. Part way through the walk, we ran out of reserves: energy bars and gels and most importantly, water. We were very hot, tired and concerned. To keep our minds off the danger we were in, we talked about all kinds of things and we sang marching songs and kept in step with each other, thinking only in the moment so as not to be negative of what could happen around the next bend.

As we reached the top of an incline in the road, we spotted a tapas bar. If we had the energy we would have run to the building due to the crushing need to buy water, but we didn't. We staggered in and bought three bottles of water. I went back outside and emptied one bottle over my head then drank the second bottle. As we stood outside the tapas bar we had two magnificent sights. One was the tall steeples of the Cathedral in Santiago; we were close, only one more night. The second was where we would sleep that night before we reached our ultimate destination. This refugio was actually one of the 1992 Olympic parks for the athletes. The area resembled a tidy, clean mobile home park. There were rows upon rows of white buildings on cement slabs.

We woke to our eighteenth day on the trail with a mixture of feelings. Our destination, Santiago de Compostela was a short walk downhill.

As in every community and city we approached; we could see the spires of a church, but the Cathedral off in the distance, towered over hundreds of roof tops. We were excited. We had made it intact, but sad that our adventure would soon be over. We stopped checking our map for directions. We just followed the many backpackers who were in the same state as we were, tired and happy. Some were actually limping or bent over from exhaustion.

We walked along narrow cobblestone roads that led us eventually to a stone arch that opened to a huge piazza. We stopped, walked into the middle and wondered if we had arrived. Where was the greeting sign or a crowd heralding our arrival? No band, no dignitaries? We looked around for some sign that this was the right place. Of course we didn't expect a greeting, but felt it should somehow happen. When we made a full 360 degrees we ended up facing the giant cathedral that we had seen from the top of the hill the day before. Its spires reached to the billowy white clouds in the bright blue sky.

We agreed, this must be the place. We had walked six hundred kilometers in eighteen days, survived and became closer as sisters and friends.

We found our way to the Camino office and showed our pilgrim's passport with all our stamps, signed a paper declaring we had walked more than one hundred kilometers of the Camino and received our certificate. We had been asked by the officials if we travelled the Camino for spiritual or sporting purposes. I decided, although I'm not Christian, this was more than adventure, this was spiritual. The Camino had given me new life, a new perspective and an understanding that I could overcome any obstacle in my way and I would succeed. This was definitely a spiritual journey. It was not only the Way of St. James. It was also My Way. From my experience on the Camino I learned a number of lessons:

1) Have no expectations, accept what is before me;
2) Listen to my instincts;
3) Don't listen to other's interpretation of the future sites, that's from their perspective;
4) Don't procrastinate, always gather what you need when it is before you, you may not have another chance;
5) Don't complain about bad decisions, it doesn't change anything;
6) Ask for what you need;
7) That I am stronger in my mind and body than I thought;
8) That I can eat to survive not for entertainment;
9) I really love being in the country;
10) That I can survive in a foreign country with a different language, food, weather and terrain.
11) that my life at home was too complicated and I wanted to make my life much simpler;
12) I had a sister who had my back and I hers . . . or at least I thought so

Outside the door was a woman who asked if we needed a room. In my research we were told not to accept rooms from people standing outside the Pilgrim office because it may not be safe. Putting caution to the wind, we followed her through the maze of narrow streets to a building with long hallways, many steps up and finally a nice clean room.

Once settled in our rooms, we left to find the main post office. Would our package be there? Would it be intact? Sure enough it was. Now I had my Santiago/London clothes. I was quite bored with what I was wearing on the trail. I noticed my clothes fit looser around my waist. I had been bringing the belt in a notch every so often during the days on the trail, but didn't know what I weighed. We found scales in a public place. I was astonished. I still weighed the same but I had lost inches and probably gained muscle mass which is heavier than fat.

After one day of sightseeing Santiago, we decided to go to a La Caruna, a coastal resort often enjoyed by vacationing Spaniards, for a few nights. The landlady agreed to hold our room and store our things and recommended a hostel. We left behind Ellen's pack with most of our belongings and I carried mine with essentials for both of us.

We took the bus and arrived in this quaint resort town. We looked over the city and the sandy bay and noticed a few outcrops of rugged rock dividing the bay almost in half. We needed to get to the other side of the bay. Instead of walking around it, we decided to walk along the beach close to the water, which would cut the distance by half, but we would have to find our way. We could either go up the beach a ways and around the rocks or we could go to the water's edge where the waves crashed onto the rocks that sat in shallow water.

One problem, the waves were high and fierce. We watched the rhythm of the waves and decided to wait until the wave was receding and run in front of the rocks. Timing was critical. It was risky because the waves were high and frequent with little time between waves. Ellen went first and made it. I waited. I had the pack so I was heavier making me feel a bit more cumbersome. The wave receded, I let that one pass, then the next one came, I made a run for it but the next wave came fast and hit me just as I was clinging to the rock. My foot hit a depression in the sand underwater and I started to get sucked out to sea. I could hear Ellen laughing, but I was getting scared. I managed to regain my footing and quickly made it to the other side. I saw the sandal from my left foot heading out to sea. A bystander swam out and retrieved it. We probably had more than one bystander watching these crazy Canucks tempt fate. The bottom part of my pack was soaked including a few rolls of film and our vitamins.

We laughed once I was out of that mess and we joked about it often for years whenever we talked about our journey in Spain.

We did the usual sightseeing and returned to Santiago in time for a festival and our final two days in Spain.

Where ever we were in Spain, we seldom passed a bakery without buying a treat. There was no pastry that came from a box. Everything was real food and made from scratch. In Santiago, bakeries were supplying samples of the city's specialty . . . almond tortes. The sample wasn't big enough. We bought a slice each of this delicious delicacy. I could not pass up the opportunity to buy more. I had never seen almond tortes like these in Canada that were as good as these. I bought a dozen small tortes to give to people back home . . . and for myself. Later we ate a scrumptious sea food dinner. By nine o'clock we realized we were too tired to get involved in the festivities that had not yet begun, so we went to bed early.

We arrived in London, checked into the bed and breakfast we had secured from Canada and headed out to see the sights. As we passed The Ritz, backtracked and went in for lunch. We chose to sit in the small restaurant next to the entrance to the hotel because we weren't appropriately dressed. In my search for a washroom I had to meander through the hotel lobby. All my senses vibrated with the elegance of this famous hotel. The Ritz had lived up to its reputation. The washroom had a wicker basket full of neatly folded cotton towels and a décor that glistened with cleanliness and money. There was nothing in here that was inexpensive. As I was leaving, a well-dressed woman entered, gave me the up and down look and passed without a word. I was wearing my hiking pants and shirt and probably looked like I didn't belong. I just chuckled to myself.

I had wanted to take advantage of the world renowned live theatre, London style. Ellen had never seen one so this was the perfect opportunity to introduce her to high quality live theatre. We sought out the theatres and came across a Lloyd Webber production called "Whistle Down the Wind", bought tickets for the matinee and took our seats. It was a great production and Ellen was in awe and hooked.

After the play we hopped on a double decker tour bus and saw the sights from above. We could have gotten off at various points but we were too tired to do anymore walking. We went to bed early that night and in the morning took a train to Liverpool to visit cousins.

When we arrived at the hotel, I realized I had forgotten to bring along phone numbers for our cousins. Without them, our trip to Liverpool was in vain. We looked in the phone book hoping we'd be lucky. Our last name was popular in England so there were several pages listed. Without an address the search was impossible. I had no alternative but to phone a friend in Lethbridge who had my house key for emergency purposes. This was an emergency. I told her where she could find my address book and next morning I called her and she relayed the much needed phone numbers. Whew!

I had not been impressed with London because it was so dirty and busy, but Liverpool gave me a whole new view of England. The city was neat and clean with lush beautiful gardens.

Cousin Ted, a retired Bobby, gave us a tour of his former beat which included the Beatles old club set in a cavern at the docks. The next day we visited our other cousin, Mabel. She brought out family photos and we showed her the two albums we brought hoping she would be able to identify family. For lunch Mabel took us to the yacht club.

We returned to London the next day and stayed at the same bed and breakfast. The next morning we caught our flight home. Two weary, grateful travellers heading home full of wonderful fulfilling memories.

A year after I got Trigo, Ellen phoned and said she knew of a sister for Trigo. She was ready for her new home. I contacted the breeder who made arrangements with friends to bring her to me. This beautiful, soft, white and beige shi tzu/bichon didn't weigh any more than three pounds. She had gorgeous big brown eyes and a slightly turned up nose. I extended my hand and she fit perfectly. I brought her to my chest and we merged into one. I was in love once more.

Trigo was intrigued. He sniffed her entire body while she timidly curled up on the floor at my feet. It didn't take long and he was the one stretched out on the floor and she was crawling all over him. She was so tiny she couldn't climb the stairs. Trigo had already chosen his spot on the bed at night, stretched out and against my body. The only spot left for Chee-chee was at my feet. Now Trigo's pack had grown and he carried his new responsibility with pride. Trigo became her protector and mine, stepping between us and an aggressive dog or person when he sensed the need.

Chapter Twenty-Nine

I wanted to get out of this city. Memories of the sexual assault were too hard to handle. Perhaps, I thought, a change of venue would help. When talking with Ellen she said she really needed trustworthy help in the family business up north. Her son was the owner of the business and she was the manager. This was my out. I liked the challenges of the north and I felt Ellen and I could work together to make the store even more successful than it already was.

My conditions were a salary plus the use of a rent free double wide trailer that my nephew owned. We all agreed to the terms and I got ready for the big move. Ellen said the big appliances were in bad shape so, I bought a washer and dryer and a fridge and stove that were all used but in excellent condition.

Ellen and I had talked about me eventually buying the trailer from her son, Zak and perhaps use two of the bedrooms for a bed and breakfast. Affordable housing was short in the town so I had a good chance of making a bed and breakfast work. But I'd have to fix it up first to accommodate guests. She thought that was a great idea and I was excited about the prospects.

Zak wanted me up there right away, but I had to prepare the house, put it on the market, and inform my clientele and pack. The earliest I could get there was in late October of 2002. At least I'd be there for the Christmas rush. I informed my gardening and clinic clients that I was closing my businesses and selling the house. My realtor came over and we signed the papers.

Within a few months the rented twenty-four foot truck was loaded with the help of a few hired young men. I piled pillows and bedding in the front seat beside me so the dogs had plenty of room and could see out the window. I had never driven a truck this size so I was nervous, especially going anywhere close to a large city. We headed out on our two day adventure.

I stopped half way for one night in a motel and pushed through the next day. There was a little snow on the ground and it was cold but the roads were clear. I stuck to the secondary highways and managed quite well, pulling into my sister's driveway late and resting for the night at her place across the street from my new home.

In the morning I went to the trailer to unload the truck. To my dismay the double wide trailer wasn't as nice as I had expected. It was going to require a lot of renovations and clean up. I could see the ground through the furnace vents and when I lifted the carpet I could see the ground between the floor boards. The galley kitchen was old and worn out.

Once I was unloaded and unpacked the essentials, I hired a handyman to knock out part of the kitchen wall to open it up so I could see into the living room and give the trailer a more modern appeal. When he was finished the rough work, I completed the job. I replaced the old counter top at an outrageous cost of $200 (when in a southern city, it would have cost about $60), attached tiles to the backsplash and put up shelving on one kitchen wall.

The living room carpet, before I arrived, had been lifted and shampooed both top and underside because the previous tenants had a dog that had peed freely throughout the living room. However, the carpet was just lying loose on the floor boards, not tacked down or placed under the baseboards. It looked awful and still smelled.

The front door was actually an interior door which would not give much protection from the winter cold making the entry way frigid. I had a proper exterior door installed and erected a wall between the entrance and the living room to create a mud room that could be closed off in the winter from the rest of the home.

I hired someone to install a wood burning stove which helped to heat both the living room and kitchen. Wood wasn't cheap and the man I bought the firewood from gave me green wood many times and cheated on the amount of cords he delivered. I painted the bedrooms to brighten the rooms and help kill the smell.

I closed off the furnace vents in the two back bedrooms because the drafts from them were too big to plug and I was losing valuable heat. To repair them would require crawling under the trailer and replacing the vents. I would have to wait until spring to do those repairs.

When the first blast of winter hit, the outside walls of the bedroom closets frosted up, damaging some of my clothes. I noticed all the walls were cold. Drywall had been installed over old wall panelling only months before I got there. The window frames were not finished after the drywall was installed and cold air was seeping in, sometimes blowing in on a windy day. To prevent loss of heat and have a warm cozy place, meant tearing out the new drywall, the wood panelling and insulating the walls.

Outside there was an extension cord that led to the heat wraps for the water pipes. When I tried to move it, sparks flew. I could see daylight through the skirting and in the dead of winter, the pipes froze despite using a fan on them. So much work to do.

I was so discouraged. I had already sunk about $10,000 into the place. If I was to continue living there I would have to repair and renovate. This would bring my costs beyond what I had expected to pay. I wasn't sure I could take on anymore expense and that meant my idea of a B&B wasn't going to work nor could I rent out rooms that weren't properly insulated and heated.

I took the dogs for walks but during winter their feet hurt from the cold so we never stayed out long enough for them to do what they needed to do. I closed in a section under the overhang in the back with a huge tarp to create an outside room for the wood pile and hoped the dogs would be able to go out there, but even then they were holding their feet up from the frozen ground. My dogs could smell the odor in the carpet left by the previous dog, so naturally my living room became their bathroom.

Meanwhile at the store, I wasn't doing well. My sister presented me to the staff as an efficiency expert, even though I wasn't. I knew how to make my environment run smoothly by cutting wasted human energy, creating efficient procedures and require accountability. But I was met with resistance. I had made a number of errors in judgement and got the staff upset with me. I had difficulty with the computer program and couldn't do the necessary work on it. Every day I'd look at the cash out from the others and it was always short. One day, I was shocked to find my till was short over $300. Because the computer program worked on rounding out figures, I couldn't figure out how to balance or find the error. I was accused of stealing the money.

I knew I was leaving. I couldn't work if Ellen and others thought I had stolen the money. Besides I just wasn't happy there nor were the dogs. Zak, who lived in Vancouver, phoned and asked me to call him back when I got home from my shift. I did and I knew quickly he was trying to get rid of me without telling me he was actually firing me. He just kept saying no one there liked me. Everyone wanted me gone. I was hurt. I couldn't imagine Ellen saying that to him or feel that way. But I discovered during the conversation that Ellen had told him everything I ever said about my feelings and my work. Nothing I told her was in private. Zak used this information as ammunition to coerce and manipulate me. I listened to him for half an hour or more at my expense and finally, I resigned. I was so angry that I had been duped into moving and helping them and to great expense to me. I also discovered that I could not buy the trailer I was in, because it was used as collateral for the business loan Zak had. That really angered me. All that money I put into that place thinking I would buy it one day. How deceptive. I felt manipulated, disrespected, hurt and angry.

Compensation for any money I put into the trailer and expenses for moving were not forthcoming, including my last pay cheque and the End of Employment slip. I had to threaten many times that I would call Labor Standards and Revenue Canada if I didn't get it in due time. Zak kept making excuses that he had to get his accountant to fill it out and he would get it to me, but it never came until it was too late for me to apply for unemployment insurance. When I did get the form, it was he who had filled it out.

When I returned to my house, which thankfully hadn't sold, I knew I had to re-establish my former business. The thought was embarrassing. But first I'd have to replace all the clinic furniture I would need because I had sold the ones I had used before my move. I had to start all over again.

I was so exhausted from all the physical work I had done up north and moving there and back within three months, plus the mental exhaustion in dealing with what I felt was a stab in the back and abuse, I couldn't work for about three months. I had to cash in my RRSP to make the mortgage and have money to live on. I could only work at rebuilding for about two hours at a time because I would get so tired I was stumbling. Then I had to rest for the remainder of the day. Eventually, I managed to build a massage/facial table and sideboards for the manicure area.

Gradually, my clientele returned, along with my energy level and gardening clients began calling me to continue maintaining their gardens. My life was back on track but I had lost a spark.

I was depressed. I had lost the friendship of my sister, $10,000 of my meagre savings renovating someone else's house, plus my RRSP I used to sustain me until I was back in business. I was fatigued all the time and was not enjoying my work. In 2006, I would be sixty-five. It would be time to retire. I would work until then.

Chapter Thirty

Time appeared to stand still. My 65th birthday felt so far away and I was ready to retire. I had begun visiting my sister Betty and her husband Ken in small town in the mountains, only five hours drive, about once a month during the summers. I felt comfortable among the mountains and greenery. I loved the reflection of the mountains and trees on the River and the always present sweet smell of the evergreens. Gardening is so much easier in the mountains. I could have an extensive garden with shrubs and flowers that I couldn't grow in Alberta. Soon I began thinking of how I could find a way to move there when I retired. The problem was; I didn't have enough money to buy a house.

The trailer across from Betty's was a rental. It had been on the market for years and never sold. The fourteen by fifty four foot old trailer was sitting on a large lot with plenty of room to add an addition and still have a yard and a garden. I made an offer on the condition that they agree to hold the property until I retired which would be in three years. It was a stretch, but hey, if you don't ask, you'll never know what is possible. They agreed. The tenant moved out shortly after and the owner put her twenty something son in there. That was good. I felt there was no danger of the trailer being trashed.

I didn't want to wait until February 2006 to retire when moving during the winter would be more challenging. Early in 2005 I put an ad in the paper selling the house and business for $100,000. I had three firm interests and sold it to a massage therapist. I packed and hired a few guys to load the rental truck. I was nervous about taking the truck through the passes in the mountains. Some of those hills are very steep and could be covered in snow and ice. And, I'd have to tow my car which I had never done before. Betty and Ken said they would come out and Ken would drive the truck. What a relief and what a generous offer.

I met them at a restaurant for lunch and on July 1, 2005; I was officially retired and said good-bye to Lethbridge. I was off to my retirement home in the mountains.

I am forever grateful to Betty and Ken for their help. Making a run like that meant they were on the road twelve or more hours with only the lunch break we had in Lethbridge.

To my dismay the owner's son had trashed the place. The owners said they didn't mind if I backed out of the deal, but they weren't lowering the price. I could look for something else, but I decided to buy the broken down trailer because I was able to see the potential of a comfortable lovely home once I did the work. It was dirty and had been abused, but no structural damage was apparent. I really had no idea what lay ahead of me.

I stayed with Betty and Ken for the first two or three weeks while I gutted the master bedroom and bathroom. There was extensive water damage in both rooms, evidenced by a water line about two inches off the floor on all four walls. I was going to replace the wallboard with gyp rock so the walls weren't a concern . . . at the time. But I discovered the damage was so severe I would have to replace the sub floor as well.

Betty and Ken talked with a friend to do the major part of constructing the addition. I met with him on my last visit before the move and he agreed to draw up a plan with costs. He said he would be available when I moved.

Ken had found the building inspector in a satellite office, so I just had to call him when I was ready with the building plan of my renovations and addition. The work was going to be extensive. I would double the size of the trailer and put on a peaked roof. When finished it would no longer be a trailer but a house.

With the plans in hand, I went to the inspector for approval. He came out to the site and wanted to know where the property line was. No one knew, not even the previous owner. The pegs weren't evident either. After measuring, he said I couldn't put a peaked roof on because the overhang on one side would be too close to the 'guessed' property line. I would have to go with a flat or sloped roof. Disappointed I had to change the plans. That was the first of many changes.

I began tearing out walls in the bathroom and discovered that the outside walls were soaking wet. An electrical plug-in was sitting in water and ants had nested in several places in the walls. When I looked at the walls from the outside I discovered that someone earlier had reroofed and didn't put an adequate overhang. This meant that the new roof fell short of the outside walls and siding so when it rained, the water ran off the new roof and inside the walls. Mold was everywhere. So off came the siding of the trailer on all sides adding to my expenses.

Meanwhile the builder was working on preparing the foundation for the new side of the house. As soon as he was ready, I called the cement company. When the truck arrived I knew the invoice clock began ticking. To avoid paying overtime, we each had a wheelbarrow to carry the cement for the supports. That was heavy work but with the help of the teenage boy up the hill, my builder and me, we got the job done in time.

Early the next morning my builder arrived late. He wanted to talk with me. He said he found a full time job and wouldn't be able to work on the project full time. He could only come on weekends. I was shocked. He had given me no indication he was looking for a full time job.

I didn't think he could work all week then come to my place and work on the weekends. I didn't know where to turn for a replacement. Plus this would delay the project considerably. I was stuck.

Working on the project weekends didn't last long. He found it too difficult and quit, asking me for money for the plans and wages for the time spent. I paid him, not realizing the plans were useless because they didn't show the unexpected changes and none of it met construction codes.

My neighbor up the hill, Max, a man in his seventies who had been doing quite a bit of construction work for a contractor, offered to help me. He was incredible. He was strong, knowledgeable and really easy to work with.

While we waited for the cement foundation to dry, we tackled the moldy outside walls of the trailer. The more we worked on it the more we realized that most of the studs and plates on the outside wall where all the water damage had occurred, had to be replaced. They were moldy, rotting and infested with ants and wood bugs.

Another neighbor was laid off for a while and I hired him to knock down inside walls and build new ones according to the plan. I also had him remove the old bathtub, washer and dryer. I hired a plumber to re-plumb the bathroom and a friend of Ken's agreed to install my new shower. It turned out he did it for free even though he'd worked several hours on it. I was grateful.

Max and I worked side by side on the rest of the building. He did the heavy work and decisions on construction and I was his helper. He'd call out measurements and I'd cut. If he needed another pair of hands, I was there. Where I didn't have the strength, he would be there. With screw drivers and hammers in hand, table and miter saws in the yard, we had a great partnership.

When it was time to construct the roof, we were having trouble figuring out how that was going to work. The inspector was adamant on how far we could place the overhang. In frustration I went to the main office, a thirty minute drive away and talked with an inspector there. To my dismay, he said we could have had a peaked roof with a normal overhang because the wall on that side of the house had no doors and therefore would not be violating code. I was so disappointed and angry at the other inspector. It was too late to change the plans again. The frame for the roof was in place. We continued with a sloped roof. If I had known the roofing problems that lay ahead, I would have torn out the roof frame and started fresh with a peaked roof.

When an extra strong body was needed, Ken willingly came over. He was awesome. He'd work full shifts at his workplace and be at my house after hours. On weekends he'd jump out of bed and be there with hammer in hand.

At every major point of the construction, the inspector would come over to check our work. He made suggestions that would help keep us to code. The concern for the inspector was the septic tank. Where was it? I knew it was somewhere near the far end of the trailer, but no one in the neighborhood knew for certain. They gave all kinds of information of work previous owners had done but no one knew for sure what condition the septic tank was in but I was assured by everyone that because I was the only one living in the house, I wouldn't be putting a stress on the system and it would be okay. So I did nothing further on the issue. Bad decision.

Autumn was coming and I was getting very tired. I had worked seven days a week about 10 hours a day. When Ken and Max where working on the roof, I was cutting boards for the roof, building a fence and leveling the yard with the help of Betty. I swung two by tens and two by twelves fourteen feet long like any guy, well, maybe not quite that easy, but I found ways of lifting them so I could cut them and pass them to the men on the roof.

It was somewhere during that time, that Betty had a health problem. At the time we weren't sure if she'd had a heart attack or stroke. She had to quit work, go on meds and reduce her stress levels. That meant she could no longer help me at my house, but she could make sure I ate properly. This was an enormous relief for me. I didn't have to stop to make meals or eat junk.

Several neighbors came when it was time to stand the fifty-two foot outside wall frame of the addition. I was unable to visualize what that was going to look like. I could see the wall bending and falling apart as it was raised, but Max knew what he was doing and up it went, intact. Next came the two end walls. I was elated. My new home was forming before my eyes.

When the roof was finished it was time to knock out the old wall that stood between the old and new part. Max worked on it and when he went home for supper I took over.

The electrician installed the new wiring for the entire house, but some of his work was lacking in quality and probably code. He hung the wiring on one wall so that it went across the studs and plate, instead of putting holes in the studs and running the wiring through them. His helper drilled a hold in the floor plate in the dining area but instead of going under the house and drilling from below she tried to angle the drill to go from above, coming close to cutting the plate in half which would expose the wiring to screws and nails during the finishing work.

I needed to get the insulation and drywall up. Cold weather was coming. I installed the insulation, caulked and taped according to directions from the inspector. Ken and Max worked on putting up the drywall while I built a wall to create a master bedroom at the back end of the addition and another wall at the front of the addition to create a mud room. Across from the master bedroom was my utility room with the washer and dryer, storage and a fourteen foot closet that I built.

I set up an office in the small bedroom of the old part which meant I could erect a half wall on the side of the room facing the living room. This would allow heat to enter from the living room and give the room a spacious bright feeling.

Max installed the wood burning stove that would heat the entire house. The bathroom and utility room had an electric heater built into the wall.

Now, most of Max's work was done. The rest was up to me. I replaced the kitchen countertops, built an addition to the counter with shelves below and built a bench against three walls that would have shelving and cupboards for storage in the dining area. Then I painted everything.

My intention in the beginning was to paint the plywood sub floor then faux paint it to look like tiles, but the rains had come before the roof was on and the plywood buckled so I had to buy laminate flooring, a huge expense that wasn't in the budget and I was getting low on energy. I taught myself how to lay laminate on 1456 square feet and install ceramic tile in the mud room where I had also built a closet. When I needed direction or strength, Max came to my rescue, but for the most part I worked on my own to finish the project, often going by trial and error as I went along.

The last big push was to put the siding on the house. But first it had to be wrapped. Betty and I had started but she needed to rest, so Ken and his friend came to help. Because of their strength and knowledge, they were able to wrap the house much quicker and easier. The extra help cost me a cord of wood.

To save money on siding I chose to put up board and batting which was comprised of half inch plywood and one by two strappings. I caulked every joint and little crack I found to keep it bug and water free. Then I painted the siding. Other than a few smaller finishing jobs, my new home was finished. I had a stack of wood piled high against the house, thanks to Ken. The entire summer building project was injury free, other than hitting my finger with the hammer a few times. But near the end of the project I broke my record.

I had loaded firewood in my wheelbarrow and was rolling it to the wood pile when the wheelbarrow hit a bump and stopped suddenly.

Like a projectile, the bucket came up to my face as I fell forward. It struck me on the upper lip. I thought I was going to pass out from the pain and the fear that my new bridge was broken. Blood began to fill my mouth and I could feel my lip swelling. Ken guided me to Betty who gave me first aid. I ended up with a split lip in a few places, and lots of bruising, but no broken teeth. Accidents happen when the body is exhausted and mine certainly was but I had one more thing to build before winter.

I needed a shed to store my bike and gardening tools so I built one in the back close to the neighbor's fence hoping to stay clear of the septic tank, wherever that was. Once that was finished, I was ready for winter.

The budget for the entire project was blown a long time ago and I had about $40,000 left to last me the rest of my life. Canada Pension cheques wouldn't be coming in until March after my sixty-fifth birthday so I was concerned. However, all the building expenses were paid and I expected no maintenance costs in the near future because everything in the house, including the house was brand new.

Days of heavy snow mixed with days of warm sun came and with that, roof problems. The ice started to build up under the roofing and when the temperature rose, it began melting and came pouring down my living room wall. I had to tear out the gyp rock and pull the insulation away and put a fan on it to dry it out, then repair the roof. I was on the roof often removing the snow hoping to prevent more trouble, but my efforts were to no avail.

The roof had to be redone at a cost of five thousand dollars. Now I felt broken and broke. That additional money would have paid for the cost of a peaked roof that I wanted in the beginning.

I had a startling discovery. I was wandering through a home improvement show nearby. I was about to leave when I heard a familiar voice behind me. When I turned around, there he was . . . . Vince. He was at a water treatment booth and was promoting his services to someone. I approached: "Vince?" He looked puzzled. "Elizabeth?". "Oh my god" he said and ran from behind his counter and hugged me. He was too busy to talk with me so we made arrangements to meet the next day at a café.

We had a pleasant visit and we brought each other up to date on what we were doing. He hadn't had a drink or a cigarette in twenty-two years and recently started up his business in Trail. We had a few dinner dates and I found him to be kind and considerate. I was hopeful that maybe we'd be able to make more of our relationship. We had a history; one full of intellectual stimulation. I missed that. As a gift to me, and perhaps part o˜his twelve step program initiative, he provided and installed a water softener and reverse osmosis system free of charge. That was a huge expense for him, and a much appreciated luxury for me.

Unfortunately, my hopes for something better for us was just that . . . hope. What happened in short time finished our relationship for good.

But first, my peaceful existence was to be broken once more time. Every morning the dogs and I walked into a small residential area where a St. Bernard lived. Trigo liked him and seemed to be happy to see him each day. They didn't really play, they just wandered around the block sniffing the same shrubs, side by side. As we approached the street where he lived, I saw him sniffing around a tree so I let Trigo off the leash to go visit. What I didn't see was a mastiff cross hidden behind the shrubs close by. As soon as he saw Trigo he approached with an arched neck and a stiff tail. Before I could tell Trigo to come, the mastiff had Trigo on his back, biting into him. Trigo was screeching, Chee-chee was barking incessantly. I picked her up to keep her safe, then I proceeded on kicking the attack dog. He wasn't fazed by my hits to his gut. Finally a neighbor came out and took Chee-chee from me. I grabbed the collar of the mastiff and pulled him off Trigo. Trigo took off, yelping. Another neighbor came and took the mastiff from my grip and tied him to a post while I went after Trigo. He was traumatized. I could see he was bleeding but wasn't sure of the source.

My leg was also bleeding where it contacted with the dog while I kicked. A neighbor took me in and gave me first aid. Then she drove us home.

I shook uncontrollably, making it difficult to dial the number for the vet. It was a long weekend and none of the vets in town were answering. I called a clinic in a city close by and the vet said he'd meet us there. Trigo couldn't keep still and no wonder; he had twelve punctures, most on his hind end, one canine tooth was torn from his mouth and more minor punctures in his chest.

The vet injected morphine into him so he could do the examination. Trigo would have to stay in the clinic until Tuesday when they could operate. When he had recovered from his surgery I picked him up. He was in a frantic state. He didn't walk, he hysterically ran. It was like he was looking for a place to hide. When I took him out to relieve himself, he pulled on the leash so hard I was certain I would fall. He tried climbing into a wood pile or behind a sheet of plywood that was propped against the fence. He was in flight mode and couldn't stop.

Finally in the weeks to come, he recovered. His wounds healed on his body, but his mind still wasn't quite right. I'm sure Trigo and Cheechee had PTSD, and for certain I did. I'd lie in bed reliving the attack over and over again. My heart raced and sometimes I held my breath until I realized the attack was over and we were all safe. The experience changed all three of us. We were apprehensive when we saw a big dog. My heart would beat faster and the dogs' ears perked and their bodies went stiff. As time passed, the walks were easier, but never the same.

I was very unsettled about my house. It had cost me a large sum of the money. If ever I had a major costly problem in the future, like the septic system, I'd be in financial difficulty. I couldn't see myself selling my new house and finding something else in the area. What the real estate market could provide me in my price range would need renovations and I didn't have the energy or money to go through that again.

A friend and fellow dog walker I met in the area, was originally from a small town on the prairies and was planning to move back. She suggested I move there where my money for a house would go a lot further. I knew a couple who lived in there. I called to find out what was available. They invited me to stay while I looked. My friends had arranged for me to look at three places. I chose the first house I looked at. It was an old two storey farm house on about a half-acre of land. The basement had two parts. The furnace and water heater were on a dirt floor in the main area at the bottom of the stairs. There was a set of shelves on one wall for storage. The other half was a crawl space.

The neighboring houses were far enough away that I felt I lived in the country. The expansive exhibition grounds across the road were an excellent area to walk the dogs. The town centre was only three blocks away. The location was perfect. I'd have privacy but be close enough to people that I'd feel safe.

Although the colors of the interior weren't mine, they were fresh and that made the house liveable until I was ready to redecorate. The outside was in need of a paint job. The grounds were full of weeds and wild prairie grass. Lots of hard labor ahead. All for $12,000 on a handshake.

I asked the owner if she would hold it for me until I got the money from the sale of my house and she agreed. I stood back looking at my soon to be house and visualized a covered wrap around porch, a big fenced in area for my two dogs, a vegetable patch and a flower garden on the other side of the fence to keep the dogs out.

I returned home and put my house on the market. It didn't take long and I had a buyer. Because they needed a mortgage, the house had to be inspected. The big hitch was the septic system. Where was it and in what condition? I hired an excavator to dig for it. When he found it, it was a collapsed oil drum! What next? I thought I'd go crazy. Now I was faced with having to use a large portion of my savings to create a whole new septic system if I wanted to sell.

The contractor came in with the inspector watching every stage of the process. Eventually the whole back yard was dug down lower than the foundation of the house. Gone were my prized roses, pond and lawn that I'd nurtured back to health. The new septic tank was placed and pipes snaked through the entire hole. When the contractor was finished the inspector said I couldn't fill in the hole! So I had this huge cavity in the back yard with these ugly white pipes. What a disaster. The buyers took the house anyway and I began my plan to move. I had enough to buy my new house and do the work to create my vision.

At my new house I had to get a fence up right away to protect the dogs. The former owners found someone to dig up the weeds in the back so I could create my flower garden. I dug the post holes and set up the fences. I had the outside of the second story scrapped and painted by a local painter.

I hired a young man who claimed to have had building experience. He built my porch, but his abilities were lacking. Fortunately, the porch didn't require inspection because it would not have passed. With the porch completed I scraped, filled cracks and painted the lower half of the house myself. Within a year I had all my plans completed.

After three years in the house, my yard looked like a private park and was admired by anyone who passed by. I had two ponds, a full flower garden with an arbor for the grape vines, a pear and an apple tree, shade trees and four separate lawn areas.

Inside I painted in my colors, built an extension to the countertop and built two small cabinets to house some of my small appliances. Eventually I would build a carport to complete my house and my needs.

I enjoyed my new home and planned on living there for the rest of my life. There was senior's housing if I was in need, a doctor and only fifty kilometers away was a larger town with a dentist, physio therapist, optometrist and small hospital. The senior's centre was active with great people in it and the residents were friendly and helpful.

When the woman who did the flower pots for the town, left, I took over. That was my contribution to the community. And when the work on my house was completed, I helped at the senior's centre, played cards on Thursdays and had many days and evenings of entertainment with new friends.

The dogs and I had all kinds of space for our walks. Trigo loved to run in the open fields, sometimes landing a foot in a gopher hole causing some pain but he recovered to do it again. Chee-chee followed. With the yard well fenced, I was confident that they'd be okay if I left the house. They had the pond for water, a dog house and covered porch for shelter, lots of shade and a huge lawn to snoop around. Often I'd find them lying on the porch perusing their land. They were content and so was I.

Vince and I talked a number of times on the phone. On one occasion he decided he would come to visit me. I had an extra bed upstairs so he was welcome to stay. I enjoyed our long walks on the country roads and sometimes we went for a drive so he could see the area; a time I didn't enjoy because I had long ago stopped taking leisure drives. He began talking about the potential to make a living in the area. Our water was hard and on the farms there was need of water treatment systems.

We began looking at houses for him. One stood out. It was an Eaton house (ordered from their catalogue and delivered in parts to be assembled by the owner). It was in rough shape. It had been moved from its original location on a farm into the town many years previous on a large sled. The move caused cracks in the plaster, the kitchen and bathroom needed total renovations and the upstairs was in bad shape. The renovations were possible, but it was a big job and needed an experienced hand. Vince didn't have that. He had excellent knowledge of water treatment systems, but didn't know much about plastering and building and definitely nothing about electrical systems. But he loved the house and decided to buy it. Vince said he would put his business on the market and as soon as the house was livable, he'd move and set up a business.

After he had started working on the bathroom and kitchen it was obvious he wasn't capable of the work. Finding experienced help was difficult. Tradespeople were busy and not interested in doing the work. I helped him fix the cracks in the plaster in the living and dining rooms, and then painted them at ten dollars an hour. Better he pay me than a stranger and I could use the money and do a good job.

But, after three years and little progress on the house, he still hadn't moved. The only thing he finished was installing the water softener, water tank and dry walled the bathroom wrong. He visited once a year, sometimes twice and most of the conversations were about his plans for his house, over and over again. I was getting irritated listening to the same story. There seemed to be little else we could talk about. I gave him advice on what needed to be done, but something was holding him back. He wasn't sharing information about himself and remained a mystery to me.

Chapter Thirty-One

My mother had been living with Ellen and May. When they decided to leave the north, mom had to find a place to live. I suggested she move close to me and live in one of the senior's suites. She loved the open prairie and the small town feeling. It was then that Ellen and I began communicating again. About once a month I'd drive three hours to visit them. We never mentioned what happened in the past.

During one of my visits, we went swimming in the local pool. I played in the water, went down the slide, did a bit of diving and finished off with a dip in the whirlpool letting the jets beat against the tight muscles in my back. The next day on my way home, my left leg became very uncomfortable to the point it was hard to keep it still. I rested that night thinking it was just a passing thing.

The next day my leg felt better but I was not pain free. I decided to finish painting the living room walls. The leg pain developed to a point I had difficulty climbing the ladder. Soon sharp pains travelled down my left leg. By the next day I could barely stand without extreme pain. I spent most of the day and evening in bed as the pain progressed to the point I couldn't roll to my side without intense pain. I could only lie flat on my back.

I went to the doctor who ordered an X-Ray and prescribed Baclofen, but it didn't help. The pain was so severe I couldn't stand for any more than a minute without falling to my knees with pain. Prior to the next doctor's appointment, I made arrangements with the secretary to take me to the examination table as soon as I arrived. I didn't pause to take off my winter coat because that would increase the pain. The more I aggravated my condition, the longer a more intense pain lasted. I asked the doctor if I should have an MRI. He said no, not yet. He ordered a CAT scan.

The pain progressed until I was in bed all the time except to go to the bathroom and prepare something quick to eat. It took me a half hour just to make tea and toast. I would set up everything I needed, return to bed and wait for the pain to subside, go back into the kitchen and put the bread in the toaster and pour the boiling water in the coffee pot and shuffle back to bed. I did that back and forth routine, until I had my breakfast. Then I couldn't sit up to eat, so that was a chore trying to eat and drink.

I returned to the doctor. I was on the examination table when he said he wanted me in the hospital. First, he then told me to take my bra off and did a breast exam. I struggled with the layers of clothes and exposed myself. I wondered, at the time, why a breast exam was necessary when it was my back that hurt. Then he told me to remove my slacks and said, pointing to my gut: "pull them down". I asked him why and he said with the force of an army sergeant: "cause I want to go inside". I told him he couldn't do that. He replied: "well I am a doctor" and threw his gloves in the waste container.

What did an internal have to do with my back and where was the female attendant that is normally present during such a procedure? My cumbersome winter clothes and my pain level made me feel so vulnerable.

He wanted me in the hospital. I had to think quickly. What about my dogs and my house? How would I get there? I couldn't drive, especially the fifty kilometers to the hospital. I had the town administrator call my mother to care for the dogs. An ambulance was an option, but I was under the impression it would cost several hundred dollars so I chose to call Ed, a dear and compassionate friend, to drive me. I couldn't sit up so he put a foamy on the floor in the back of my van. With his support, I hobbled into the van and he covered me with a pile of blankets.

After being admitted, I was put in a single room with a bathroom and a television. The doctor ordered Oxycontin, Gabapentin and Baclofen. He said he wanted to get the pain under control. Well it didn't work. The only thing all those powerful drugs did for me was to fog my brain. I couldn't see or think clearly. I had little if any energy to look out for my needs. The pain was still as intense as it was when I first went to see him. To shower or sit on the toilet was excruciating. One time I had just finished my shower when I had a sudden urge to vomit. I went down on my hands and knees to the toilet and hung my head in the bowl while I heaved and heaved. With each heave I felt an extra electric shock down my leg. The exertion used to vomit was so violent that it caused me to pee on the floor. There I am on my hands and knees, naked, heaving and peeing at the same time; urine draining out of me, all over my legs and the floor.

When I recovered somewhat, I cleaned myself as best I could, put my pyjamas on and returned to bed. I called the nurse and told her what had happened. She looked quite disgusted with me and went about cleaning up the bathroom.

A neighbor from back home came to the hospital to visit an old friend and dropped in to see me. He asked if I wanted anything from a restaurant. The food in the hospital was so terrible, the thought of something tasty was tantalizing. I told him I'd love my favorite dessert; a rich chocolate cake with creamy frosting. He was such a darling to have done that for me. I ate half of it and within the hour, I knew I was going to vomit. To avoid vomiting in my bed, I turned to my side and violently threw up in the waste basket just in time. With each heave the pain was like a burning electric shock from my buttocks to my big toe.

When the doctor visited later, he said he heard that I had vomited and with the same demanding voice that I experienced in his office: "why did you do that?" As if I had done something to cause it.

One night I woke, very disturbed. I'd had a nightmare. I remember only segments of the dream. I began to cry. I called the nurse. I looked at the door, waiting to see her. *What I saw was terrifying. I saw a dark menacing figure. I thought it was my abuser. I became confused and for a split second I wasn't sure where I was.* When the nurse came closer I realized I was hallucinating and told the nurse I had a flashback. Another nurse came in and between the two of them they calmed me down and I fell into a fitful sleep.

After about a week, one of the nurses told me what I really needed was an MRI, that a CAT scan won't show enough. I knew my doctor didn't want to order one so I lay there dealing with the drugs and the pain. Each time I had to get up to go to the bathroom, to shower, change or use the toilet, I would go down on my hands and knees to alleviate some of the pain. When I returned to bed, the pain would be worse than before and would take an hour or so to subside to the earlier level of pain. I thought I was going to go mad. I wanted to cry, but that just made me hurt even more.

The meals were terrible and I was lonely. Television was my distraction. My mother could only visit when someone else was coming to the hospital to visit a friend, which wasn't often. After all, it was winter and the road conditions made driving those fifty kilometers difficult if not impossible at times.

After two weeks the doctor sent me home to await the CAT scan. I was no better than my first day in the hospital.

I was back in my own bed watching television all day, eating poorly and being alone most of the time. I was having hallucinations of strange forms in my room and believed that my mother was out to get me. I had a splitting headache most of the time and didn't sleep well. Nausea was always present. I needed an opinion.

First I called the drug store and asked the pharmacist if these drugs could cause these problems. His first remark was "why would he give you so much", and then he said my symptoms could possibly be from the drugs.

I didn't want to continue this way so I called Ed to drive me to the emergency ward of the hospital in yet a larger city farther away, again with me lying on the floor of my van. The doctor did a brief examination while I told him about the hallucinations and asked if the drugs were at the source of the problem. I told him I didn't want to take them any longer. To describe the pain, I told him that it was like a dentist had drilled a hole in my tooth and then constantly blew cold air in the hole. When I had to get up, the pain increased. He said my condition was severe and wanted me to return to the hospital closer to home until the CAT scan. He suggested Tylenol three and phoned the hospital and ordered total bed rest, only to get up to go to the bathroom.

My new room didn't have a television or a shower and the hardness of the mattress was equivalent to sleeping on the floor. I couldn't see myself looking into the ceiling all day. Fortunately the television room was a very short distance down the hall from my room. My doctor wasn't in the building at the time so I asked the on call doctor if I could walk to the television room. She agreed as long as I lie down right away. I had no problem with that. The sofa was across from the television and that's where I lay during the day and only rose for meal times and the bathroom. But doing this was to my detriment. The staff decided I wasn't in that much pain if I could walk to the television room.

That meant a number of changes in my care. During my previous stay, when my mother phoned, they'd bring their remote phone to me. During this stay they insisted I use the patient phone in the hallway. Then they wanted me to sit up to eat, but I told them not to raise the head of the bed at all because it just caused more unbearable pain.

On my first day back in the hospital, a nursing aid brought my tray. I asked her what was in it as I couldn't see the food from my point of view. She told me, in a voice loud enough that everyone in the ward to hear, "your demeanor had changed". I said: "of course it has, I'm not drugged". She didn't agree and left me to struggle with my tray of food that was on a level higher than my head and to the side of the bed at an awkward angle.

They almost tossed the bowl of water and cloth at me so I could bathe in bed. After a week my doctor ordered me to use the shower, that I was no longer on bed rest. Obviously he didn't agree with the emergency doctor's diagnosis. The shower this time was a distance down the hall. I had to lean against the wall to hold myself up as I struggled to get to the shower, clean myself and get back to bed quickly.

Surprisingly, there was one day when I was actually feeling relief from the pain. I started walking up the hall with new found confidence, then half way there the pain struck like lightning and I was once more hunched over, breathless and on my hands and knees in the shower all the while puffing like I was giving birth.

Tylenol and codeine worked better but I needed it on a regular basis so the pain didn't have a chance to rise between doses. Most times I got them late and I'd be in intense pain all over again. It would take an hour for the pain to subside. I felt that everything I asked of them was an imposition.

I'm not sure of the cause but I'd wake during the night and had no saliva in my mouth. It was impossible to swallow. I reached for my jug of water but it had been taken away to be cleaned and replaced in the morning with fresh water. Finally, one early morning I was awake when the staff did their rounds to remove the water jugs. I asked the woman to please leave me a jug of water. She was annoyed but left it for me for the remainder of my stay.

The doctor was going to send me home to wait for my CAT scan and he wanted me to try Lyrica. A nurse gave me the pharmaceutical book so I could read the side effects which were worse than what I had been taking. I was shocked that the doctor would even consider this drug after the problems I had with the other ones. I told him I didn't want any prescription drugs and asked what I could take that is over the counter. He looked frustrated and told me ibuprofen and acetaminophen with codeine. Then he said something that was so outrageous. "if you get addicted to codeine, don't come to me for help". This was the guy who had me on Oxycontin which is highly addictive! I didn't care what he thought; I was not going on heavy drugs.

Ed drove me to the city for the CAT scan which showed nothing abnormal. I wasn't surprised. I needed an MRI. That was the only thing that would show any abnormalities in soft tissues. When I got back home I lasted only a few more days and needed to find someone who could help me. Ed again drove me that same one hundred kilometers to the city to see a female doctor. The pain was so bad I asked Ed to go into the clinic ahead of me to see if they had an examination table available so I could go right to it and lie down. There was no way I could sit in a waiting room. When they were ready for me, he got a wheelchair and quickly steered me to her office, where I immediately laid on her examination table. I told her about the "care" I got from the doctor back home. She told me I should report him to the College of Physicians and Surgeons. She recommended an MRI and if I paid for it myself I'd get an appointment sooner. I asked her to make those arrangements.

I returned home to await my MRI in Calgary March 12th. The over the counter meds were helping but not enough that I could stay up for more than a minute.

I was so lonely. The only interaction I had was with my dogs and the odd visit from Ed and a few times with mom. It was winter and the roads were slick. It was too risky for her to walk the three blocks. Mom couldn't come to help me with meals or clean my house so I arranged for home care to come in a few times a month and daily meals-on-wheels for supper. After three meals I cancelled. The last straw was a dried up hamburger patty with cold mashed potatoes no gravy and canned soggy mixed vegetables; worse than the hospital, if that was possible.

I watched television from my bed all day and into the night and sometimes during the night when the pain was so bad I couldn't sleep; always lying on my back. Even reading was difficult. I tried. From a lying position I had to prop my head up to see and hold my arms up to hold the book. That caused the muscles in my upper back to tighten and that transcended to my lower back. My body was best lying flat on my back.

Ed agreed to go to the store and buy a laptop for me, using my credit card. I thought I could surf the net and play games, but that was equally difficult. To keep from drowning in my misery, I used to imagine the universe sending healing rays. I could feel the light engulfing my body and calming the nerves down. I didn't get any relief to the pain, but I felt hopeful that one day it would help. This was a way of staying positive.

Mom had decided to move closer to Ellen. She had a few men move her furnishings and the rest was going in my van with Ed driving. On the day she was moving, mom asked if I'd like to go along for a visit with Ellen. With mom in the front seat, me lying down in the back with my two dogs, we headed out.

During my visit, Ellen and I talked about the difficulty I had being alone at home, unable to do much of anything for myself. She offered to let me stay with her until my MRI appointment, then she'd drive me to my MRI appointment three hours drive away. During the day I laid on Ellen's couch watching television and at night we shared her queen size bed. I'm sure I kept her awake most nights with my restlessness and I think snoring. But she didn't say anything. She made my meals, cut my meat and brought me treats. She really stepped up to help and support me at a time I was feeling helpless.

To deal with the pain I was popping 1200 mg of ibuprofen plus acetaminophen with 16 mg of codeine, five or six times in a twenty-four hour period. The pain was unrelenting. One day I couldn't take it anymore and called an ambulance to take me to the hospital. One of the paramedics was so kind; I broke down and cried in her arms.

When I calmed down, they gently helped me get onto the stretcher. At the hospital, I lay in the emergency room for a long time before the orthopedic surgeon came. He asked me about my condition and ordered a shot of Demerol and gave me a referral to a neuropath. Ellen was working so I had to manage a taxi back to her place. I thought I was going to pass out from the pain. I found the Demerol made my head fuzzy so I didn't give a darn, but it didn't relieve the pain.

Ellen drove me to my MRI appointment while I lay on the floor of my van. I had the MRI and waited for the results. I had disc problems between L4-5 and between L5-S1 including a mild case of osteoarthritis . . . . No wonder I was in so much pain. And that wacky doctor back home didn't believe me.

Surgery was a possibility, but not my choice. I still needed to see what the neuropath had to say. Meanwhile, I had to find an alternative to surgery. I phoned around and discovered a Chinese trained acupuncturist in a nearby city. A phone call to a friend and I had a place to stay while I had treatments. When I arrived, I immediately went to my friend's sofa and lay down. She drove me to my first appointment while I sat squirming in pain in the seat next to her. By the time I reached the clinic I was gyrating with pain. I asked to be put into an examination room immediately so I could lie down.

After the treatment, I walked out upright. I still had pain and I was very weak, but the pain was much less. The second treatment gave me more relief. Then a horrific snow storm hit the city. It was difficult to see across the street for the heavy snow fall. My friend asked me when I was leaving because she forgot to tell me that I could only stay for a maximum of two weeks and that time was up! I was devastated and felt my mere existence was annoying to her and her husband. I also felt trapped. Where did she think I was going to go in this storm?

It was difficult enough for me to get into a car to go to my appointments let alone register at a hotel and get in and out of taxis. Not to mention the cost. The problem became overwhelming. I phoned my friend Marion just to vent because I didn't know what I was going to do.

She called me back shortly and said her sister who lived in a condo made arrangements for me to stay in one of the rental guest rooms and

I would eat with them in their suite. They picked me up, took me to the condo, found a small television and I was set to stay there for a few days anyway.

I was able to walk a little, but because I'd been in bed for four months, my body was very weak. I couldn't walk a block without extreme fatigue.

I made one more appointment with the acupuncturist using the taxi and after that, I decided to go back to Ellen's on the bus. The quilt I had brought with me served as a soft pillow so it was more comfortable to sit for the two hour trip. I still had pain, but it had been reduced to a dull ache with jabs of sharp pain down the leg, but it was tolerable.

My appointment with the neuropath was due. The doctor looked at my MRI results and suggested a few treatments of cortisone with a fluoroscope. I was nervous about needles going into my back, but the doctor said he'd freeze the area before he injected the cortisone. I was certain I was going to feel pain. An assistant held my hand and walked me through the procedure to help me cope. To my relief, I felt only pressure. I had it done a second time and that gave me even more relief.

Ellen was having extreme financial problems and after careful consideration I told her I'd pay her debts with my Line of Credit. Her interest and payments would be considerably less. She cried when I had finished making the arrangements. I knew she would never get out of debt otherwise.

My back was getting better by the day. I could walk upright for longer and longer periods. My challenge now was to get stronger. I was still very weak especially in the left leg. I would have to take my time and not tax my body until I regained my strength.

I decided I was going to write that letter to the College of Physicians and Surgeons as well as the College of Pharmacy because of the combination of drugs and high dosage the doctor had given me. The CPS wrote me with a copy of their letter to the doctor, then a copy of his response and finally a letter with their action. I didn't keep those copies after the issue was all over so I don't remember all that was done, but I think he had to act more professionally. It felt like he got a slap on the wrist, but, I was satisfied knowing that his name was in the forefront of the Colleges and if any similar complaints were made there could be more stringent consequences.

I didn't know at the time, that this whole experience with the level of pain and its duration, the incompetence and inappropriate behaviour of the doctor would develop into Post Traumatic Stress Disorder and add to my existing PTSD I'd been experiencing for years prior to this event.

Chapter Thirty-Two

When I tell women I'm going to travel alone, they are so amazed. They usually say something like: "I could never travel alone". But for me, it's always been about new experiences and sites, putting myself forward and finding what resources I have hidden deep in my soul. And, there aren't many women I know who want to do the things I do when I travel. I understand their hesitation. When I left Monty, I had to learn to deal with banks, landlords, buying a car, booking a holiday. It wasn't easy, but if I wanted something, it was up to me to get it.

I wasn't reckless when I travelled. I researched the area, the hotels, hostels, local transportation, and food. If I was hiking, I wanted to know about the wildlife in the area. One client who was an RCMP officer and loved to travel said she would never go anywhere where she didn't trust the local police. I remembered that each time I chose to travel.

I think the Camino was the greatest challenge for me, because I wouldn't be able to book the rooms ahead. To not know where I would stay for the night was a little unsettling but also part of the adventure. My sister and I had to trust that we'd find something at the end of each day on the Camino. And we did. So when I was planning the Italy trip, I knew again that reservations weren't always possible, and this time I was alone. I had to learn to take chances and trust that I would never sleep on the streets and never go hungry. And neither has ever happened and it wouldn't this trip.

I wanted to do one more big trip before I stopped travelling to faraway destinations. I wanted to know if my body could handle travelling. Would my back support this trip? Would sciatica return? On September 21, 2009, leaving my dogs with my sister Ellen, I boarded a plane to Italy to hike the Cinque Terra and other parts of Italy with a full back pack.

I used Rick Steve's book on Italy as a resource for where to stay and the sites to see. It was invaluable. If I had a lot of money I wouldn't be so concerned about accommodations because I could afford almost anything, but I had a budget and had to know what was available in my price range. His book gave me that. I made reservations at key places beginning in Milano, then Santa Margherita and the last in Rome. Anywhere in between, I would have to find a room when I arrived. My plan was to stay in each village two nights so I could get a better feel of the communities. I didn't want to rush this trip.

I boarded the plane heading for London, then to Milano where I'd stay overnight and board a train to Santa Margherita.

For five Euros, I boarded a bus at the Milano airport. It arrived in the city at the Centrale Trano, a huge station with trains and buses going in all directions and doors leading to the streets on all three sides of the building. According to Steve's book, the Hotel Garda was only a few blocks away provided I exit the correct door. After a few tries I opened the main entrance and walked to the hotel.

I registered and dropped my pack in the room, then asked the concierge where I could find a nice place to eat. He recommended Giovanni's Trattoria and gave me directions. I had an incredibly delicious meal with a glass of fine wine and walked back to the hotel for an early sleep. I wanted to be fresh for the next leg of my trip, where I'd stay for three nights to acclimatize and see the sites.

Walking back to the hotel along the dark Milano streets I could feel the liveliness of the social life. The calm humid air was filled with the aromas wafting out from the many restaurants and cafes. Music and chatter made the setting complete for what could be a romantic night.

On September 23rd, after a restless night (probably from the coffee at Giovanni's), I walked to the travel agent at the end of the block and purchased my train ticket to Santa Margherita. I returned to my hotel for the continental breakfast of croissant, cream cheese, jam and a double espresso. Deliciouso! Then onto the internet to email folks back home. The train wouldn't be leaving for a while so I browsed the kiosks in front of the train station. There were all kinds of antique treasures from books to chandeliers. They were all tempting, but I was backpacking so any purchases at this market would have been too heavy to consider.

It was time to board the train and this is where I got nervous. The dozen or more trains were lined up in their bays with a long line of cars for each train. This meant I was walking a block back and forth in search of my carrozza (car) and wondering if I was even looking at the right train. There was no staff to help me. The carrozzas weren't marked well and the computer screen overhead read one number for the track and my ticket said another. A kind English speaking couple helped me and I boarded the train. Once seated in my cabin, I relaxed. A couple from Huston sat beside me which was perfect because they had travelled Italy often and were able to give me advice.

The train glided along to its own rhythm while I watched the countryside roll by: small villages, rolling landscape, ongoing rows of seasonal vegetables, familiar forests and flowers, and homes scattered across the land just like at home on the prairies.

At 3:15pm, the train pulled into the leisurely seaside vacation city of Santa Margarita, where the soft beige sand in the bay meets the Mediterranean blue waters of the Ligurian Sea. Above me mountains reached to the sky and houses painted in pastel colors, sat on terraced land among olive groves and vineyards that were generations old, many looking neglected. I discovered the younger members of the families are not interested in being grape and olive keepers. They wanted to work in the service industry or left for the larger cities.

I followed the passengers from the train and in short time, I climbed the meandering road up to the yellow and white Hotel Nuevo Riviera, the B&B recommended by Steve. I was given a skeleton key and a request to leave it on the board in the hall when I went out. Mmmmm, why bother locking my door? I trusted all would be well. I rested for a while then ventured out to find shops and eateries.

Photographs of this city fail to absorb the beauty that surrounded me: ancient ornate churches, large piazzas, many lovely restaurants for fine dining, interesting people and so many fresco painted buildings. Someone told me university students made a study of the fresco and they discovered over seven hundred different designs within the city. The work was so well done that from a distance, I found difficulty knowing what buildings were fresco from the others that had designs carved into cement on the outside walls.

For the next three days, I wandered through the city: eating at lovely cafes and restaurants; swimming for the first time in the warm Ligurian Sea and enjoying the outdoor market, which was several blocks long. There I bought cheese, pastry and grapes to take to my room.

My first evening there, I walked in the residential areas uphill. As the sun set on the horizon, I realized it would soon be dark and I needed to return to my hotel. I was totally lost. I knew I had to go downhill, but which hill and what branch of the road? I was getting nervous as the night settled in, but eventually I recognized a few buildings and knew where I was.

My greatest challenge was getting use to the eating hours. Breakfast was okay because it was at the hotel and was served over a two hour period, but lunch had to be eaten before the shops closed between 2 and 4pm for the afternoon break when families came out to play in the piazza. Supper was served after 7pm at which time the city came alive with aromas of pasta, fresh baked breads and the chatter of people over dinner. I quickly grew to enjoy the change and once I did, I fell into the relaxed state of the locals.

I was so impressed with the taste of the food . . . . and the wine. I fell in love with their focaccia, simple pasta dishes, fish salads, gelato and pastries. I felt like a kid in a candy store and told I could have anything I wanted. Everything was delicious.

The heavy tomatoe rich sauces, familiar in North America, were non-existent. Instead, pastas and salads were drizzled with olive oil, locally grown and pressed. The herbs were grown in the chef's garden. Nothing was phony, especially the desserts. There were no 'edible oils' or frozen desserts that were thawed before serving. They were all real natural ingredients. It would be easy to gain a lot of weight in Italy. The wine was made locally and every bottle was exceptional.

On Sept 26th, at ten o'clock in the morning, I said ciao to my gracious host and boarded the local train; a milk run and filthy. I didn't want to sit or touch anything. Monterrosa, the beginning of the Cinque Terra, lay ahead. Cinque Terra was known for its challenging trail in places, but I had faced many obstacles on the Camino and I could do it again. So far my back was doing very well. About eleven o'clock I stepped off the train, embraced the warm breeze and looked at the colorful houses appearing to rest one on top of the other nestled in the steep mountain.

The place Steve recommended was booked so I had to find another hotel. Slight panic. The 'what if's' kicked in. Onward and upward. I would find something. I walked up the cobblestone street and found Albergo Al Carugio. At the registration desk, a couple were requesting a room for the night, but the owner didn't want to book just one night at eighty euros. The couple walked away. I stepped up and told him I wanted a room for two nights and would pay seventy euros. He agreed. Yeh, victory! I had such confidence in myself. It's tough bartering, but if you don't try you'll never know how much less you could have paid.

I dropped my pack in the room and with camera in hand I investigated this lovely village by the sea.

While dining that evening I saw a young man carrying a huge overstuffed suitcase and looking lost. He wasn't lost, he just wasn't sure if he could seat himself or wait to be shown a table. I looked around and there were no tables available. I asked him to join me. He was an engineer in the auto industry in the United States, heading for a church function in southern Italy. We had a wonderful time until darkness descended and I grew weary. We said good-bye and he went about searching for a room for the night.

Most times I ate alone, but occasionally I enjoyed the company of others from various parts of the world who spoke English. We'd chat for a while then go our separate ways.

Everywhere I went I was snapping pictures unaware that my battery was running low. And to my dismay, I had forgotten to take my battery charger. The next morning I couldn't leave Monterossa as early as I wanted because I had to find someone who could recharge the battery. The first trail was going to be difficult and I wanted pictures. Thankfully, the man at the hotel desk agreed to charge it. I had breakfast and walked around one more time and by eleven the battery was charged and I was ready to hit the trail. I was concerned that if I arrived in the late afternoon in Vernazza I would have trouble finding a room. But I couldn't worry about that; I had a huge challenge ahead.

On Sept 28th, camera charged and a full pack on my back, I began to hike the Cinque Terra. The hike to Vernazza was only three kilometers, but it was the roughest of all the segments of the trail. I needed to be sure footed and not hurry to avoid falling. The trail is carved out of the side of the mountains by local volunteers and sometimes the steps up or down are jagged rocks. At times the rough trail was narrow and on a very steep incline with no fence to prevent a fall several hundred feet to the sea. About half way to Vernazza, a man sat at a small table by the trail selling fresh squeezed lemon juice and the local liqueur, lemonchello. I stopped for a break and allow younger hikers who didn't have a full pack pass me. It was a hot and humid day. The ice cold lemonade was just what I needed and it was delicious. I placed the lemonchello in my pack and continued on. As I rounded the corner of the trail, four hours later, I looked down at Vernazza; a quaint fishing village straight out of a travel magazine. It had a small bay with a breakwater that held a sign warning not to go out there on stormy days as people have been known to be swept away by a rogue wave.

My legs were sore. I was hot and tired as I walked into the piazza but I had to keep moving to find a place to stay. I met with a gruff matron at a bar (Steve warns about her) who turned away people before me, but told me to follow her. Perhaps they wanted a room for only one night. We weaved through the narrow streets, climbed many stairs (da ja vu the Camino) and finally to my room. The room was spacious enough and clean for fifty euros a night.

I ate seafood I thought I'd never consider trying back home. It was fresh and well prepared to stimulate the taste buds. I savored the mellow homemade wines. I discovered a number of exceptionally friendly places to eat, or sometimes coffee or wine at an internet café. I stayed for my planned two nights and on the 30th of Sept, I headed for Corniglia which turned out to be my favorite village; probably because the managers of the rooms spoke English and were very friendly. The room was also much cheaper at forty euros, complete with a view of the sea.

I checked my emails at the café's internet. One came from my friend Naomi who had just been diagnosed with cancer. I was so sad. I needed to talk to someone, to share my feelings but there was no one. I went to the church because I thought it would at least be peaceful and I could sit and grieve. But there were too many tourists. I went to my room and cried for my friend of thirty years.

I discovered that my money wasn't going as far as I had planned. Just because these villages were small didn't mean they didn't charge high prices. I probably could have found meals that were cheaper if I spoke the language and purchased at local grocery stores. I had to settle for a lot of pasta in the restaurants.

The days were filled with hiking and seeing the sites of the town. It was the evenings that were long. Fortunately, I brought a book with me for my evening entertainment until it was time for bed, which was usually about nine o'clock.

I decided to change my plans slightly. After my two nights in Corniglia, I would stop in Manarola long enough to look around, have a snack, then move on to Riomaggiore, the last village of the Cinque Terra. There I would stay overnight and catch the morning train to the Etruscan/medieval town of Orvieto, only an hour north of Rome by train.

The trail was much easier and quicker between Corniglia and Riomaggiore. On Oct 2nd I arrived in Riomaggiore where I found a room for fifty euros. I had been washing my clothes by hand, but when I opened my pack the stench was repulsive. The Laundromat was just as disgusting was double the price at home but, I was desperate. At least my clothes would be clean and smell pleasant.

Two women from Atlanta sat with me for a while. We shared experiences over a glass of wine. They headed back to Vernazza by boat. I was on my own again. I bought a bottle of wine, went to my room and after pouring a glass I went outside onto a common area that looked over the sea.

The air was sweet and warm. Branches of the trees and shrubs bent gracefully in a gentle breeze. Over in one corner of the patio two French speaking women conversed over a glass of wine. When they went to their room, I was left to myself. I looked up to see a brilliant moon and a sky filled with dazzling stars and the blinking lights of a plane heading north. I lowered my head and gazed over the calm Ligurian Sea mirroring an image of the moon. This for this moment was all mine. I felt full. At peace. I went back to my room leaving the serenity of the night to others who wanted to claim it.

I'm Still Here

The train left for Pisa at nine in the morning on October the 3rd, then on to Florence where I would change trains and continue on to Orvieto. The five hour ride passed by quickly because I sat with an English speaking local who was most informative about the Italian culture and sites to see in Orvieto. Upon my arrival, I could see a colossal mound of red volcanic rock towering above the train station. I would have to ride up the cliff in the funicular (cable car) one thousand feet where I'd then be in Old Orvieto. I purchased my ticket and boarded. Once at the top I walked up the cobblestone road to the heart of the city and my hotel.

Steve's book had recommended the Hotel Posta at thirty euros a night. It was the best rate during my whole time in Italy. The hotel was once a private home that had been converted. Heavy ancient doors opened into a large sitting room. At one end was a marble staircase that climbed two stories where I'd find my room. It was perfect. I had a single bed with crisp white sheets and a large bathroom.

The registration desk was staffed by a lovely older woman who was very helpful and kind. Each morning, I established a habit of washing the clothes I had worn the day before, and then I'd hang them to dry in the bathroom. The rest of the day was eating and sightseeing. When I returned to my room at the end of each day, my clothes were either out on the clothes line or folded neatly on my bed. When I left I bought her a flowering plant for her desk.

Orvieto is an amazing place. The Etruscans created tunnels and work areas under ground. Tours led through the tunnels to the ancient cemetery, olive presses and many other archeological finds. Moving ahead in time on the surface, one section of Orvieto is of medieval architecture. When I looked down the long weaving narrow cobblestone road lined with two and three story stone buildings, I could imagine victorious knights in shining armour entering the city.

For three centuries a magnificent Duomo (cathedral) was constructed beginning in the thirteenth century. Walking into this enormous ornate cathedral is overwhelming. The detail is stunning and takes a long time to study it all, inside and out.

In my search for fine dining, I discovered a lovely small restaurant, which was also a chef school in the back. My meal was exquisite. For my last night in Orvieto I felt the need to celebrate the end of my hike and adventures with the experience of fine dining at a restaurant close to my hotel, recommended by Steve's book. When I was finished this most delectable meal, I received a complementary liqueur because I told them Steve sent me.

Orvieto is one place I would like to revisit.

After my three nights there, I took the train to Rome, my last stop and my departure city. I had reserved a room in a hostel close to the train station. This was not on Steve's recommended list, but the only hostel that had a room. This should have been a red flag.

When I entered the huge very busy station I had difficulty finding my way to the correct door that would lead me to the street and the hostel. Finally, when I exited the station I faced this ancient city with all its many wondrous sites. However, the station is in a grungy part of the city. I was uneasy walking about and grateful it was still day light. The hostel wasn't far away, but it was still in this shabby area. It reminded me of Hastings Street in Vancouver, only busier.

I entered the building. Directions said the hostel was upstairs, several flights. There was an elevator, but it was a very old model and didn't look safe or clean. As I climbed this filthy, dusty and poorly maintained marble staircase, I wondered if I really wanted to continue. Perhaps this was actually a seedy "bed by the hour" place. I decided to move on to see what the hostel was like, hoping it would be acceptable; otherwise I had no idea where I would sleep that night. Finally, after four floors, I reached the hostel. When I entered through the door I was reassured. It was much cleaner. My room was basic, no frills and a shared bathroom.

When I was settled in my room, I emailed my family and friends from the complimentary computer and internet services in the common room. The front desk provided me with a map of the city and I ventured out onto the street. I wanted to get somewhere that looked more inviting. I had developed a cold and so I had little energy to investigate anything on foot. Not too far away I stumbled across a line-up for open air tour buses, bought a ticket, climbed to the top of the bus and collapsed into a seat. This way I could get oriented and I would be able to find my way around.

I had expected the ancient buildings and museums to be in the same area, but instead were scattered across the city. And to my dismay any ancient structures from the Roman Empire days were surrounded by roads and housing. I ran the bus tour twice because I was too sick to walk around. All I wanted to do was sleep in a nice clean bed with fresh sheets and a soft pillow. I stopped writing in my journal. The way I was feeling and what I saw just didn't feel worthy of the bother.

I searched for a hotel but Rome is expensive, so I stayed where I was. The food around the hostel looked questionable. I settled on a hotel restaurant thinking that might be safer. The pasta was covered in what tasted like tomatoe paste straight from the can. I returned it and walked out.

The woman at the desk of the hostel told me if I wanted authentic good Italian food I had to go to a certain area that was quite a distance away. I didn't go because going there for supper meant it would be dark and I wasn't comfortable walking around on my own and I had little money left to use taxis. So I had really bad food in cheap places. I couldn't wait to head home.

On my second day I felt a bit stronger and found a good café with outdoor seating looking out onto a road with a magnificent fountain in the middle. It was close to Trevi fountain and the tour buses. When I finished breakfast, I boarded a bus for the Basilica, museum and the Vatican; an incredibly beautiful and amazing piece of architecture. I was disgusted by the wealth of the Vatican knowing that so many followers were in poverty. I returned to the café and noticed that in the area was Via Museo della Terme. I was amazed to find the works of Galileo and see the detailed scientific studies and discoveries by this remarkable man.

Rome was anti-climactic. Other than the tour of the Basilica, its museum and Galileo's museum, I was disappointed. Perhaps it was just time to go home, I wasn't feeling well, I had had enough travelling and being on the go all the time. After two nights, I boarded the train to the airport, flew back to Ellen's for an overnight stay and collect my dogs and go home. I was ill prepared for what I'd find back home.

It felt good to be in familiar territory and I was looking forward to relaxing in front of English speaking television, sleeping in my own bed cuddled with my dogs and eating my own food. My body and mind had been through a lot, mostly good things, but still stressful and I was still recovering from a cold. Rest was the prescription.

The October temperatures chilled the air and my house. I turned the furnace thermostat to a medium heat and proceeded to unpack. In short time I realized the furnace hadn't kicked in. Perhaps, I thought, the pilot had blown out from a wind storm while I was away. It had happened before. I knew this was going to be an ordeal. The pilot was hard to light and I was so tired.

As I opened the basement door I was shocked beyond belief. The basement was flooded with about two inches of water. All the storage containers, that once were full of precious items, had obviously been floating and tipped over, emptying their contents into the brew of mud, laundry detergent and paint. Nothing was spared. The furnace pilot was out, but also the water heater. It was obvious that water had been running down the side of the water heater. I discovered that the release valve had not closed and the contents of the heater emptied into my basement. Fresh water continued to drain into the heater and out the release valve. The flood line indicated that water levels rose three feet before the release valve finally snapped back into place. At least that's what the plumber told me when he came the next day.

I had to get all the water out of the basement to prevent mold setting in. About four of the storage containers that had lost their contents, had flipped upright and were full of stagnant water.

I went to a neighbor and borrowed their shop vacuum, but once the bowl in the vacuum was full, it was too heavy for me to carry upstairs (no drain in an earth basement floor). I called a local man who had once cleared my sewer pipes. I knew he had a pump. He looked down the stairs at the mess and said it wasn't worth his while to haul his equipment in. He said I should just let it soak into the already saturated dirt. But, I told him, many of the storage containers were full of water. Nope, he wasn't doing anything for me.

Angry, disappointed, frustrated, exhausted and alone, I gathered the water into small pails and carried them up the twelve steps to throw the contents into the yard. I climbed those stairs a hundred times at least, or it felt like that. By the time I had finished cleaning up the mess I could barely walk. I was cold, hungry and exhausted for so many reasons. I collapsed into my easy chair wanting to cry but I was too tired to bring tears. I sat stunned at what just transpired and felt quite sorry for myself. Then the phone rang.

"Hi Judith, it's Vince, I just got into town". Well that was the last thing I needed was company, especially the kind that didn't want to talk about anything else but renovating the house he bought four blocks away.

I told him what had happened in the basement and that I had just returned from my trip, had jet lag and I recovering from a cold. He came over, looked at what remained of my treasures once stored for protection in the basement and sat down in the living room and proceeded to tell me what was happening in his life and what he was going to do to his house, again.

I sat in my chair; stunned, zoned out, annoyed that he wasn't sensitive to what I was dealing with. I heard him talking but I wasn't listening. This was probably the last straw for me when it came to Vince. He knew that I had spent four months in bed, only a year ago but he didn't call or give me much support. And now, here I was, having gone through all this and sick as well. His interests were only him and that was a reminder of what it was like when we were married.

I told him I couldn't help him anymore but I could offer suggestions and guidance. After all I had torn down, remodeled, built and decorated three houses. I had some idea of what would work and wouldn't. Most of what I had to say wasn't useful to him. He listened and went on doing what he wanted to do even though it created more work for him or was illogical from a renovations point of view.

Next day the plumber came and replaced the water heater valve and thermostat, cleaned out the furnace and lit the pilot. Finally I had heat and hot water.

For the next week I struggled to regain my strength, and within a few weeks I managed to put together a slide show of my Italy trip, create a movie night for everyone to enjoy at the senior's centre once a week, play cards and have fun with friends.

Eventually I felt stronger, inspired and renewed and went about building a carport. It would likely be the last big thing I'd build. One of the locals brought his auger and dug the post holes for me, another brought dirt to build up the bank. This was a huge challenge.

I didn't know how to construct the roof to make it squared and aligned with the house; which was not on even ground or square itself. Even when I asked people who knew about construction, I couldn't make it happen the way it should be. I needed an extra pair of hands and that wasn't available. But I did it. It may not have been the prettiest construction job, but it was secure. When the last screw was in place and the roof was on, I rolled my van into the carport with plenty of room to spare and just in time for winter.

Now the house was complete. I had a deep covered porch on three sides, a fenced in beautiful yard and flower garden, a vegetable patch that had fresh compost and manure worked into the soil ready for spring planting, newly planted fruit trees, a freshly painted shed to match the newly painted house, and a place for my above ground sixteen foot diameter pool for the summer. There was nothing left to do but reap the benefits of my hard work and creativity.

I visited Ellen about once a month. I'd pile the dogs and a suitcase into the van and three hours later I was at her doorstep. We had good visits, talked about flowers, gardening, the Camino, enjoyed meals out and movies. We began talking about her financial situation which was still not good and my issues. I knew my energy and strength were diminishing. I was getting tired of working so hard around the house. What if I needed a new furnace or roof, and that was inevitable; would I have the money to pay for it? Would I have the physical energy and strength to do any minor repairs, not to mention the needs of my huge yard? Travelling to the larger centres for acupuncture and physio was costing me about $250 a month in gas.

I thought how vulnerable I was and who I would see for any medical issue. I knew the doctor in my town wasn't acceptable. The doctor I found in a larger centre was too far away. Chances are, I might have to seek the services of the local doctor in an emergency and that was undesirable. The thought made me cringe. I wanted and needed to be in a city with good medical care.

As Ellen and I discussed these issues, we came to the conclusion that we'd put our houses on the market and when they were sold, we'd find a rental house that would accommodate her daughter, Ellen and myself.

However, I was faced with leaving my house that I had worked so hard to improve. This move began to feel like a number of losses. I was giving up the peace and serenity that living in the country gave me. I would leave the friends and activities I enjoyed. I'd lose my privacy that was sacred to me. I would have monthly payments for accommodations that I hadn't had since my mortgage was paid off in 2002. I would have to ask a landlord permission to do anything to the house or yard. Not a pleasant thought. How was I going to cope with all these losses?

The biggest question in my mind was how would the three of us; Ellen, her daughter May, who had Asperger's manage, knowing we had different lifestyles? I was uneasy. Finding my own place wasn't an option at the time because I felt the cost of an affordable apartment would leave me with little money each month. Perhaps we find ways to live together without conflict.

When I returned home, I placed "house for sale" signs in key places in town and in short time, a couple answered my ad and gave me an offer. I was asking $40,000, they talked me down to $30,000. We agreed that I would forgo the down payment in exchange for letting me stay until March when the weather was more predictable and safe for driving. Winter came in its usual blustery frigid way and I began packing what I could and making plans to move.

Chapter Thirty-Three

In early spring Ellen called to say she had found us a house and emailed pictures. I liked what I saw. It wasn't old and broken down. The lawn and the shrubs were in bad shape due to neglect but we could fix that. The house was across the street from the dog run, had a fenced-in backyard for the dogs and a single attached garage. It was a four level split with a completed basement with two bedrooms useful for May's suite. There was a bar in the main room that I could make turn into a kitchen for her. With a hot plate, an electric frying pan and a fridge she could cook her own meals and put her dishes in the dishwasher upstairs. I bought May a fridge and for her privacy, I bought a screen that would act as a door to her living area at the bottom of the stairs. May could enjoy some independence and responsibility, but still have her mother available to continue monitoring her care.

Ellen and I shared the main floor consisting of a kitchen, dining and living room. The upper level gave us an office, a bathroom with two sinks and our own bedrooms.

In the beginning of March, my next door neighbor and one other fellow volunteered to help load the rental truck. It was a cold and blustery day and my helpers worked hard and steady. I was so grateful. There was one problem. When we finished loading I discovered the truck had a flat tire. I called the garage. Tim was so helpful and kind. He came over and was able to repair the tire and off I went. I was on the move again and hopefully for the last time in my life. Well . . . maybe not.

Ellen and May had already moved in when I arrived. With the help of a young man to help May and me, we unloaded the rental truck.

Once settled, Ellen and I cleaned up the badly neglected yard and flower beds and tried to deal with each other's idiosyncrasies. It wasn't easy. Our lifestyles were in direct conflict. We thought this would be something we could iron out in time. Monthly meetings were planned so we could talk about problems, but that didn't last more than three meetings. It didn't take me long to realize this was a huge mistake, but

I couldn't see that I'd be able to find a place I could afford on my own, so I decided to stay with this situation until I could figure out something else that would be more healthy.

The love I have developed, in these recent years for my dogs, knows no boundaries of emotion. When I look into their eyes, I feel warmth and trust. When I watch them play, my heart is light and I laugh. When they are unwell, I fear the worst. And the worst arrived after a number of trying times with Trigo who was in and out of the vet's clinic with numerous issues that sometimes were not resolved. And he would endure whatever discomfort he had.

I had Trigo for nine years when it was clear after several operations and medications that something else was not right. I could see he was hurting. When I picked him up, he'd groan or cry. He was in pain and there was nothing that could be done. He would stand in the middle of the room staring into space and just bark. He was trying to tell me something. One evening, I knew when I looked into his eyes, it was time. I called his doctor and Ellen and I took Trigo in for his final medical visit.

As he lay between us on the leather sofa in a private grieving room at the clinic, Trigo drifted off and away. I was relieved he was no longer in pain, but what remained for me, was guilt. Maybe I was too hasty in my actions. There's always that self-doubt when this kind of decision is made. If they could only talk our language. But deep in my soul I knew he had completed his job on earth. He had lifted my spirit, taught me more about raising a dog than I could have imagined, protected Chee-chee and me, made me laugh, loved me and let me love him. I have missed him beyond what I have felt for any other dog I owned. There was something special that is difficult to put into words. A photo of him in a typical pose hangs on the same wall with Frenchy's photo.

Chee-chee and I grieved for months. I'm sure she was looking for him, waiting for him to come home from the hospital. She seemed to be lost. It took her a year before she discovered herself. She became the perfect respectful loving dog. She developed expressions that helped me learn what she needed and when. Chee-chee learned to follow my lead whether it was my voice, a noise I make with my mouth or my hand signals. She has come into her own and is a wonderful companion in her late years. As of March 2013 she is 12. She will be my last pet. I will satisfy my need to love animals by walking the rescue dogs at the local SPCA.

Chapter Thirty-Four

I had a lot of time on my hands and one of the things on my "bucket list" was to help at the police station in Victim Assistance. Jenna, the trainer, invited me to go to the station for an interview. Before I left, she introduced me to the administrator of the unit.

The next step was the polygraph. I was given a form to fill out with details of who I was and information about my life. This was an indication of what the polygraph was going to be like. There were questions about my children. I didn't want anyone to discover that I didn't even know how to get in touch with them and that we'd been estranged for over twenty years. This was too difficult, too embarrassing. I called Jenna and told her I had to withdraw. She assured me that I wasn't the first person in my situation and she felt I was a very good candidate. Reluctantly I went for the test. The three hours or more slowly and painfully passed. The personal questions brought tears. I hated this part but if I was going to be of service to victims, I had to do this. I passed as not being a "very good liar".

I began training shortly after and have become an asset to Victim Assistance. I had developed strength and understanding of what had happened to me over the years and felt competent I could support the victims of violent crimes. I still had moments of anxiety, but I understood their source and the feelings would subside. What happened next shook my foundation and self-assurance.

My level of anxiety had been high for months. Living with my sister and niece was difficult. I knew leaving my peaceful home and sharing a house in the big city would be a big adjustment but I had no idea how it would affect me. Adjusting to the loss of my independence and my own house left me emotionally vulnerable.

Christmas was nearing and with that came the Christmas fair with all its colorful booths in festive décor. People filled the fair as soon as it opened. We were shoulder to shoulder. *I began to feel anxious. I felt like the place was closing in on me, people became a blur, my breathing became rapid, my head was spinning and I felt the need to run. I couldn't get out of the building fast enough. I was frightened by this experience and didn't understand where* it came from. I sought help from a psychiatrist. After giving him a brief history, he said the experience at the Christmas fair was part of Post Traumatic Stress Disorder (PTSD) and prescribed an anti-depressant. He said it would help to keep me calm. I have not had much luck with these medications because the side effects are worse than my mental condition. Months later, PTSD raised its ugly head again.

One evening I needed to drive somewhere. *I got in my car and put the key in the ignition and was about to turn the motor on when a voice said "I don't understand the command". I stopped breathing for that moment. The message repeated. Deciding to go along with what I thought was a gag, I said: Start the car"; nothing but the same message. I was frightened. What was going on? I wondered if I was imagining the voice. Shaken, I started the car and drove away.*

I told the doctor about this incident and he said people with PTSD can have hallucinations both visual and auditory. I guess I looked concerned because he immediately said not to worry, there was no indication that I was schizophrenic. That was a relief but what kind of power does this PTSD have over me? He referred me to a social worker, who specialized in victims of sexual abuse.

Seeing her, has been one of the best things I've done to help myself to begin living a fuller, more peaceful life. I knew from the beginning, Grace and I would work well together. She is compassionate, kind, wise and a great listener. Our weekly appointments went on for several months. The feelings of being overwhelmed began to subside and the flashbacks had diminished. I had a stronger sense of myself and how I became the person I am today. She helped me realize what was real. I had come to a point where I didn't feel the need for her help any longer and I said good-bye for what I thought would be the last time I saw her professionally.

The pills had removed the anxiety and the ugly thoughts that crept into my mind every day, but they also made me lethargic, gave me a headache and my hair was falling out. I didn't care about anything and had no desire to do anything. Whenever Ellen's family came over, I went to my room because I couldn't handle the confusion and noise. Two months passed and I had not felt better. I went off the pills, began seeing Lee again.

The following spring brought excess rain causing flooding throughout the area. People were losing their homes and other homes were threatened by rising waters. I wanted to help. I had the time. I called the Red Cross. I was invited down for an interview and quickly put to work in the human resources unit at the command centre which was at the College.

My jobs were varied. But mainly I assisted the human resources person with filing, recording data and anything else that would help make her job easier. When I had time, Logistics, the unit that provides supplies for the operation, including food for the volunteers, asked if I could help. In a few days I managed to have a full week's supply of meals ready for pick up when they were needed. It wasn't all that exciting but I knew my little bit of help made it possible for Red Cross volunteers in the field to continue doing what was needed. When the flooding was under control the Red Cross was no longer needed and that is when I began the training classes.

Meanwhile, the saturated soil in our neighborhood couldn't handle any more rain and it began seeping into our basement. We complained several times to the property manager who sent someone different following each call for help and with each visit came a different "solution", yet the basement kept flooding. We had to consider moving if the problem wasn't resolved soon.

I had just completed Red Cross basic training when several forest fires broke out and suddenly the Red Cross was pulling people from across Canada. I volunteered and was accepted to work in Human Resources in the Red Cross House. Most volunteers are asked to stay three weeks. I stayed for six. In the fall I volunteered for a second deployment of another six weeks. It was an incredible experience . . . . I was asked to submit a paper on the differences between my first deployment and the second. What I wrote would be published in the Red Cross magazine. The following is what I wrote:

When I was a young girl, my world reached no farther than my home, school and interests. As I matured, I read how others lived and sometimes suffered from personal disasters that far exceeded my experience. The fires created a disaster deep into individual's lives where, in many cases, their very situation had left them homeless, unemployed and owning only the clothing on their backs and debts.

I heard on the news of the fires and knew in my core that I had to help. I had recently joined the Red Cross with only the basic training, but I was accepted to deploy to Human Resources.

Upon arriving at the Red Cross house, I was struck by the chaos in the halls and the sheer volume of people moving quickly from one room to another, the conversations on critical matters, decisions made in a moment's notice, human energy that consumed and overpowered the weight of the building. I had to shift my head from retirement mode, long after being involved in the business world, to mounds of paperwork, unfamiliar procedures, forms, finding information from the correct people, a sense of expediency, people coming and going and performing at a pace I had left behind prior to retirement. My duties were to process the paperwork required to ensure volunteers arrived and deploy them to various locations and ensure they returned home safely.

I returned home six weeks later, to my comparatively quiet lifestyle, unknowingly, mentally and physically exhausted, but enriched with a sense of satisfaction that I had made a difference in something far greater than myself. Memories overflowed. All those days of pandemonium, people looking after people, the smile at the office threshold, the spontaneous hugs, the "candy man" who made sure any one volunteer was rewarded with a candy lifted from someone else's stash and the gratitude by a stranger from the afflicted area. And eventually, wondering when I'd apply for deployment a second time.

Oct 30, 2011 I arrived at the Red Cross House once more for a six week stay in Human Resources. I knew this deployment could be quite different, as now, the numbers had changed. There were far less volunteers and greater numbers of contract paid employees. I was struck by the calm, quiet and subdued airs of the second floor. No longer were decisions and conversations carried in the long halls. Personnel were stationed in front of computers in their respective desks concentrating on bringing the mission to a successful end. The chaos was gone, but the passion and dedication to the Red Cross principles was paramount in everyone's mind. The respect for one another and concern for self-care was still intact.

Through the piles of past paperwork, came the memories of familiar names and who they are and their long ten to sixteen hour days of dedication to the victims of the fires. How could I not be humbled by these people and the experience?

Chapter Thirty-Five

Sharing a house with Ellen and May was a bad idea from the beginning and I ignored the gut feeling that we would not survive this living arrangement unscathed. The three of us were different: the way we decorated our space, the foods we ate, the way we cooked, groceries we bought, how we cleaned the house, how we organized our space, how we managed our money, how we gardened, our social lives and entertainment. The only common ground that was solid was the care and love we had for animals. Other than that, this was a formula for discontent.

The water problem in the basement was getting worse. I had told the first contractor that the problem with the flooding water in our basement was due to a collapsed draining tiles or non-existent ones. But no one believed me. May's bedroom was the hardest hit. The so-called expert renovators had removed about three feet of drywall and lifted the brand new wet carpet, exposing the concrete with no plans to renew anything. We decided to move. Sharing a house was the most affordable, since my niece and I were on fixed incomes, Ellen had a low income job and we had pets. We needed to keep in mind two things as we searched: we had to find a house with a basement suite that I could live in. If I was physically removed from their lifestyle then perhaps, I thought, this arrangement would work for all of us. The second concern was our pets. I had two dogs and they had a cat and a dog. We had to have a fenced in yard and a landlord that would accept all our animals.

We began looking and were dismayed at the high cost of rental houses that should be condemned. Fortunately on one of Ellen's drives around town she stumbled onto a for rent sign. She approached the tenants who were moving out and asked if she could look inside. She called me, all excited that this was the perfect house. And it was. It had three bedrooms and two baths upstairs and a two bedroom suite downstairs. I would have to buy a stove. The only physical connection we'd have was sharing the laundry facilities which were in the basement and the front door for access. We contacted the owner and signed the lease the same day.

There was a lot of work ahead, considering we had two households to move. There was also the condition of the old house. After many attempts to talk with the landlord and being manipulated by the property manager, we finally were in touch with the landlord and he was very concerned about his house. I told him what I thought the problem was. He hired a contractor to dig along one side of the house. Before the contractor came the landlord told us if we wanted to save the plants we had bought and planted in the front, we should remove them soon. We began lifting plants and putting them in pots and storing them in the back yard. We had to dismantle the greenhouse that I had just spent arduous hours affixing a permanent roof. Ellen was limited to what she could do, so it was up to me to do most of the work. If I needed an extra pair of hands or more strength I could ask May.

The activity in the greenhouse over two seasons had damaged the lawn in a few places so that had to be repaired. There were some plants in the front that we didn't need or want so I prepared a bed along the side of the back fence and planted them. I didn't want the landlord or the property manager to find any fault in the condition of the house and yard. We needed and wanted our deposit back in full.

When the contractor dug up along the side of the house it was evident that the tiles had collapsed and they hadn't been installed properly.

I knew I had to pace myself. I wasn't able to push myself as I had done in the past, so I began packing a little everyday so that when we were about two weeks away from moving, I would have little left to do. I packed items in the kitchen and bathroom cupboards, leaving only the bare necessities. When a cupboard was empty, I cleaned and in some cases, repainted the inside so they'd be fresh and clean and spot painted the outside of the cupboards. Where pictures hung I filled the holes and spot painted.

May and Ellen had barely begun. They had a lot more to pack than I did. I was concerned that if they didn't begin packing soon they would run out of time. But they said they'd be ready.

Nine days before our move, Ellen fell, breaking her foot, hurting one arm, a concussion that caused extreme headaches and a nasty gash on her head that required stitches. She could do nothing to help with the packing and the move. I was in shock. How was I going to manage all this . . . moving two households on my own?

May was unmoved when I urged her to increase the tempo of her packing. The carpet cleaner was scheduled and her things had to be out of her suite and into the garage before he arrived in a few days. But she refused to pack any faster and was on the verge of a meltdown almost every day. I understood that she was traumatized by her mother's injuries so I reluctantly left her to do what she could. Ellen was in bed most of the time with pain. But still they didn't want me to pack their things.

My friend Maggie, at the Red Cross, arranged to have a number of Red Cross volunteers to help us move, along with a considerate neighbor. Ellen contacted a local moving company and for about $600 they loaded a truck and moved us. There was plenty of help available now and that was a relief for me.

However, on moving day I had more to do than I had expected. I was constantly finding more things that needed packing and things that needed to be taken to the front lawn to ensure it was loaded on the truck. My experience has been that movers don't always do a scan of the property to ensure they've loaded everything.

We moved into our new home by about five o'clock that afternoon. Ellen had arranged for a cleaning company to go to the old place. Because I had done so much of the cleaning beforehand, there wasn't much for them to do except clean the stove, fridge, bathrooms and the floors. They had been told May's suite didn't have to be touched except for the bathroom. I didn't have the energy to check her suite after the moving truck made its last trip, but wished that I had.

The next day the walk-through with the property manager was scheduled for noon. When I walked into the house about eleven thirty, I discovered May's suite was not tidy or clean. There were pieces of paper and other debris scattered on the floor, the storage box for firewood hadn't been vacuumed or cleaned by the carpet cleaner, one of the bedrooms had a few pieces of clothing on the floor and the garage needed cleaning out. There was still a lot of work to do before noon. I just couldn't do it. I picked up what I could, but there was nothing left in me to do any more cleaning.

The property manager wasn't happy with us because we had caused them a lot of grief over the flooding and they had lost the account with our old landlord because of their incompetence. As a consequence during the walk-through they found all kinds of things that were wrong, including damages by previous tenants who had painted the living room walls a ghastly color without permission and we were being held responsible. Our damage deposit was not going to be returned.

We contacted the landlord and explained what was happening. He assured us that he had seen the place before we moved out and was very happy with how we had looked after his property and he would support us in any way he could to make sure we got our deposit back. We had to threaten with legal action against the property manager. We had pictures of the place before we moved in and a supporting phone call from the landlord. A few weeks later we received a cheque for the full amount of the deposit. To say it was a stressful time was an understatement.

I loved my suite. It was spacious, quiet and freshly painted. When I finished settling in, I had an apartment that was very comfortable and attractive.

Our problems didn't go away just because we had a different living arrangement, but it was better. If I stayed out of their way and their business I thought, we would be okay. But then, another drama developed. My life began to unravel again. I returned to my therapist, Grace.

We were in our new house less than a year when Ellen said "heads up, Andrew is coming down for a couple of weeks in February before he leaves for his new job in Europe. He needs some "time to study". I told her that was okay by me. I can handle having a man in the house for a few weeks. He was going to bring some of his things down and store them in the garage. When he arrived, he came with a U-Haul truck, furniture, boxes and all! I was not happy. He was moving in and not for just "a few weeks".

I knew Andrew was a night person, so I was concerned his activities would be disruptive during the night. My bedroom was below his bedroom and the computer room. May was also a night person and had learned to keep her noise level down when she was on her computer during the night. When Andrew moved in, the two of them played computer games well past midnight and when that wasn't happening, Andrew talked on the phone for hours in his bedroom, well into early morning. He spoke so loud I could understand every word he said. The activity above me was too disruptive. I felt invaded. I had to keep reminding myself that this would only last a few weeks.

Ellen and I went out for breakfast and after chatting about unimportant things she said Andrew would be staying for a few months. Now I was really upset. She denied that she had told me "a couple of weeks", saying: "what's the difference"? I explained that my name was on the lease and I had a say in who lived in the house. She saw the situation differently. She felt the upstairs was her domain and she could do as she wished in her living space.

I told her I would think about this situation and if I still wasn't happy I would be moving out. I put my name in the local Housing Authority for subsidized housing. I was placed on a minimum two year waiting list. After talking with Lee, I knew I couldn't wait any longer. I was depressed, anxious, angry, feeling alone and physically ill. I began looking for an apartment that would take a dog.

I had to ask myself, 'why was I uncomfortable with Andrew?' This was unsettling. After all, he was family, he had never hurt me. I barely knew him. But he was a man living in my house and the presence of any man, made me feel uncomfortable. He never smiled at me, and the odd time he spoke to me, he was disrespectful and he never volunteered to help me.

The other reason is more physical. When we had a leak in the furnace room and water was spraying on the walls, Ellen, Andrew and I were trying to find ways to fix it. The furnace room was small and compact. I turned and bumped into him. We were nose to nose. It was like hitting a wall of muscle. Immediately, I felt as if I was hit in the stomach. The next encounter was when I had begun to unlock the front door to go out just as he was turning the handle from the outside.

When he walked in we were once again, face to face. Both times my immediate reaction was an intruding male. A force I couldn't stop. My body stiffened and my heart beat faster, I held my breath and I wanted to run.

Andrew's presence meant I had to wear my housecoat at night when I went upstairs to let Tibbs outside. I didn't like the idea of him coming downstairs to do his laundry when I was in my bed clothes. Life was freer when we were just women sharing a house.

Logic told me he wasn't a menace, but he felt that way to me. These feelings were created from my experiences in the past, but understanding didn't remove the feelings I had when he was around. His presence was foreboding. He reminded me of Darth Vader . . . big, dressed in black and serious.

This situation was more than the presence of a man in my house and more than Ellen letting him move in without consulting me. This was an enormous betrayal by manipulation.

I did what I could to reduce anxiety. I put up a curtain across the archway to my living room anyone coming down to do their laundry couldn't see me. I made a fountain in my bedroom hoping the sound of bubbling water would distract me from the noise upstairs. It helped a bit, but I still wasn't happy. I didn't feel safe and my peace had been dismantled. Ellen had betrayed me and a man was living in our house.

One more issue occurred next that accelerated my search for my own place. But before that occurred, I had a remarkable discovery.

I began thinking it was time to earnestly find my children. Apart from not knowing how I would find them, I was also afraid. Afraid of being rejected, hurt and lost. I also didn't want to disturb their lives. I thought they might have created lives of their own that were peaceful. To contact them could be upsetting.

I was afraid that if I died without making contact with them first, they would not have the opportunity to ask me questions about our past, or to tell me how they felt about me. If they were angry with me, I didn't want that anger to go unresolved if it was at all possible while I was still alive to make a difference for them. They needed to know what had happened from my perspective.

I had known for some time what province my daughter lived in and that she had a son, because I accidentally met them at a restaurant when we were both visiting in the same place. It was clear to me that she didn't want my company. After that brief meeting, I didn't know how to get in touch with her or if she was married and lived under a different name.

I had no idea where Vern was. His friend spoke to my sister Betty from time to time and she would relay Vern's whereabouts, but there was never a definitive location given.

In more recent years I met Les's mother-in-law, Faye. She brought me up to date on Les and Mandy's lives. They had a daughter and a son. When she showed me a photograph of my grandchildren I asked if I could make a copy. On the back of the photographs, I wrote their birthdates. When the forest fires threatened many homes in Les' home town one year, I called the Red Cross to see if they had registered. The volunteer gave me Les's phone number. I left a message, but didn't get a reply.

I was seriously thinking of hiring a private detective. When I spoke with Grace, she suggested I try Facebook. I was unfamiliar with Facebook or any other social media. It was worth a try. Facebook was popular and could be easier than hiring a detective. I opened an account with Facebook, but navigating on that site was foreign to me. At my next session with Grace, I told her of my difficulty. She gave me a few pointers. I went home to find my children.

It was February 27, 2012, my eldest son's birthday. I keyed in his name on Facebook and a few contacts of the same name appeared. My eyes were drawn to a photo of a man that looked a bit like Vern, but I just wasn't sure. He didn't quite look like I remembered him, but then it had been twenty-three years. My heart began beating faster. Could it be this easy? I sent him an email to confirm.

Then I keyed in my other son's name. A link led me to a business and his name appeared. Without a photo I wasn't sure. I emailed him.

He responded: "Hello. It's been a long time. Hope you are well. My contact info is below . . . Les"

Feeling apprehensive but also excited, I gathered a bit of courage and replied. I wrote a little about myself and where I was living.

He replied: "I always wondered when or if we would ever connect again. Mandy's mom had given me some updates as to where you were some time ago but no other details". He then went on to fill me in about his family. Relieved, tears rolled down my face. There was no anger in his words.

This experience was overwhelming. I had one more child to locate. Dare I hope? I keyed in her name. Again, I got a link to a business and there she was with a photo and contact information. I emailed her.

I barely slept that night and woke early. I went directly to my computer and found an email from Vern! And just like the email from Les his comment was the same: "hope you are well". I shook so much I could barely type. My reply was a brief history about myself.

Then he responded, telling me about his recent marriage to Meg and their life and how busy he is and that he didn't have a lot of time to spend on the computer. He had a managerial position in a resort and this was high season. I understood and didn't want to press him to continue emailing when he really didn't have the time. Of course, I wanted to chat with him for hours, but that wasn't possible.

My life was expanding exponentially. An email from Lynn: "I have thought of you a little more recently. I think you just had your 70th birthday, did you not? I hope you are well." She told me she was glad I had tracked her down because she was thinking of me recently. She also told me if I had contacted her 10 years ago, she would not have responded so favorably. She went on to tell me her son, Roger, who was then 22, had malignant tumors in his neck and mental health issues. She ended her email with "love, your daughter, Lynn". I sobbed.

My life had now taken an enormous curve. I had searched them on the internet and phone books many times over the years to no avail. And in one day, one morning, I had located all three. Tears poured from me for a long time. During the day, I would break into tears just thinking about how lucky I was to have found them so easily and that they were not hostile toward me. There was hope.

It became clear that Vern wasn't ready to meet me. I had to accept his decision. Lynn and I emailed and talked on the phone a few more times. She offered to be my executor for my estate. When I edited my current Will, I sent it off to her. She suggested we meet for a holiday in the mountains in the near future. I was elated. How much better could my day be?

As suddenly as my connection with Lynn happened, it was over. She emailed and said she had a growth on her thyroid and was seeking treatment. I offered to fly out to be with her, but she told me that with her health issue and now more issues with her son, she couldn't handle anything else. She said, as she had several times during our conversations, that she has been on her own all her life and she can do this on her own. I haven't heard from her since.

Les and I have emailed a number of times and the communication lines are open with both boys. I just have to be patient and hope a closer connection will develop and Lyn will reconnect.

I searched my photo albums and asked the boys if they would like copies of their childhood days. They both agreed. Vern's wife Meg asked for more and I sent them as well. A stronger connection was developing.

I made the best of this living arrangement with Ellen through the summer. Mom's ninetieth birthday, September the sixteenth was coming, and it was time to make plans to celebrate. Ellen and I had talked briefly about doing something special, but had never made any decisions. Or, at least so I thought.

I asked Ellen to come downstairs to my place so we could talk about the celebration. She suggested a birthday card that would circulate among family members who lived in other cities and she wanted dinner at a steak house. I suggested we have a picnic at one of the parks in the area because fine dining would be boring for the young children that might attend and they would be restless. At a picnic they could play on the swings and run around. We could all chip in with food since cost was an issue for most members of the family. The planned date was September the fifteenth.

I suggested I send an email to our siblings to see what they preferred. I gave a copy to Ellen for approval. Later in the day she said to hold off on sending the email. Then she told me she had, weeks before our planning meeting, poled the siblings and grandchildren and the decision was fine dining! She told me Betty didn't want me involved because she said: "I would change everything".

This meant that the whole time Ellen and I were discussing possible venues, the decision had already been made and I was not given any voice or participation in the planning. I had been manipulated and deceived again. I was livid and very hurt. I felt like a leper in my own family. Old feelings of not being important or heard welled inside me. My stomach bloated, I slept poorly, I was on edge all the time, I angered easily and the slightest thing, I couldn't eat because it upset my stomach and my head hurt. I felt like I was drowning. I told Ellen how I felt and that what she did was hurtful. She didn't understand. Nothing was resolved and a deeper division between us.

Ellen told me days later, that she would likely be moving when the lease came due in May. I wasn't sure if I believed her. Perhaps she wanted me out and said that to get me to move or she had plans that she was not going to share. I didn't want to wait until she made a decision on what she was going to do. I couldn't trust her. I was motivated to find something right away. I had already looked at a number of places and they were repulsive, filthy, shabby and expensive.

I went to Kijiji one day and found a promising apartment. The rent was a stretch for my budget, but not impossible. Fortunately, I was able to view the apartment the same day. New life breathed into me. There was hope. I was going to be on my own for the first time in two years and away from the stresses of sharing accommodations and the problems between Ellen and me.

The brick "adult only" apartment building was small, containing only six suites. This meant the building would be quiet. It was also a "no pets" building, but I was able to convince the landlord that Tibbs was not going to be a problem. I followed the landlord to the third floor. As soon as I walked in, I could see the room was flooded with light coming in from very large windows and a patio door that led to a small balcony facing west . . . perfect for plants. The apartment was clean and the cupboards inside were freshly painted. The Red Cross building, the police station and downtown were all within walking distance and the dog run was at the end of the block. It was perfect. I signed the lease papers and gave the deposit.

I advised Ellen and gave notice to the present landlady. I asked her to come to the house to view my suite so she knew I was leaving it in good condition. She was pleased. Now I was free to get out of there. Ellen would give me my share of the deposit right away and agreed to buy my stove. I left the counter I had built.

A team of friends helped me move. They were great and I was in my new home in a few hours. I am eternally grateful to them.

My only concern was my dog. She had never been on her own in her life and I didn't know how she would behave when I left her to go shopping or volunteering. Would she bark a lot? Would she bark at the other tenants as they moved about in the hallways? Would she pee in the apartment out of anxiety? I found out soon enough. One day, while out shopping the landlord came to the building to work in the yard. He said she barked the whole time he was there. Now what do I do? I was concerned. I began by taking her everywhere I could, but sometimes that wasn't possible. I decided to get an anti-barking collar; not the vibrating or painful one that gives them a shock when they bark, but one that gave a sharp high pitched sound. It worked like a charm. I put it on her twice and never had to use it again.

Chee-chee settled in to our new life beautifully as we developed our daily rhythm. She had been a little hyper in the former house, but within a few months she was like a new dog, calm, obedient, didn't pee in the apartment and was connecting to me like never before. To ensure she doesn't have an accident in the apartment, I take her out four times a day. She walks well with and without a leash as never before. She has managed to win the hearts of everyone in the building, especially one neighbor. She treats him like her second owner. I could not have asked for anything better.

Mom's birthday was only weeks away. Betty phoned and hoped I understood why she was making all the arrangements. She said she wanted to do something for mom on her own. I told her that wasn't what I was told. She didn't respond to that comment. I told her I understood and left it at that. It was too late for me. I was hurting and anything Betty had to say was not believable.

Then she told me the designated date of the dinner party was backed up because of a conflict with her husband's work schedule that could not be altered. Fortunately, I was leaving on my trip to visit Les the day before the dinner, which meant I could attend.

The little I was told about the party was that it was to be a surprise. Mom didn't know who was coming, nor did I. She only knew that someone would pick her up at one o'clock Saturday and take her to the park for pictures. My plan was to take mom to her hair appointment in the morning, than take her to my place for lunch and to change into her party outfit and wait for someone to pick her up.

At twelve fifteen, Ellen calls to say mom has to be ready by twelve thirty. Mom was barely dressed and we had not eaten. I was not sure what I was supposed to do. I assumed they were taking her to Ellen's for a quick visit then to the park. This didn't sound right, but I wasn't about to interfere. I would arrive at the time I had been told weeks before, which was just before one o'clock.

When I arrived, which was exactly when I was supposed to, everyone, including mom were already there and gathered for a group picture. I had missed mom's surprise. Mark and his family arrived just a few minutes later and almost missed being included in the family picture. Pictures were taken in various groupings, always with mom.

I was hurting. I was the only one who didn't have my family present. I felt even more of an outsider. It wasn't anyone's fault but mine and there was nothing anyone could have done to change that. Mom was beaming she was so happy and that was the most important thing.

When the photo shoot was over, mom drove off with family members. I wasn't aware that lunch was being served at Ellen's. But it didn't matter. I had to pack, load the car and fill the gas tank before the dinner party. I wanted to be ready to leave the next morning by six o'clock to visit my son and his family. I had not seen him in over twenty years and I was nervous. I had not driven long distances in a number of years. I was travelling a highway that was not familiar to me and I had aged enough that long distance driving made my body stiff and took a few days to recover. As well, I didn't know what to expect when I arrived. How would they greet me? Would there be emotional reservations?

When I arrived at the steakhouse, Betty asked me why I wasn't at Ellen's. I reminded her of my trip and the need to prepare.

The restaurant had moved the necessary tables in a 'U' shape in a corner. It was a perfect setting with crisp white linen, low lighting and soft music. We were the first to arrive. Some family members chose the salad bar, drinks were ordered and served. Shortly after, the table servers took our orders for our meals. Time passed and our meals had not been served. We began to wonder what was taking so long. The children were restless and fidgeting. This was obviously not a pleasant time for them. Finally our meals came, followed by a few short speeches, the birthday cake and singing the birthday song. I felt embarrassed that our speeches had invaded other patron's solitude. This was not the atmosphere for such things.

After mom had said good-bye to everyone, I drove her to my place. She was staying in my apartment while I was away. This was an opportunity for her to see if she could live on her own and get out of assisted living where she had been for the past three years. Chee-chee was going to stay at Ellen's because I didn't want mom going up and down the stairs four times a day to take Chee-chee out. I said good-bye to mom, took Chee-chee to Ellen's and I was on my way to unfamiliar highway territory.

I had travelled through the mountains for many years, but this part of the Rockies was different. The highway was narrow, the shoulders were almost non-existent in many places and the drop from the highway was sharp and long. My full attention was needed. I was going the speed limit but still drivers passed me on the double lines. A transport truck was so close his grill was all I could see. I would have taken a breather if I could have stopped safely at a roadside rest stop, if I saw one.

I had something else to be even more concerned with. I was half way to where I would stay the night when I heard a disturbing noise coming from the brakes. Every time I went down a steep hill, and there were many, my brakes squealed loudly and the steering wheel vibrated. I had just had the car in for maintenance and asked them to check the brakes. The service person said everything was okay. I did not know that I had to tell them to check the rotors as well.

I knew there was something seriously wrong. I had to sweat it out until I pulled into where I had a hotel reservation and hopefully I could find a mechanic. Fortunately, a block from the hotel was a dealership. Early the next morning, I walked over and asked if they could check my car. They did and I needed new rotors and brake pads. Four hundred dollars and two hours later, I headed out onto the highway and to see my son and his family.

The visit with Les was with mixed emotions. My desire was to be invited into his family and begin a role as mother and grandmother. I knew that was a dream, and not very realistic. There were too many years between us and an unhappy story. I decided to let our meeting unfold, taking direction from him. He greeted me at his office with a hug and we sat down and enjoyed a few hours, bring one another up to date on our lives.

It was obvious he had a very successful marriage, family life and career. He was also protective of his family and wasn't about to let me enter right away. I accepted his decision. I had to if I wanted to gain his trust. He helped me find a motel on the strip that was in my price range and I agreed to call him next morning to see what might happen next. I called him just before noon and he suggested we meet for lunch. Again, we had a very pleasant visit over a fine meal. He said he would leave communications between me and his children up to them. If they chose to contact me, it was their decision. He and I would stay in touch. We said our good-byes. He returned to work and I headed home on the familiar easier but longer route.

I cried the next hundred kilometers until finally, I found a place to pull over where I could be alone. So many stops were flooded with people. I sobbed until there were no tears left. I was relieved that I wasn't shut out of his life entirely, but sad and disappointed that I couldn't have more of him and his family.

After several hours I realized how exhausted I was and needed to stop for the night. I could have gone to Betty's, but I was still upset with her, so I pulled into a broken down road side motel. After a good night's sleep I headed home. At least this highway was familiar and not nearly as frightening as what I had experienced only a few days ago.

When I returned from my trip I stopped to pick up Chee-chee. Andrew answered the door. I called Chee-chee to come and waited. Then I called again. Finally she appeared from behind the sofa, walking very slowly, cautiously. At first I thought she might be stiff from lying down for a long sleep. There was more to her condition. Her body was hunched over, she was low to the ground and her head hung low.

I watched her as she carefully came down the stairs to me. My little Chee-chee was in pain. What was wrong? I began walking across the lawn to the car, but she wasn't following. I urged her and finally she slowly moved toward the car door. As I picked her up, she gave out the most terrifying blood curdling cry. I was mortified. Something terrible had happened.

When I got home I phoned Ellen. She said Chee-chee was like that the day I dropped her off. When she and May went for a walk that morning Chee-chee was straggling behind. When May picked her up she cried out. How could Ellen allow Chee-chee to remain in such pain for a full week without medical attention was beyond my understanding. When I had left Chee-chee there, she had a mild eye infection and had to have ointment applied for three more days. I had noted that on the container. It was obvious she was still getting the antibiotic cream in her eyes. Did Ellen not care to look at the container to see what the dosage was and read my note? I always believed that no matter what happened between us, Ellen would love and care for my dog as if it were her own.

I phoned the vet who said it sounded like a back problem and prescribed an anti-inflammatory. Later that day, I began searching for a chiropractor for animals. I found a massage therapist to horses who agreed to try her techniques on Chee-chee with no promise of anything. With the medication and the massage Chee-chee was walking much easier by the evening. The next day she was fine and back to her lovable carefree self. I vowed I would never leave Chee-chee with Ellen again.

In May 2013, I finished writing this book and set it aside for a while. I needed a break from it and I needed to begin making preparations to visit my son, Vern and his wife Meg. I was excited, apprehensive and scared. What kind of greeting would I get? Will he and Meg like me? Would Vern and I spend quality time together to reconnect? Would I have time with Meg to learn who she is? Again, just as it was with Les; I had to let the visit unfold according to their wishes and what was comfortable for them. I arrived May the 12^{th,} very tired from the long journey and on. After what seemed to be hours, I was processed through Immigration and Customs.

As I went through the doors to the hot humid air outside, I looked from my left to my right, scanning the crowds of people and cars. As my eyes moved toward the right I saw them. Vern and Meg. As if a magnet drew us in, our eyes met. It was like magic. My whole body vibrated, I could barely breathe. He smiled, that familiar broad warm smile and pointed me out to Meg. I felt my movement was as if I were in one of those romantic movies where the camera slows down as the two bodies merge. Vern was holding a puppy in his arms and quickly passed it to Meg. He held his arms out wide and we embraced. I could feel the tears coming. He asked me: "are you okay?" I said: "yes, I am now". Then Meg grabbed me, held me close and kissed my cheek over and over again and welcomed me. This couldn't have played out any better. Our meeting was more than I expected, but had dreamed. They introduced me to their little pup, Little Guy and we proceeded to the car and drove to the condo Vern had arranged for me. Vern and Meg took a day off to show me the sights and on several occasions we enjoyed dinner together.

I wanted to talk about the past, but withheld because I didn't want to start off this relationship on a sad note. I would wait and take their lead. Vern and I had two wonderfully intimate talks. The first was an update on all he had done since I last saw him in 1988. He had many adventures including hiking many summits in Canada, climbing to the base camp of Mt. Everest and living in Thailand for nine months.

Our second time together was about the past. He recalled the beatings I received from Monty, but he remembered one beating I have no memory of. He said he was about three years old and saw his dad hit my head with a heavy glass ashtray, drawing blood. I was shocked. What a terrible thing for a child to see. He said he wondered at the time when it would be his turn.

When I left, Monty took his frustrations out on Vern, sometimes with a closed fist. Vern had many days when he didn't want to go home after school. The beatings on Vern ended when he was about seventeen. His father had raised his fist to come down on Vern, but instead, Vern grabbed his father's fist and told him that he would never hit him again. Vern was nine when I left, he was seventeen when Monty stopped beating him. I was so sad for Vern. What a terrible life. No wonder he ran away to live with me. I had to tell Vern how sorry I was before he hurried off to work. I couldn't let this memory of violence go by without saying something. I went to him, looked him in the eye and told him I was sorry. He hugged me and said: "it's not what this is about". I was so relieved at his response that I didn't ask him what he meant. I took it as forgiveness.

As for Meg. She is delightful and I told Vern how special she is and how happy I am for him. He looks at her with such adoration and love, it warms my heart. She is special and she loves my son.

When we were out sightseeing, I took a number of pictures and one of them is Vern and I standing before the soft blue waters of the sea, his arm around me, both of us smiling. The two weeks there were a mixture of fulfillment, joy, shock and sadness. But in the end, this was an incredible journey toward freedom from guilt.

Now I had my two sons who displayed no animosity toward me. The only one left is my daughter who has yet to contact me after that brief reconnection. I will give her time and hope she will want me in her life one day.

Chapter Thirty-Six

Writing my story has been one of the most difficult things I have ever accomplished. I had to re-live emotions and pain at their deepest levels to remember details. There were memories that triggered terrifying sensations and I'd feel as though I was back in the abuse with all the symptoms; petrified, frozen and vulnerable. My mind and body became sensitive to any situation that didn't feel healthy, supportive or was threatening. Many times, I would feel I was getting sick but, when I finished that part of the story, I felt better. Other times, my mind resisted, barely able to focus mentally and physically. I'd get very sleepy, unclear and unable to articulate my thoughts. When I felt that way, I would shut down and seclude myself, not wanting to be in contact with anyone for a few days and do something enjoyable, or, I'd bite my lip, allow the tears to come and write anyway because I didn't want to lose the details of what I was remembering. Lack of sleep was a big enemy. Many nights I would wake after only three hours sleep, with horrifying feelings and images in my mind. Nightmares left me uncomfortable with no clear image or significance. Occasionally, I would have vivid auras of violence or the familiar snakes. When I finally finished this last chapter, it took about two days and I was sleeping six to eight hours non-stop every night.

A few friends questioned whether or not I should continue writing. They wondered if I was being self-abusive. I wanted to tell my story in detail from my perspective and to impress on anyone reading this—**never give up—the path to self-discovery is difficult, but there is light ahead. The important thing is to never give up.**

People have asked me if writing my story has been healing. I don't say I am healed, because that implies I have no symptoms of Complex PTSD, no vivid memories filled with emotion or physical reactions. Loud constant noise, harsh smells, chaos, feeling ignored, abandoned, overwhelmed, a confrontation with someone, being with more than one person at a time, lack of money are all triggers that produce the symptoms that can stop me in my tracks. My belly will swell, my heart rate increases, my face will flush, inner trembling, headache, sleep disturbance, ugly thoughts, exhaustion and stomach upset are a few of the main symptoms now.

The sense of smell was a difficult one for me to understand. When I was in group therapy at the Rape Crises Center, I realized that the smell I encountered that came from nowhere but my body, was the smell of siemen. The smell of freshly sawed wood was the smell of my Uncle Arnold. I haven't figured out why perfume draws the same reactions, but it's likely something from my grandparent's bedroom where grandma had her perfumes or the scent I wore when I lived with Monty. Maybe someday I will understand that.

These triggers come from my memory of traumas. I'm not aware of the memory at the time of a trigger. It just happens. As a person who has experienced all that I have, my mind and body are super sensitive to the triggers. These reactions are not as intense as they use to be and because I understand their source, I can remind myself, that I am okay, that this too will pass. As a result of my willingness to see where all this behaviour is coming from, I take a deep breath or two and I calm down much sooner.

When I first began writing, I saw my past as cheerless and full of apprehension. Instead, I discovered there were periods of complete joy and freedom that were overshadowed in my mind, by the dark side of my life. I was loved and I had my own version of giving love. I cherish the times with my children when our world seemed to be in balance for a moment. We did fun things together. I taught them how to use empty boxes, blankets and kitchen chairs to create imaginary trains and club houses; I played my classical music and danced with them; and they enjoyed putting pins and rollers in my hair. I cooked their favorite dishes and made special cookies, providing they had not pilfered my supplies of chocolate chips. My favorite memory is when I sang bedtime songs lulling them to sleep. I had forgotten all those times until now.

I had questioned my parent's feelings toward me, especially by my father. As I unraveled my negative feelings, I felt their love for me. My parents did their best to protect and guide me through my early life. They used what tools they knew.

As I neared the end of writing this book, I became aware of something insidious. I learned through therapy and research that if

I could accept who I was and release the guilt I carried for so many years I would be free of this burden. But, I was not willing to let go. To release the past seemed to me, to pardon what I had done to my children and what I did not do for my children. Anything I did to feel less guilty was never enough. I resisted. I didn't want to let go, because I was serving a self-imposed life sentence and didn't deserve to be set free. After all, they were living their lives with painful memories that I helped create.

There were numerous incidents as a youth that led me to believe there was no one I could trust: Shorty and dad touching me; dad's friend molesting me; Monty beating me. If what my mother said about 'Uncle Arnold when I was between four and seven years old and the situation with my grandfather when I was ten months has any validity, then I couldn't trust them either. The memories of all these experiences were repressed, stored away and almost forgotten. Those were the years when emotional impoverishment began to develop. Without competent help, those awful nightmares of snakes continued to creep into my sleep, creating endless anxiety and the effects of future traumas by Vince, Norman, Vlad and some family members were compounded.

The emotional pain of these compiled abuses has felt like a broken bone that hadn't yet set. I couldn't find a comfortable position where I could get relief if only for a moment. But it wasn't a broken bone, I was broken. My whole body screamed to be comfortable. I was in pieces, unable to put myself back together. I didn't know what being whole felt like because the traumas began at such an early age. I was constantly trying to survive. Often, when the pain became too great or my sense of self-worth was inadequate to make changes, I was exhausted by the struggle and I stopped trying.

I am amazed and confounded by my actions. I endured years of abuse without fighting back but, when my life was threatened by myself or someone else, I found the courage, strength and determination to live. Where did that strength come from? I didn't want to die. I just wanted the fear and pain to stop. At the time, the only way I knew how to be free of pain was to flee, either physically or emotionally and endure the consequences.

It was as if there were dark foreboding clouds on the horizon all the time threatening any balance and peace I had amassed. When the storm clouds covered my sky, I was on full alert to any danger. My world was full of fear and pain. I could think of nothing but to dive into the depths of despair or find a way to survive. At some point, the storm would pass and the sun would shine for a short time. Always the storm clouds laid waiting on the horizon.

My life was a contradiction. I was anxious and on alert for danger, yet I put myself in harm's way. The roots of this contradiction are a pattern of how the mind processes untreated abuses. I was unable to see the red flags because my mind shut down. The emotional intimate relationships I had with men and others were all dangerous in some way from the beginning and I was not aware of the danger.

I often asked myself: "how is it that other battered wives leave and they take all their children with them?" "What is wrong with me, that I didn't do that?" I know I had been emotionally bankrupt and functioning on an unconscious level, void of emotion, unable to feel or understand anything I was doing or what was happening to me. How could I possibly help my children or myself in that state of mind? I couldn't. I proved that when I had Lynn and Vern living with me. I just knew when I felt my life was threatened; I had to survive, no matter what the cost.

I came to realize, I had to find a way to 'accept' the behaviour of myself and those who abused me if I wanted to put the past to rest. I learned that the abuse wasn't personal. The abusers had their own story of pain that caused them to lash out on the vulnerable. I did not do anything to the abusers that could create the kind of frustration, inconsideration, self-destruction and violence they expressed.

Monty's face would contort with rage when he was beating me. His face turned red and the veins in his neck protruded. He wasn't aware, at the time, of what he was doing. That's why he could not remember what he did to me the night before. He was rabid. He had this fire in him, from his own story, building over days or weeks. The pressure rising from his anger became uncomfortable for him, maybe even painful. As if switching on a light, he lost control of his rage and it had to be released, somehow. I was available, I was vulnerable and I was willing.

Vince had a different way. He was also in survival mode. He had his story of pain. He needed to be in control so he could predict how his life would unfold. He didn't have to hit me, he controlled and manipulated me, probably on an unconscious level.

Norman also had an early history of pain and another method of control. As a psychologist, he had the knowledge and training and he used it to keep me in line. In the end when he felt he was losing his hold on me, he turned to violence.

For these men, there is nothing to forgive, only to accept that they too were in extreme anguish. But, their behaviour was not something I had to tolerate just because they had a painful history. Unless they could see they needed help and were hurting innocent people, then they were and are not people I want to be around.

I am uncertain when I think of Vlad. He is a dangerous predator. I suspect he has his own story of pain and he has his way of dealing with it. Eventually, I suppose I will find a way to 'accept' him for who he is and let go of my antagonism toward him.

I did not feel anger toward these abusers until later in my adult life. I broke all those dishes, not because I was remembering, but because there was this rage in me that felt like I was going to explode. I didn't understand at the time. I just reacted. Most times when I remembered the traumas and the deep destruction created in me, I would ease those moments of anxiety by thinking of what I would do or say to them, if I had the courage and opportunity. Those feelings and images were paramount for years, other times, I just had to lash out and release the pain. What a waste of my energy. The abusers had no idea I was angry or sad. They carried on with their lives . . . so why couldn't I? I came to understand something fundamental when it comes to anger and abuse.

Richard Chamberlain writes in his book "Shattered Love": *"If I burn my hand in a fire, the flames are not to blame. I am not wronged by them and there is no need to forgive the flame. It is a flame and it is dangerous . . . . The abuser is just like the flame. That's the way he is. What the abuser does to the victim is not personal."* P201. The abuse I received from the abusers was not personal. I was handy.

Buddha once said: *"Holding on to anger is like grasping a hot coal to throw at someone else; you're the one who gets burned".* I have been angry at myself and the abusers for years. I was putting myself in the hot coals.

My responsibility in these scenarios was to give the abusers permission to continue abusing me when I didn't leave after the first sign of abuse, when my instincts said "flee". However, I also know: I always believed I was to blame; that I did something to provoke the abuse; that I trusted the abuser knew what was good for me, and I could not see a way out that felt right.

I also 'accept' my behaviour over the years as inappropriate, insensitive and abusive. I did not set out to withhold my love or to inflict pain and fear on my children. It was not a conscious decision. When I threatened, hit or screamed at them, I was voicing my fears and frustrations that were building from the abuse. Perhaps I was unconsciously reacting to the tension building within the abuser at the time and I reacted from fear. I needed to expel the conflict in me, just as the abusers had done. I did not know any other way to deal with my tension. I did what was familiar.

Did I, at the time I lived with my children, justify my behaviour to myself? There was no forethought, no calculating my behaviour. I reacted. I was 'unconscious' mentally and emotionally. My pent up energy had been spent and my children paid the price. I just did not know how to fix what was wrong with me or my situation. I was just me trying to cope.

I didn't have a 'delete' or 'edit' key. I spoke without thinking of how others would feel or what they would think of me. My world was very small and its boundaries didn't include anyone around me. When someone was talking I'd interrupt and talk about me. I was never comfortable in social gatherings and I was frustrated that the topic of conversation was not something I could contribute. I would try to include myself by a feeble attempt to be funny; almost always offending someone and embarrassing myself.

There wasn't any one person who created me. It was all the: abuses as a child; a father who was emotionally unsupportive; parents who didn't teach me how to set boundaries and have respect for myself; social services that were thoughtless and didn't show me a sustainable option; incorrect diagnosis of my mental condition; the unnecessary electro-shock therapy; incompetent and ignorant doctors and therapists; lack of funds for real professional help; the lack of training to sensitize primary doctors and police; the lack of awareness by society; the lack of information on the effects of various forms of abuse available to the abused and family.

My life could have been immeasurably different had these things not happened. I would have become a different person and avoided the violence and self-abuse in my life and the loss of my children. I could have had a much healthier life and as would my children. All these participants and issues became accomplices for the state of my mind and consequently, my behavior. In a sense I was groomed to be abused by a society that was ignorant and unwilling to talk about family violence and sexual abuse.

I have been enlightened by my research, writing this book and the effective therapy Grace provided, but this does not mean I now breeze through life. With my new found tools and skills I make my way through the chaos of life; striving to seek beauty to enhance who I am and how I see the world. I have overcome many challenges and I have developed into a useful, confident (sometimes) woman with a sense of self-worth (most of the time).

I now understand that a glance at the past is comparable to looking in the rear view mirror of a car on the highway. What is behind is gone. I can see the past but I have no influence over it. In front are a myriad of challenges and opportunities. Where I am now, on this highway, is all I will deal with. I have moved on and use my new skills of life to deal with the challenges before me.

I have a small trunk that sits on my bureau. Over recent years, I have put all the momentos of the good that has happened: beautiful cards with encouraging loving messages; winning medals for running competitions; poems of support; defining words of who I am in the eyes of others. When I feel low, I look at the contents of this trunk and know that I am loved and respected by many. I think back to a letter I received from a young woman in the Women's Liberation Movement, who wrote to thank me for being a mentor to her and giving her skills to live a fuller life. I read that with pride and a few tears. I discarded that note because at the time, I didn't accept that I had any influence of someone's personal life. I thought of the note as very sweet but I had nothing to do with shaping her life. But I must have, if she took the time to write.

To my children, I hope I have answered questions you may have. I hope you now have an understanding of our early life together and later as adults when we first attempted to re-connect. I hope you can accept me as I am and know I never intended to hurt you. I tried, I really tried to make a good life for us and thought I had at the time. I am truly sorry for what happened and what you did not have.

The storm clouds are still there on the horizon, and storms will come and go, but I am no longer on guard for them or overreact to them as I did in the past. My symptoms of Complex PTSD and my reactions to them are more subdued and fade away much quicker because now I have new and better skills and an understanding of how to respond to them. I see my symptoms as an opportunity to grow while I watch the sun filter through the clouds as they move on . . . . just as I will, because I'm still here.

Thank you to my chiropractor who gave me compassion and help at a time of crisis in my life; to Marion for hanging in there even when I was a jerk over our twenty-two years as friends; to Naomi who has watched me grow over the past thirty years and still considers me a friend.

Thank you to: my parents for their love and doing the best they knew how; Monty for fathering three beautiful, loving children; to Vince for introducing me to the wonders of the world through education; to the police officers who took my sexual abuse statement for their sensitivities; to the Rape Crisis Centre counsellors for their compassion; to my fellow Victim Assistant for giving me the idea and the title for this book; to Jenna of Victim Assistance, who saw in me something I could not see and encouraged me become a VA; and to my dear friend and current therapist, Grace, for helping me find my children and see my truth, comprehend who I was and reminding me of how far I have come; to all who have supported me when I needed your help. I could never repay any of you but please know that I am 'paying it forward'.

Books I've Read to Help Me Write This Book

Peter A. Levine, PhD: "In An Unspoken Voice"

Gabor Mate, MD: "When the Body Says No"

Pattie Mallette: "Nowhere But Up"

Norman Doidge: "The Brain That Changes Itself, Stories of Personal Triumph from the Frontiers of Brain Science"

Pat Baker: "The Child was Me"

Fmr. Capt. Luis Carlos Montalvan with Bret Witter: "Until Tuesday"

Theo Fleury: "Playing With Fire"

Louise Hay: "You Can Heal Your Life"

Mary Beth Williams, PhD & John Sommer Jr: "A Look at Trauma: Simple and Complex"

Engel, Beverly, M.F.C.C.: "The Right to Innocence: Haling the Trauma of Childhood Sexual Abuse": Ballantine Books 1989

Drs. Mary Beth Williams and Soili Poijula: "PTSD Workbook"

CPSIA information can be obtained at www.ICGtesting.com
Printed in the USA
LVOW06s0505250913

353937LV00003B/23/P